THE CANOE IN CANADIAN CULTURES

251

FOREWORD
Kirk Wipper

PREFACE
John Jennings and Bruce W. Hodgins

EDITORS
John Jennings
Bruce W. Hodgins
Doreen Small

NATURAL HERITAGE/NATURAL HISTORY INC.

John Jennings, Bruce W. Hodgins, Doreen Small, Editors

Canadian Cataloguing in Publication Data

The canoe in Canadian cultures
Includes bibliographical references and index.
ISBN 1-896219-48-9

1. Canoes and canoeing — Social aspects — Canada.
2. Canoes and canoeing — Canada — History. 3. Fur trade — Canada.
4. Voyageurs.* I. Hodgins, Bruce W., 1931 - . II. Jennings, John, 1941 - .
III. Small, Doreen.

VM353.C345 1999   386'.229   C99-930517-4

Front photo: Early morning on the French River (canoe from a Temagami out-
fitter). Photographer, Toni Harting.
Back cover: Top: High water on the French River. Artist, ©Neil Broadfoot.
Lower left: Nootka whaling dugout canoe, early nineteenth century.
Photographer, Michael Cullen.
Lower right: Early nineteenth century western Arctic baidaraka model, with
loops for hunting implements. Figures are wearing ceremonial costumes.
Photographer, David Rankin.

Cover design by Blanche Hamill, Norton Hamill Design, Toronto.
Text design/production by Gringo Design, Toronto.
Printed and bound in Canada by Hignell Printing Limited, Winnipeg,
Manitoba.

THE CANADA COUNCIL | LE CONSEIL DES ARTS
FOR THE ARTS | DU CANADA
SINCE 1957 | DEPUIS 1957

Natural Heritage/Natural History Inc. acknowledges the support received for
its publishing program from the Canada Council Block Grant Program. We
also acknowledge with gratitude the assistance of the Association for the Export
of Canadian Books, Ottawa.

TABLE OF CONTENTS

FOREWORD *i*

WORD FROM THE EDITORS *iv*

DEDICATION *viii*

1. THE CANADIAN CANOE MUSEUM AND CANADA'S
NATIONAL SYMBOL
John Jennings 1

2. BEING THERE: BILL MASON AND THE CANADIAN
CANOEING TRADITION
James Raffan 15

3. EXTREMELY CRANKY CRAFT: THE JAMES W. TYRELL KAYAK,
BIG ISLAND, HUDSON STRAIT
Kenneth R. Lister 28

4. BARKLESS BARQUES
Eugene Arima 43

5. THE DAO OF PADDLING
Bert Horwood 62

6. TRADITIONAL LONGBOATS OF ASIA PACIFIC
Adrian Lee 74

7. THE CANOT DU MAÎTRE:
MASTER OF THE INLAND SEAS
Peter Labor 92

8. MANUFACTURE OF BIRCHBARK CANOES FOR THE
FUR TRADE IN THE ST. LAWRENCE
Timothy Kent 100

9. THE REPRESENTATION OF ABORIGINAL CULTURE WITHIN THE
CANADIAN CANOE MUSEUM
Shanna Balazs 144

10. CANADIANS AND THE CANADIAN CANOE IN THE
OPENING OF THE AMERICAN MIDWEST
Ralph Frese   *161*

11. PADDLING VOICES: THERE'S THE POET, VOYAGER,
ADVENTURER AND EXPLORER IN ALL OF US
Alister Thomas   *175*

12. THE CANOE AS A WAY TO ANOTHER STORY
Bob Henderson   *183*

13. HISTORIC CANOE ROUTES OF THE FRENCH RIVER
Toni Harting   *199*

14. THE DARK SIDE OF THE CANOE
Gwyneth Hoyle   *212*

15. THOUGHTS ON THE ORIGINS OF THE CANOE
Kirk Wipper   *224*

16. CANOESCAPES AND THE CREATIVE SPIRIT
Becky Mason   *233*

17. THE CANOE AS CHAPEAU: THE ROLE OF THE
PORTAGE IN CANOE CULTURE
Bruce W. Hodgins   *239*

18. R.M. PATTERSON'S PADDLING PASSION
David Finch   *247*

ENDNOTES   *254*
BIBLIOGRAPHY   *274*
VISUAL ACKNOWLEDGEMENTS   *277*
INDEX   *281*
CONTRIBUTORS   *297*

FOREWORD

In the interval between the first Canexus Conference at Queen's University in 1988 and Canexus II, held at Trent University in 1996, much has happened. It is rewarding to review what has transpired in so many directions in the world of paddling in Canada, the essence of which is captured so ably through the range and depth of the essays in this volume.

The Canadian Canoe Museum, under the banner of a "Museum in the Making" has moved sharply forward with its carefully planned objectives. In all cases of this the public has responded enthusiastically to the developments taking place. The specimens now on display in the Garfield Weston National Heritage Centre in the Museum have captured the imagination of many visitors, near and far. Shortly, an original Hudson's Bay Post will be installed to add to the interpretation of a unique and colourful Canadian heritage. A talented staff, led by Bill Byrick, the Museum's Executive Director, along with a dedicated Board of Trustees, an Advisory Council and an outstanding corps of volunteers are responsible for the excellent progress made in this major project.

The Canadian Recreational Canoeing Association now has a home in Merrickville to provide improved service in canoeing and kayaking across the nation. National standards are in place. An inclusion program for the disabled has been presented under the slogan, "Canoeing and Kayaking is for Everyone." Innovations have been developed for those who have not been included in the paddling fraternity. The "Flame of Hope" is for urban youth who, through this program may paddle with police, fire-fighters, ambulance workers and emergency task force members. This program contributes to a much better understanding and appreciation of other community members.

The Canadian Heritage Rivers System and Rivers Canada have made important inroads into the preservation of nominated rivers across the country. This program is significant not only for contemporary users of those rivers, but especially for future generations who will be assured of cultural and wilderness experiences of high quality.

Media attention is at an all time high. Films, videos, radio commentaries, newspapers, magazines and journals and advertising have all focused on the canoe and kayak in a variety of ways. Authors, too, are devoting attention to small watercraft making this Canexus publication most timely as it is about to be made available to the public.

A number of intriguing watercraft designs have emerged in the paddling world. Craft for slalom, coastal paddling and all forms of competitive water activity are but a few examples of such proliferation. The "rocker" canoe has been introduced again for white water activity. These craft may be related to the birchbark canoe of aboriginal origin. Propelling devices also have become diversified and include the increasingly popular bent shaft paddles and poles, as well as the employment of new materials including graphite, metal and fibreglass.

The virtual explosion of the use of fur trade replica canoes, the canot du nord (North Canoe) and the canot du maître (Montreal Canoe), have given to paddlers a group experience which has, for many, a singular attraction. In these large watercraft, one can begin to feel something of the pulse of the fur trade. The introduction of Dragon Boats also presents a group paddling experience in the competitive realm of canoeing.

Re-enactments of historic events, festivals and pageants have become an important means for interpreting and experiencing the story of Canada. Some examples of historic figures that have been featured are: Alexander Mackenzie, David Thompson, Simon Fraser, and John Graves Simcoe. These portrayals give the public a new insight into what has gone on before.

Outfitters across the nation have become much more visible in the cultivation of skill and safety sensitivity as they present a broad range of adventurous experience in outdoor places. My own recent experiences with outfitters have given me a renewed enthusiasm for the welfare of the environment we use in our journeys into the wilderness. They are demonstrating in their practices a real difference between adventure and sheer foolhardiness. Today, there are, fortunately, more reliable outfitters by far than when the first volume of Canexus was published. According to all reports, they are making a distinguished contribution to paddling in Canada.

In the period since 1988, the canoe has emerged as the true symbol of Canadian culture and heritage. Moreover, it is, at the same time, an important catalyst for Canadian unity and, as such, a symbol of fundamental significance in these times. The articles here reflect a diversity of thought, experience, and observation not heretofore presented in Canadian canoeing literature. This volume gives cause for reflection, appreciation and inspiration, all of which make this publication a joy to read.

Kirk Wipper

WORD FROM THE EDITORS

This collection of essays has its origins in a conference held in Peterborough in May 1996, sponsored jointly by the Frost Centre for Canadian Heritage and Development Studies at Trent University and by the Canadian Canoe Museum. The conference and the publication of these writings represent the first important academic collaboration between Trent and the Canoe Museum – the first, it is hoped, of many such collaborations in the future.

The essays in this volume, most of them with their roots at the conference at Trent University, are varied, some concentrating on the act of canoeing, others on the craft itself. It is hoped that, collectively, they will give the reader some fresh insights into the evolving world of the canoe. As well, it is hoped that they complement the papers of the first Canexus publication, which emerged from a similar conference held at Queen's University in 1988.

Collectively, these two volumes go beyond the usual canoeing literature and some of the essays even enter the realms of philosophy and spiritualism. Anyone wondering what could possibly induce canoeists to risk their lives in the furthest corners of canoe country at the height of bug season should read this volume, and then its companion. Together they evoke the sense of adventure that compels canoeists to seek new territory and the sense of peace, sometimes described as religious experience, to be found in unsullied nature.

This volume also discusses the historic role of the canoe and the historic art of canoe building. To a large degree the canoe dictated the borders of Canada. It was the Native birchbark craft, transformed into the majestic canoes of the fur trade, that spanned the continent and forged a nation. The canoe, perhaps, is the closest thing Canada has to a national symbol.

One difference that has occurred since the publication of the first Canexus volume becomes obvious in this volume. The Canadian Canoe Museum, formerly the Kanawa International Museum, is established solidly in Peterborough, Ontario now, and was central to the creation of this collection. Several essays in this book are specifically about the Canoe Museum. Others are written by people closely connected to the Museum. Kirk Wipper's extraordinary collection is now becoming the focal point in Canada for the celebration and study of a uniquely Canadian symbol. Canada exists because of the canoe, and the Canadian Canoe Museum is dedicated to joining Canada's rich canoe heritage to the present and future stewardship of her vast and magnificent "canoe country."

Trent University, through its Frost Centre for Canadian Heritage and Development, was also very important in the collaboration that produced this book. Trent was the first university in Canada to develop programs in both Canadian Studies and Native Studies. Now a collaboration has begun between Trent and the Canoe Museum which, some day, will result in the establishment of the world's foremost centre for the study of the canoe and "canoe country."

The main purpose of this volume, and of the conference from whence it came, is to continue the themes that the first Canexus began. This, the second Canexus publication, will have served its purpose if it has informed readers, in an interesting fashion, of some fresh elements in the story of that craft which helps to define Canada.

Regrettably, as with the first Canexus volume, there is no Aboriginal author included here and the lone French-Canadian voice is somewhat disguised. This is a situation that must be rectified in the sequel! However, former chief Gary Potts of Bear Island did give an oral presentation at the conference in which he spoke of the importance of the canoe and the role

Fall Paddle

of canoe culture in the history of his people, the Teme-Augama Anishnabai. Tim Kent, who documents the crucial role of the French-Canadian canoe builders of the St. Lawrence Valley to the North American fur trade, is himself the descendant of a number of these builders.

To coincide with the conference and a special opening of the Museum, the Canadian Canoe Museum organized a canoe trip from Ste. Marie-among-the-Hurons to Peterborough, to commemorate the 1615 voyage of Champlain and his Native allies to Peterborough, and to other lesser points. The conference and the Canoe Museum were honoured especially in that, among the crew of the Montreal Canoe making the trip, were two Wendat (Huron) paddlers from Loretteville, the Wendat community near Quebec City. They had come on the trip to recreate some of their own history and were joined in Peterborough by others from their community who came to present their tribal flag to the Canoe Museum and to perform a drumming ceremony to bring luck to the new museum. The group then went on to Ste. Marie-among-the Hurons to spend some time with their ancient roots.

Special thanks go to Erik Hanson, who did much of the organizing of the conference, to John Wadland, current Director of the Frost Centre at Trent, to John Marsh, his predecessor, and, especially, to David Wesley of Norflicks Productions, who has been so instrumental in supporting publication of these papers.

In the period between the two Canexus conferences and the publication of the Canexus volumes, the canoe world has lost a great canoeist: Bill Mason. He is greatly missed, but his spirit is at the core of this book, as it is at the centre of the explosion of canoeing, not only in Canada, but around the world.

John N. Jennings
Bruce W. Hodgins
Doreen Small

In memory of Bill Mason (1929 – 1998)
for his leadership, his vision and his renowned contribution
to the world of canoeing.

Bill Mason on the Petawawa River.

THE CANADIAN CANOE MUSEUM AND CANADA'S NATIONAL SYMBOL

John Jennings

The canoe is a symbol unique to Canada. It is one of the greatest gifts of the First Peoples to all those who came after. It is the most powerful symbol joining the Native Peoples to the two founding cultures of Europe – French and English. It is a symbol of exploration and discovery, of individual courage and of partnership, of heroic enterprise and of a quiet harmony with Nature. It is a symbol of our history, and it can be a symbol of our future, a symbol of confidence, of community, of paddling together toward a renewed Canada.

To paraphrase somewhat the words of Bill Mason, one of Canada's greatest paddlers: God first created the canoe and then thought up the ideal country to go with it. Thus did Canada come into being. Canada contains roughly half the fresh water of the world. She also has the longest shoreline of any country in the world. Rivers are at the heart of Canada and, for those who travel them by canoe, they become living things that speak to the soul. Canada is perhaps unique in the world in having a system of rivers and lakes that so completely links all parts of the country. To a great extent, landscape defines a people; a country's essential character is formed, in part, from the relationship between its people and its land.

I know a man whose school could never teach him patriotism, but who acquired that virtue when he felt in his bones the vastness of his land, and the greatness of those who founded it.[1]

Pierre Trudeau, many decades ago, wrote an article on the wilderness canoe trip in which he described the trip as a metaphor for life. Anyone who has travelled through the vastness and haunting beauty of Canada's North instantly recognizes Trudeau's sense of awe for the canoeist's communion with this land. Canadians used to define themselves as a northern people. Though Canada is now one of the more highly urbanized countries in the world, her wilderness is still there, much of it just as pristine and sparsely peopled as a century ago, and it beckons perhaps with increased intensity to those who feel that they have lost their connection with it. The symbol of the canoe can provide the link between wilderness and the deep yearning of so many in cities for a closer bond with nature.

Every city dweller in Canada lives within a few hours of unblemished nature; the symbol of the canoe connects those in cities with images central to the Canadian identity – the wilderness, natural beauty, the splash of a beaver tail, Canada geese etched on the evening sky, the echo of a loon at dusk, the gentle hum of the mosquito! As David Suzuki has observed, "Cities disconnect us from nature and each other." In the big cities of today, it is all too easy to lose a sense of place, a sense of uniqueness. The shopping malls of Mississauga are rather similar to most others in North America. But, in a world becoming startlingly cluttered, Canadians can have it both ways. They can enjoy the many benefits of city life and also retreat quite easily to the tranquillity of nature.

The canoe of the Native Peoples, developed over several thousand years, is perhaps the ultimate expression of elegance and function in the world of watercraft. All its parts came from nature and, when retired, it returned to nature. Except for the tribes of the Plains, the canoe was central to all Native cultures. Each tribe was defined by the distinct shape of its canoes or kayaks. The canoe was not only the principal means of transportation, but was also central to almost every facet of life. The Native canoe builder held one of the most revered positions in society.

Today the canoe continues to be important to many Native cultures. For instance, the revival of the building of the great sea-going canoes on the west coast, beginning with Bill Reid's *Luu Tas* (Wave Eater) in 1986, is central to a sense of rebirth and renewed pride among west coast First Nations. For many of them the canoe is a spiritual symbol – the healing

Haida sea-going dugout, commissioned by the Kanawa International Museum, forerunner of the Canadian Canoe Museum.

vessel, a metaphor for community and for life's journey. This revival of canoe building has become the central symbol in a resurgence of their cultures which now has taken the shape of canoe gatherings of thousands of west coast Native People every few years.

The canoe is perhaps the greatest gift of the Native Peoples to later cultures. Through honouring the canoe as one of Canada's most important symbols, the centrality of Native Peoples to Canadian history can be emphasized. The symbol of the canoe can do much to bring the Native People back to the centre of Canadian culture, rather than leaving them on the margins, where they all too often reside.

What symbol could better represent Canadians abroad than the magnificent sculpture The *Black Canoe: The Spirit of Haida Gwaii* by Haida sculptor and canoe builder Bill Reid, which now resides in place of honour at the Canadian Embassy in Washington. And what theme is more fitting than the Native legend of humanity after the Flood, paddling into the future in a mythological canoe. The *Black Canoe* has become one of Canada's most famous sculptures, chosen to represent Canada to the world. It represents the present, but is pointing toward both the past and

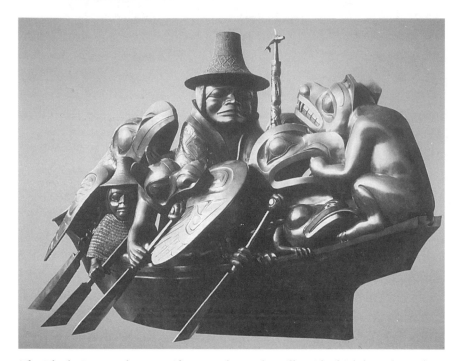

The Black Canoe, *the magnificent sculpture by Bill Reid which has place of honour at the Canadian Embassy in Washington.*

the future, and the multiplicity of its passengers is stunningly caught with irony and humour. Many willful differences are represented, but all, after a fashion, demonstrate a mutual recognition and are paddling together in the same direction. Most of the figures are part human and part animal; the distinction blurs and there is no condescension toward the natural world. The most powerful message of The *Black Canoe* is that all aboard must listen to the language of the others; jumping overboard is not a sane option. The *Black Canoe* is an extraordinarily powerful metaphor for Canada as she enters the next millennium. The multiplicity that is Canada, too, can maintain individual distinctiveness as they direct Canada into the future. Mutual recognition will be one of the most important elements in Canada's survival.

Canada exists as it does today because of the canoe. In the United States it was the horse that determined national boundaries; in Canada the canoe. Some Canadians claim that Canada is a young country with little history. Nonsense! The ancient water routes that link the country each have their history, passed down from one generation to the next over many centuries before the arrival of the Europeans.

When Europeans arrived in the New World, they quickly adopted both these water routes and the Native craft, so wonderfully adapted to inland travel. European craft were abandoned at the Lachine Rapids, the first major impediment on the journey across the continent. Europeans were quick to recognize not only that the birchbark canoe was the perfect vehicle for traversing Canada's inland waters, but that vast fortunes could be made from harvesting the seemingly unlimited supply of wildlife. This search for fur led to the development of the fur trade, the most important partnership in Canada's history between the Aboriginal Peoples and the two founding peoples of Europe – French and English, with the canoe being central to this collaboration. It was the following of Native water routes across the continent and the extension of the fur trade by these routes that essentially shaped Canada and determined her borders.

The canoe is the symbol of the extraordinary expansion of New France in the seventeenth and eighteenth centuries. At a time when the American colonists hardly had poked their noses over the first serious hill, the French had travelled by canoe almost to the Rocky Mountains and to the mouth of the Mississippi, thus laying claim to the entire Ohio Valley. Names such as Champlain, who travelled to the Great Lakes in the early 1600s, Jolliet and Marquette and then La Salle, who descended the Mississippi, La Salle all the way to the mouth in the late 1600s, La Vérendrye and his sons, who persevered through the unrelenting Shield country to explore the Plains country beyond – these are but the best known of legions of French adventurers who spread New France's influence over half a continent. Before the end of New France in 1759 at the hands of the British fleet, the canoe had been the key to consistent French military dominance over the American Colonies.

The French settlers from earliest days established trade partnerships with Native groups, based on the canoe, that were very much at odds with the usual patterns of conquest and subjugation throughout the Western Hemisphere. There seems little question that the French, in their curiosity to see what lay to the west and south and in their development of the fur trade, went more than half way in embracing Native customs and technology. Fortunately for the history of relations between the Native

Peoples of Canada and European immigrants, the social patterns of the French fur trade were extended to the British fur trade after the Conquest. The result was a continuing relationship throughout Canada's frontier period which produced a Canadian frontier history completely at odds with the rest of the hemisphere.

And it was by canoe that the French of New France sped across the continent to establish enduring Francophone communities in both Canada and the United States. There still remains much work to be done by historians in tracing these major migrations across the continent. For instance, how many know that three quarters of the fabled mountain men of the American West in the nineteenth century were actually French Canadians and Métis, most of them former voyageurs in the North American fur trade? The canoe is the obvious symbol to remind French Canadians of their extraordinary role in building Canada and extending French culture across the continent. It is a symbol that puts Quebec at the centre of our history.

Canada is not an artificial creation; she exists, not in spite of history, but because of it. The essential shape of Canada was determined, above all, by canoe exploration and the fur trade, first by French Canadians and then by the Scots traders and French and Métis voyageurs of the North West Company and the Hudson's Bay Company. At the height of the fur trade empire, the Hudson's Bay Company controlled almost half of present day Canada. But what is more important than sheer size is that the HBC, today the world's oldest continuous commercial enterprise, was responsible for keeping the Canadian West from falling into American hands. And this vast fur empire was held together by the canoe and by the cooperation that existed among the main participants: the Scots traders; the Native Peoples, who provided the furs and guided fur traders and explorers; and the French and Métis voyageurs, whose skill, toughness, courage and, most importantly, whose cordial relations with Native Peoples paved the way for a relatively harmonious interaction between the Native Peoples and Europeans. This cooperation was in striking contrast to race relations on the American frontier. Here, in the fur trade, is the most notable example of collaboration between the Native Peoples and the two founding peoples of Europe. Using the Native craft and the Native wisdom of the wilderness, Canadians were able to fulfill their "magnificent obsession" of creating a nation from sea to sea.

And it is not stretching the point to claim that in this era of the fur trade is to be found the foundation for a later multicultural nation. The standards of cultural cooperation that were laid down in the fur trade era and continued into the relationship between the First Nations of the West and the North West Mounted Police effectively shaped the evolution of the Canadian West and left a deep impression on the Canadian identity.

The era of the great voyaging canoes of the fur trade is now a distant memory, but Canada's canoeing traditions are still very much alive. Today millions of Canadians continue to paddle – 2.1 million to be exact – according to the latest statistics of the Canadian Recreational Canoeing Association. Membership, including provincial and territorial affiliates and two hundred and fifty clubs, numbers about 60,000. There are approximately 1.3 million canoes and kayaks in Canada, making canoeing in Canada a very active pastime, from wilderness and recreational paddling to marathon and sprint racing up to Olympic level. Interestingly, the only Olympic sport named for a country is the "Canadian," a canoe race.[2]

Recently, there has been a huge increase in recreational canoeing, especially that associated with wilderness rivers and, since the 1970s, a Heritage River System has been established by Government with the aim of protecting our historic rivers. As Pierre Trudeau has told us, there is no better way to find our sense of being Canadian than to discover our rivers and, thus, the magnificent diversity of Canada.

Another canoe sport that recently has exploded on the national scene is the Dragon Boat race. The Dragon Boat adds the Pacific Rim to Canada's canoeing fraternity and helps to portray the canoe as an increasingly multicultural symbol, a symbol that is inclusive of many recent Canadians, and one that introduces them to this country's heritage, sport and recreation, and vast open spaces.

Nations in time of trouble need to dig deep. In the depths of the London Blitz, it was Churchill's brilliant evocation of shared beliefs that rallied the British people. In moments of national crisis people reach out for symbols that are held in common.

For instance, the most powerful symbol thus far in American culture emerged from a period of perceived crisis. The romantic image of the cowboy was invented in the 1890s in response to what one eminent American historian has termed a "psychic crisis" in that country's history.

There are some important parallels that can be drawn with Canada's present situation.

The romantic image of the cowboy, which so caught first the American imagination and then that of the world, was created by three men at the end of the nineteenth century: Owen Wister, the author of the first famous western novel, *The Virginian*; Frederic Remington, the best known western artist and sculptor of the time; and a future president, Theodore Roosevelt. These three friends self-consciously set out to create the image of the cowboy. Their motive had much to do with their extreme anxiety over the state of the country, an anxiety clearly echoed in the current Canadian situation.

Previously, the image of the cowboy had been that of a rather scruffy and dissolute character in dime novels or the one dimensional extras in Buffalo Bill Cody's Wild West Show. Then, in the 1890s, the time and the image came together. Suddenly, Americans realized that they no longer had a frontier. A great many of them were dismayed by massive immigration, which was changing the face of the country, and by the rise of industrial cities. Add to this a serious economic recession. A very large number of Americans viewed the future with apprehension.

It was in this atmosphere of rapid change and uncertainty that the new image of the cowboy was born. The motives of the inventors were clear; they were anointing their mythical cowboy, through literature and art, with the qualities that they thought had made America great – freedom, courage, initiative and a connection with open spaces.

The reaction of Americans to this new image was instant and profound. The writing of Wister and the art of Remington struck a deep chord in Americans at a time when Americans needed an image that represented shared beliefs and aspiration. The symbol of the cowboy, of course, has remained central to the American identity. It has become one of the central images of a highly urbanized people, a people who still identify strongly with a romantic past and images of space.

Canada, today, is in urgent need of comparable symbols as the country goes through a period of crisis, symbols that can remind Canadians of what we have collectively accomplished in the past and what, together, we can achieve in the future.

Canada is short on unifying symbols. The maple leaf is not found universally and, in itself, does not represent our history or our qualities as a people. The Mounties and hockey are strong symbols, but the Mounties are not loved by significant numbers of Canadians and hockey, in an era of expansion franchises, is no longer particularly Canadian. What is left? Certainly commitment to the world order, as reflected in our peacekeeping role, and our belief in tolerance and diversity as represented in our policy of multiculturism. But these ideals have yet to be represented in a nationally accepted symbolic form.

Canada, today, is faced with many issues that are centrifugal – political devolution, multiculturalism, Native self-government, a stress on regional identity. Individually, all have great merit but, collectively, they pose a threat to Canada if there are no strong counterbalancing forces at work to draw us together and remind us of the things we hold in common. The one unifying symbol unique to Canada, the Canadian parallel to the cowboy's horse, a symbol that links us with our history, with adventure, with heroic deeds, with nation building and, most importantly, with a unique Canadian landscape is the canoe.

Canadians, today, need things around which to rally. On the face of it, a canoe, a dead piece of wood perhaps does not seem an obvious choice. But it is not so much the canoe itself that is the symbol; it is the connection that the canoe makes with so many aspects of the Canadian identity. The canoe is the carrier of our myths and our images of landscape. And, as Simon Schama has so brilliantly argued in *Landscape and Memory*, societies are influenced profoundly by landscape and a country's landscape is, itself, the carrier of memory. The strength of this argument is certainly clear to the Québècois and to Canada's Native Peoples and to anyone who has followed the great Voyageur Route, which first knit the country.

The canoe reaches deep into our history and extends into our future as the symbol of our stewardship of the land. It conjures images of things that, according to surveys, Canadians collectively hold dear – images of wilderness: of the mystique of the North; of space and tranquillity; of the Group of Seven – Canada's best known canoeists; and of a Mountie singing in a canoe! The canoe is the link with all these things. And the canoe is not only a symbol that connects Canadians to these things; it is also the best means of experiencing them. These images are ones that all Canadians can share, no matter what their background.

How can this symbolism be used? In the hands of the modern equiv-
alents of those who etched the cowboy on the American psyche, the
symbol can be presented to Canadians with considerable power. The
Canadian Canoe Museum itself is the embodiment of that symbol and
the keeper of a vital part of Canada's unique story. Its development as the
premier museum of its kind in the world can be a great source of pride
for Canadians.

The Canadian Canoe Museum is the only museum in the world solely
dedicated to the canoe and kayak. Its 600 craft, one third of them
Aboriginal, constitute one of Canada's most important heritage treasures.
And the location of the Museum in Peterborough, Ontario, is an ideal
one. It was in the Peterborough area in the 1850s that the modern canoe
was first invented and Peterborough, for a century, until the appearance
of fibreglass canoes in the 1960s, was the canoe building capital of the
world. As well, Peterborough has a university with a national reputation
in the field of "canoe culture."

Trent, perhaps of all universities in Canada, is the ideal one to be
involved with the Canoe Museum. It was the first university in Canada to
develop a program in both Canadian Studies and in Native Studies. Its
recently launched doctoral program in Native Studies is the first in
Canada. The Archives of the Canoe Museum are on permanent loan to
Trent and it is the intention of the Museum to create, in cooperation with
Trent, the world's foremost research institute for the study of North
America's canoe culture.

The Museum also has strong links with Sir Sandford Fleming College
and has benefited greatly from its museum and conservation programs.
Many of the Museum's small artifacts have been wonderfully restored in
Fleming's Conservation program and interns from the College have been
very helpful in developing exhibits. As well, the Canoe Museum currently is working with the College in developing a high-tech system to
make the Museum's information available across Canada and, indeed,
around the world.

The Canadian Canoe Museum originally was the Kanawa
International Museum, created almost single-handedly by Kirk Wipper at
his youth camp, Camp Kandalore, in the Haliburton region of Ontario.
Professor Wipper will be remembered as a great Canadian for his tireless

search over many decades for this vital part of Canada's identity. The vast collection he assembled represents virtually every important aspect of Canada's canoeing heritage. In 1990 he transferred the Kanawa Collection to Peterborough and, at that time, the museum was renamed.

Now this extraordinary collection can be used to instill in Canadians a sense of pride and understanding for their past and a sense of awareness of Canada's vast and very special landscape. The Museum's primary mandate is to create a heritage centre that vividly will bring to life one of our most important national icons as a tribute to the Canadian spirit. What better model of this spirit, for instance, than Sir Alexander Mackenzie, first across the continent by canoe, whose simple and unassuming inscription, "From Canada by Land," juxtaposes his extraordinary achievements. His life is a wonderful example of the courage, endurance and devotion of those who laid the foundations of a great Canadian heritage.

As well as telling the stories of those peoples whose culture and heritage centred on the canoe, the Museum is dedicated to keeping alive the great canoe and kayak building traditions of both the Aboriginal Peoples and the European craftsmen who developed the modern canoe. Already the Museum has begun the careful documentation of building techniques that are in danger of becoming extinct.

Walter Walker (above) was the first Canoe Builder Emeritus installed in the Canadian Canoe Museum's Hall of Honour.

It is intended that the Canoe Museum be situated on two sites. At present, only one site is being developed, the former Outboard Marine Corporation office complex and factory which have been donated to the Museum. This site consists of two buildings, the 40,000 square foot National Heritage Centre and the 100,000 square foot Millennium Centre. Collectively, these two buildings will be developed to tell the story of Canada's relationship to the canoe and to display the entire collection. When this site has been completed, the Museum then will develop its second site, four acres of waterfront property in the heart of Peterborough, which was donated by the City of Peterborough and the Otonabee Region Conservation Authority. Here, a pavilion, along with a boat house and dock, will be constructed to accommodate the Museum's summer activities and programs on the water. Eventually this property will be the site of major gatherings of canoeists, for regattas, pageants, canoeing courses, as well as canoe building rendezvous. Ultimately, the Museum intends to launch a series of wilderness canoe trips on famous voyageur routes and to use this waterfront property for training and orientation.

Currently, the Museum is in the midst of a major fund raising campaign to make this Museum the focal point of Canada's most all-encompassing symbol. And the foremost challenge, beyond actually acquiring large amounts of money, is to create exciting exhibits and develop stimulating programs that will bring Canadians together. Always the intent is to build an understanding of a shared past and to instill both a sense of pride in Canada's past and a sense of connection to Canada's vast terrain. Above all, the Museum will make it clear that Canada is, without question, the supreme canoe country of the world.

The new museum in Peterborough is fortunate in starting with an extraordinary collection already in place and a clean slate from a planning perspective as it sets out to create a new museum at both its Outboard Marine and waterfront properties. With the world of museums changing dramatically, the Canadian Canoe Museum can be at the forefront of these changes. The Museum has struck a design committee. Half of its members are from the Museum's Board of Trustees and the other half are from representatives of Native and Métis communities, in recognition of the centrality of the canoe to Métis and Native cultures and the centrality of Native craft to the Museum's collection. What will emerge, we hope, is a museum full of life that will excite, educate, provoke, and cause many to rethink old assumptions. Above all, the Canoe Museum will be a place of discovery, discovery of our history, of the spirit that built the country and of the Canadian landscape that is canoe country.

In an era when the Canadian school system has shortchanged its students in a shocking fashion concerning our national history, the Museum has a clear mandate to help plug a gaping hole. A country without a sense of history is extremely vulnerable to the forces of disunity; the Canoe Museum can play an important national role in enabling Canadians, specially school children, to learn about themselves and about their history.

And, in an age of cyberspace, the Canoe Museum can be at the forefront of redefining the way a museum functions. Much of what the Museum represents can be exported across the country in a compelling way. The Museum, in effect, will become the repository of one of Canada's most important symbols and the catalyst for the dissemination of that symbol across the country.

The Internet, computer-generated simulation, 3-D imaging, all now make it possible to transmit information in ways unimagined even a few years ago. Already some museums, such as the Canadian Museum of Civilization, are experimenting in "virtual museums" that can be accessed anywhere in the world. The possibilities to produce interactive material seem endless, especially material that can be placed in every schoolroom in the country.

Canada today represents the best hope for the future of the world. For the fifth year in a row the United Nations has informed Canadians that they live in the best country on the planet. Even if this rating is somewhat mercurial, it reflects an important truth. Canada is perceived in the outside world as a standard on which to base society. Canada is, indeed, a very real country! But Canadians must regain some of the spirit of 1967, the year, according to Pierre Berton, that was our last good year. Though Canada is stronger now than in 1967, in all important indicators – her economy, arts, literature, sports – she seems less than the sum of her parts. She needs to redefine her vision from that of being "as Canadian as necessary, under the circumstances." It is time to stop devaluing ourselves and to forge a new national spirit.

Canada, more than any other country in the world, is the blueprint for

Late nineteenth century board-and-batten wide board canoe made in Peterborough by the William English Canoe Company.

the future. She is the world's first truly multicultural society. Just as the United States in the Revolutionary period ushered in the democratic state, Canada today is the test of whether the next great advancement of mankind can endure. Canada is the multicultural state of the twenty-first century – a model of diverse people living together in relative harmony under a system of tolerance and respect for minority rights, equality before the law, a sense of obligation to the world and, above all, of a pragmatic federalism able to adjust to the occasion.

So Canada matters enormously. Her breakup would not be just a local tragedy. It would signal to the world the failure of the world's foremost experiment in human relations. Her failure would be "a sin upon humanity," the defeat of the most important political and social idea of the next century, the belief that diverse societies can coexist without the destructive tensions and racial and ethnic hatreds everywhere so evident.

As Canada enters an era of great uncertainty and of great promise, Canadians need to be armed with all the resolve they can muster to counteract complacency and pessimism. Symbols are vital to that resolve and to a sense of who we have been and who we can become. The symbol of the canoe can do much to bring Canadians together by reminding them of their heritage and of their quiet passion for their land.

BEING THERE: BILL MASON AND THE CANADIAN CANOEING TRADITION

James Raffan

The extent of Bill Mason's hold on the public consciousness as a paddler and wilderness man is well known, especially in canoeing circles. There are people who were better technical paddlers than Bill Mason; there are people who knew more about the craft; there are people who made more substantial contributions to the development of instructional programs for canoeing in Canada; and there are people who were much more widely travelled, in a pioneering sense, than ever was Bill Mason. But there is no one who is better known or more identified as a Canadian canoeist than the man in the red canoe.[1] His films for the National Film Board, especially the instructional "Path of the Paddle" series, have been borrowed, bought and viewed more than any other film in the history of the NFB. His instructional guide, *Path of the Paddle*, has been translated into French and German and, along with his other books – *Song of the Paddle, When the Wolves Sang* and *Canoescapes* – has become ubiquitous in North American canoeing circles, and in Europe. Films about Bill Mason have been translated into several languages and currently are playing in more than fifty countries around the world.[2]

The curious thing about Bill Mason's popularity was that he was the most unlikely star. He was the first to admit that writing did not come easily, and yet his books became best sellers. He was not the most articulate speaker, and yet as a public story-teller he was peerless. He was without formal training in film, consistently breaking just about every rule of filmmaking, and yet he became the recipient of just about every

Bill Mason preparing dinner in front of the wilderness tent that he helped to design.

possible film award (including two academy award nominations and two British Academy awards). He was bullishly self-reliant and collaborated only when he had to, and yet he was the envy of his film colleagues across Canada and around the world. He was physically very small and was sick much of his foreshortened life, and yet he became emblematic of the robust wilderness voyageur.

What is argued here is that the most significant factor in Bill Mason's popularity, and the aspect of his being that is most instructive in illumi- nating the importance of the canoe in Canadian culture – besides the intrinsic and unimpeachable quality of his work – is the unwitting way in which he accessed for his devotees a set of national and universal themes. Mason set out simply and without pretension to tell stories and to share his love for the wilderness and for the canoe, but somehow in doing that he became emblematic of much larger and complex themes of which he was only vaguely conscious, if at all, or so it would appear. This paper sug- gests that when people responded to Bill Mason they did so to the face value of the work and perhaps, more significantly, to the deep and abiding human themes symbolized by Mason and his work – notably his absence of fear in the forest, his affection and familiarity with rivers, and his powerful sense of wilderness spirituality. As such, Bill Mason, perhaps even more in death than when he was alive, and more than any other person affiliated with the canoe, was and is, synonymous with the canoe in Canadian culture.

Toronto broadcaster, Seth Feldman, has called the canoe a "perfect machine," one of those objects that has been around so long that it has become part of who we are, a vehicle that has shaped our history just as we have shaped it.[3] A canoe still ensures free passage, lockage and camping for paddlers on the Rideau Canal. And it's not all that long ago that regular fare on any Canadian passenger train included space for a canoe in the baggage car. For years, the image on our highest denomination of coin, the silver dollar, was of a European coureur de bois with an Indian bowman in a classical Dogrib or Chipewyan birchbark canoe with its high bow and stern to protect against heavy seas on large lakes. Venerable Canadian canoes are in museums and under cottages, in literature and on beer labels. They turn up in works of art by the Group of Seven, in voyageur paintings of Frances Anne Hopkins, in ubiquitous textbook etchings of C.W. Jefferys and, again, as many of these images are encultured in philatelic art.[4] A little white frame church in Moose Factory has a red canoe in one of its stained glass windows; and, in advertising – the religion of everyday life – canoes have been used to flog everything from Export A cigarettes and Canadian Club whiskey to bottled water, fresh air and healthy vacations in the Canadian wild. We have aboriginal tales of Glooskap, the Mik'maq magician, arriving near Digby, Nova Scotia, in a stone canoe from overseas; of Nanabozho, the mythical forefather of the Algonkian, inventing the birchbark canoe on Manitoulin Island; and of Hiawatha, the best known of all canoeists of North American legendry, being told to Indian Agent, Henry R. Schoolcraft, which, when passed on again, became the substance of Henry W. Longfellow's famous poem, "Song of Hiawatha." There is a magic flying canoe in the Québècois folk tale "La Chasse Galerie;" on CBC radio there is the Frantic's bumbling super hero, Mr. Canoehead, who derived his extraordinary powers when his aluminium canoe accidentally was welded to his head by an errant bolt of lightning; and of course, there is the ribald definition, often attributed to Pierre Berton, that a Canadian is someone who knows how to make love in a canoe.[5] Philip Chester avows that this is incorrect; *anyone* can make love in a canoe, says he, a *Canadian* knows enough to remove the centre thwart.[6]

Prime Minister Pierre Trudeau celebrating Canada Day on the Rideau in a Malecite canoe.

Canoes figure prominently in our collective consciousness, just as the people who have paddled them over the years have become national icons. The Indian presence in this tradition is well known; however, had it not been for Longfellow's celebrated rhyme "Song of Hiawatha," the Aboriginal canoeist would have been more or less anonymous.[7] The coureurs du bois and voyageur heroes would have been equally obscure, had it not been for the likes of Étienne Brûlé, Pierre-Esprit Radisson and his brother-in-law, Médard Chouart Sieur des Groseillers, whose exploits made it into print. By contrast, the European paddler lineage is much better documented and, as a result, to paddle a canoe today is to invoke the traditions of a long line of explorers, surveyors, clergy, prospectors, artists, industrialists and ramblers; from Jacques Cartier, the first European canoeist, to Susanna Moodie, David Thompson, Frances Simpson, Ernest Thompson Seton, Elizabeth Taylor, Tom Thomson, Mina Hubbard, Archie Belaney, Agnes Deans Cameron, Sigurd Olson, Eric and Pamela Morse, Kirk Wipper, Pierre Trudeau and, of course, the inimitable Bill Mason.

For the longest time in our history, the canoe was merely a vehicle, a functional means for getting from one point to another on a line from the

Atlantic to the Pacific coast (with tangents to the north). As one writer has observed ". . . neither . . . coureurs du bois, explorers, voyageurs, traders, nor surveyors, saw value in the canoe other than what it allowed them to do largely because they did not have the written language, education, time, energy or inclination to do so."[8] There is nothing particularly romantic about dying young of a strangulated hernia on the trail, drowning in a rapid, or freezing in the icy waters of Lake Superior. What changed the perceptions of the canoe and canoeists in our history was the evolution of language. Slowly, inexorably, as people had more time, energy and education to write about experiences in the Canadian wild, the canoe moved in consciousness from a *vehicle* on the east/west axis to a *symbol* in the centre of a multi-dimensional landscape of the imagination. With very few exceptions, our canoeing heroes were paddlers *and* writers.

Canadian critic, Northrop Frye, describes three types of language: language used on a daily basis to express ourselves; language to categorize and describe; and figurative language–the stuff of poems, plays and novels. It is only when we move away from describing the world as it is, in the manner of the explorer or surveyor, toward describing the world as it might be, in the manner of a poet or interpretive writer, that language moves into the imagination and "becomes a mental construct, a model of a possible way of interpreting experience."[9] Looking at the way in which the canoe surfaces in Canadian literature, one could argue that it made the progression from a vehicle to a symbol in Canadian consciousness through language.

As more and more people wrote about their experiences paddling across Canada, the canoe became much more than a vehicle. It became a way of interpreting experience. In the landscape of the imagination, the canoe connects us first to the land, to the Aboriginal people, to the explorers and then to more illusive notions like freedom and possibility. Veteran contemporary canoeist, Kirk Wipper, illustrates the importance of the canoe in this respect:

The canoe carried aboriginal people for thousands of years, followed then by the explorers and the missionaries and the engineers and the surveyors . . . until in modern times it gives us the gift of freedom. The canoe is a vehicle that carries you into pretty exciting places, not only into whitewater but into

the byways and off-beaten places. . . . You are removed entirely from the
mundane aspects of ordinary life. You're witnessing first hand beauty and
peace and freedom – especially freedom. . . . Flirtation with the wilderness is
contact with truth, because the truth is in nature. . . . I like to identify myself
with something that is stable and enduring. Although [nature] is in a state
of flux, it is enduring. It is where reality is. I appreciate the canoe for its gifts
in that direction.[10]

When Wipper talks of canoes, flirtation with wilderness, freedom and
possibility, he is drawing from the canoe as symbol in an interior landscape. His love for the canoe is informed by first-hand experience as a
recreational canoeist, but it is situated within a culture rich with canoe
imagery, that includes fictional literature in which the canoe serves a symbolic function. Poets like Bliss Carman, Isabella Valancy Crawford,
Archibald Lampman, Duncan Campbell Scott, E. Pauline Johnson, Alan
Sullivan, Laura E. McCully and others, all have wound verse around the
idea of the canoe in its many dimensions.[11] Douglas LePan's poem, "Canoe
Trip" celebrates the restorative qualities of canoeing and points out the
way in which it integrates psyche and soma:

But here are crooked nerves made straight,
The fracture could no doctor call correct.
The hand and mind, reknit, stand for whole work;

The fable proves no cul-de-sac.[12]
Archibald Lampman's "Morning on the Lièvres" captures the dawn
majesty as experienced in his canoe:

Softly as a cloud we go,
Sky above and sky below,
Down the river, and the dip
Of the paddle scarcely breaks,
With the little silvery drip
Of the water as it shakes
From the blades, the crystal deep
Of the silence of the morn.

Bliss Carman's "Low Tide on Grand Pré" rhapsodizes imaginative possibilities of bucolic paddling at the end of the day:

The while the river at our feet –
A drowsy inland meadow stream –
At set of sun the afterheat
Made running gold, and in the gleam
We freed our birch upon the stream.

There down along the elms at dusk
We lifted dripping blade to drift,
Through twilight scented fine like musk,
Where night and gloom awhile uplift,
Nor sunder soul and soul adrift.

Novelists too, though not in such numbers, yet,[13] have also brushed canoe imagery into their stories. A case in point is Hugh MacLennan's protagonist "Jerome" in his novel *The Watch That Ends the Night*. The boy finds his brutally murdered mother and runs to the river. In the journey through the darkness that follows, he undergoes a transformational adventure or rite of passage in his birchbark canoe. On the river, he is headed for the sea, for eternity, finding his adult future in the act of canoeing:

He gave two more thrusts and pointed the bow downstream, and at once he began to move fast on a river wide, firm, silver and alive bearing him down past the silent camp, utterly alone for the first time in his life, bearing him down under that wide open sky through the forest to the open sea which he knew was at its end.[14]

Twentieth century scholars like W. L. Morton and Harold Innis, in exploring the centrality of the Canadian Shield as a dominant physiographic region and the fur trade as our first industrial staple, have circumstantially illuminated the importance of the canoe in Canadian culture. But other more contemporary writers of non-fiction have explored the mythic and psychological dimensions of canoeing and, in doing so, have affirmed the gradual elevation of the canoe from a utilitarian transportation device to something symbolic and much more significant. William C. James advanced the notion of the canoe trip as a religious quest,[15] drawing from the work of Joseph Campbell. By separating himself or herself from the known, encountering dragons and unspeakable dangers and returning to tell the story, according to James, the canoeist fits the pattern of the fairy-tale hero. For many paddlers, hungry to understand why the canoe seemed somehow so significant in their lives, this was a highly resonant idea. And among those who took this idea further was paddler and writer, Bert Horwood, who wrote of the canoe in yet another symbolic fashion:

The canoe is dialogue with a river, opening opportunities for wonder, both in contrasting the power and tranquillity of the world experienced at first hand, and in the penetration to explore more fully the meaning of that wonder.[16]

Margaret Atwood, the literary *bourgeois* of Canadian canoeing, has provided an even broader context, suggesting that survival—*la survivance*—is the single unifying and informing symbol at the core of Canadian consciousness.[17] America, says Atwood, organizes itself around the idea of the frontier; England, the island; and Canada, the unifying theme is survival in the trackless wilderness to which, inevitably, one must attach the image of the canoe. The canoe might even function as an organizing principle in a system of beliefs which, attached to Atwood's survival theme in Canadian literature, ". . . holds the country together and helps the people in it cooperate for common ends."[18]

Most Canadians may not be aware of the symbolic role of the canoe as adhesive in some kind of national "cooperation for common ends." In all but the quarters of recreational canoeists and paddle-minded historians, the binding qualities of the canoe are at best subliminal. If one believes Frye and his contentions about patterning in human experience, the undeclared glue may be the most important:

Man lives, not directly or nakedly in nature like the animals, but within a mythological universe, a body of assumptions and beliefs developed from his existential concerns. Most of this is held unconsciously, which means that our imaginations may recognize elements of it, when presented in art or literature, without consciously understanding what it is that we recognize.[19]

Tom Thomson on Canoe Lake, Algonquin Park.

As such, it was only a matter of time before someone would come along who would crystallize the canoe in Canadian consciousness. One of the first to do so was the painter, Tom Thomson, whose technical prowess in a canoe was surpassed only by his loving and artistic sense of the wilderness land in which he paddled. Most of Thomson's enduring images – *Northern River, Petawawa Gorges, Yellow Sunsets, Tea Lake Dam, The Pointers* – are all painted from a canoeist's perspective and, when

Thomson died mysteriously on his beloved Canoe Lake in Algonquin Park, a visual tribute to him painted by his friend, Jock Macdonald, featured the bittersweet image of an empty red canoe. And though there are other people since Thomson who have come to be identified with the canoe – Grey Owl, Sigurd Olson, Eric Morse, Omer Stringer, Kirk Wipper, Dan Gibson and a host of Liberal politicians – none has captured the essence of canoeing in the Canadian imagination like Bill Mason.

But I suspect with Mason this hold on the collective consciousness goes beyond national borders and touches universal human themes. Mason's affiliation with rivers illuminates one aspect of this unspoken universal appeal. This was a man who took his canoe and frolicked in the riparian tumult of rapids on the Canadian Shield. In doing so, Mason anchored himself in not only Canadian history but also in the public consciousness as keeper of the universal river theme. Attached to rivers as he was in life and as he remains in his books and films in perpetuity, Mason's message takes his public, as F. Colwell writes:

> . . . beyond the frontiers of our certainty to essay its wider and deeper mysteries where familiar demarcations no longer hold and are critically challenged and reconstituted. The river landscape [read Mason's message] is not simply geographical but profoundly psychological and metaphysical. It is, perhaps, no accident of history that western philosophy rose with the cities of the Meander plain. The river's passage to the sea rehearses and indeed may have inspired the entire range of philosophic inquiry: cosmogony and autogeny at the source, the problems of ontology, being and becoming, palpably rendered by its passage, the telos of the estuary.[20]

The simple way in which Mason loved his red canoe and the riparian places it took him captivated people in inexplicable ways, some philosophically, others more literally or spiritually. Simon Schama makes the argument that civilization's attachment to rivers was more deeply symbolic but in ways different from those just described. Drawing readers back to Plato via the work of 18th century philosopher, Joel Barlow, Schama writes:

> Were [rivers] not figured as bodies of water because since antiquity, their

*flow was likened to the blood circulating through the body? Plato had
believed the circle to be the perfect form, and imagined that nature and our
bodies were constructed according to the same mysterious universal law of
circulation that governed all forms of vitality. Barlow knew that to see a river
was to be swept up in a great current of myths and memories that was strong
enough to carry us back to the first watery element of our existence in the
womb. And along that stream were borne some of the most intense of our
social and animal passions: the mysterious transmutations of blood and
water; the vitality and mortality of heroes, empires, nations and gods.*[21]

Although it may seem a touch grand to suggest that Bill Mason did
anything of the kind, the unprecedented and fantastic popular success of
what were, after all, largely instructional films about canoeing cannot be
explained solely by an audience hungry for better ways to do the J stroke
or even to negotiate rapids on their way to the heart of the Shield. Mason
touched a chord with people, and in a variety of ways.[22]

Schama goes on to make the point that "... water courses are not the
only landscape to carry the freight of history,"[23] and therein lies another
possible connection between Mason and universal human themes.
Schama contends that the *first* human story or myth is about the essential
conflict between civilization and wildness. The texts of human history,
broadly conceived, illustrate that Canadians were not alone in distinguishing between the world of the city and the square, the street, the
world of geometric architecture and the random, curved and capricious
natural world, the dark forest. The woods have always been a place of
terror, a place defined by the absence of civilization.

So along came Bill Mason, a man who appeared totally at home in the
wilderness. For him the woods were not something against which a palisade wall must be built but a phenomenon to be embraced. Unlike his
predecessor in conservation, Grey Owl, whose dark and sturdy cabin rein-
forced the illusion of hidden terrors in the woods, in spite of claims about
befriending certain of its less ferocious denizens, Mason got in amongst
the wolves and when he camped, he did so in an open-fronted canvas tent.
In this respect, Mason's beloved Baker tent was an important piece of evidence for people looking to corroborate his claims about being at home in
the woods. Mason, like his tent, was open to the teachings of the wild; he

Grey Owl at Riding Mountain National Park, Manitoba.

defied the age-old human predisposition to be fearful of the dark woods. At some very deep and perhaps even subconscious level, this characteristic of Mason piqued many an imagination.

And in coming back to tell the tale, whether in person or in film or in his books, Mason put a face and a body to anyone and everyone who had ever done this in the past, including his environmental predecessors, like Henry David Thoreau and John Muir, who had said, always in the abstract that ". . . in wildness is the preservation of the world." Mason knew of these writers in the romantic wilderness tradition, but he himself was not a great reader and, if he did read Thoreau and Muir in detail, it mattered not to his public; Mason lived and breathed the wilderness tradition and lived to tell the tale. There is a universal message in Mason's comfort in the woods; perhaps this is why his films and films about him play so well in many languages in many countries around the world.

A third and final theme embodied in Mason's work was also one that can be tracked back to Muir, Thoreau and beyond, even to North America's Puritanical past in the writings of Jonathan Edwards and Ralph Waldo Emerson – pantheism.[24] Like his predecessor, Jonathan Edwards, who had blurred the Calvinist distinction between God as being *in* nature and God as being one *with* nature, Mason moved from a solid funda-mentalist Christian foundation to assert the belief that wilderness was the divine on earth. Whiffs of this perspective arise from all his works, but it was not until his final film, "Waterwalker," that he actually makes an overt statement about his views on wilderness spirituality. And although actu-ally espousing what had been intuitively evident in all his work turned some people off, there was always for many people a reassuring ring of authenticity and numinosity that came from Mason's reverence for nature. This sense of wilderness spirituality did much to add to his unspo-ken appeal in the public consciousness.

The curious aspect of these claims about universal truths and connec-tions in Bill Mason's work, and the reason why he might be likened to Peter Seller's engagingly naive character, Chancey Gardener, in the film "Being There," or to Tom Hank's portrayal of a similarly enigmatic, all-knowing, and appealing character in the contemporary film, "Forest Gump," is that in the end it is impossible to ascertain whether Mason in fact knew of and/or cultivated his following. Was he a naive prophet? Or was he a charismatic self-promoter? Or was he something or someone in between? Who knows? But none of these ever had anything like the following and popularity of Mason. In this larger picture, Bill Mason is but one element in a national scene. Of one thing, however, we can be certain: to understand the canoe in Canadian culture one must now, always, not only examine the craft but also the themes and patterns of which it is emblematic and this, in the fullness of time, will be impossible without touching the life and work of one man.

EXTREMELY CRANKY CRAFT:
THE JAMES W. TYRRELL KAYAK, BIG ISLAND,
HUDSON STRAIT

Kenneth Lister

By way of introduction, Canadian poet, Al Purdy, sets the scene with a poem titled "Eskimo Hunter (New Style)" written while gazing over the waters of Cumberland Sound, Baffin Island:

In terylene shirt and suspenders
sun glasses and binoculars
Peterborough boat and Evinrude motor
Remington rifle with telescope sight
making hot tea on a Coleman stove
scanning the sea and shore for anything
that moves and lives and breathes
and so betrays itself
one way or another . . .

but over the skyline
where the bergs heave and glimmer
under the glacier's foot
or down the fiord's blue water
 even under the boat itself
anywhere the unhappened instant is
real blood
 death for someone or some thing
 and it's reassuringly old-fashioned[1]

"Reassuringly old-fashioned" is a revealing phrase and in the context of this poem it exposes the poet's lament for the change that has taken the Inuit from a traditional, land-based life to a more contemporary, centralized one. Reading into the soul of the poem engenders a vision of Purdy sitting on the ocean shore fully aware that death by traditional or modern means is irrelevant to the victim, and perhaps even to the hunter, but his mind's eye is soothed knowing that the act of death itself is a constant and an unaltered touchstone to the "old ways" of the Inuit culture.

Although he sees "terylene shirt and suspenders" in his mind's eye, he beholds sealskin parka and boots. In place of "sun glasses and binoculars," he sees ivory snowgoggles with thin eye slits. The "Peterborough boat with Evinrude motor" fades to a skin-covered kayak with a double-bladed paddle. The "Remington rifle with telescope sight" gives way to toggle-headed harpoon with attached sealskin float. And finally, "making hot tea on a Coleman stove" is supplanted by soup warming over the narrow flame of a stone lamp fuelled by seal oil.

This vision of the mind's eye, however, is and can only be ephemeral. Culture, and its supporting technology, is not static and if we shift our perspective to view the noun "culture" as a verb – "culturing" – then culture is characterized as one of change, mutation, and accommodation.[2] The Inuit adoption of the "Peterborough boat and Evinrude motor," as elucidated in Purdy's poem, is such an example of "culturing." In its wake, however, the sealskin-covered kayak has been left to linger in the back of fading collective memory.

In the eastern Canadian Arctic, the kayak was a fundamental element in the traditional Inuit harvesting-oriented technology. Carrying various weapons on its deck – harpoon, bird spear, and lance – the kayak provided the transport necessary for armed hunters to approach within striking range of targeted animals. For all of the significance the kayak held for the Inuit, however, due to socioeconomic changes during the nineteenth and twentieth centuries, changes that included the Inuit adoption of the whaleboat and gun, the kayak has now been eliminated from the Inuit material system.[3]

The introduction of the whaleboat and gun into Inuit technology affected the scope of Inuit activities.[4] The gun, for instance, increased harvest efficiency with the result that the need for group interdependence became less acute. As noted in the 1920s for the Caribou Inuit,[5] perhaps the most noticeable, if not the most immediate, effect of the gun was the discontinuation of the communal caribou hunt where kayak hunters equipped with spears chased swimming caribou. The gun allowed the taking of caribou on a more opportunistic basis.[6] Similarly, the adoption of the nineteenth century whaleboat and later the motorized canoe provided the Inuit with increased opportunities for efficiency. Tununirusirmiut elder, Andrew Oyukuluk remembers his father's enthusiasm for such an opportunity:

They were having that [boat] *and I remember they were chasing narwhals with it. They got eight narwhals in a matter of hours so my father* [said] *throw* [away] *the kayak, we'll have that* [boat].[7]

Likewise, for the female members of the family, the new boats eliminated the substantial amount of skin preparation and sewing that was required in order to keep kayaks functional. With this positive impact on female labour we can appreciate Tununirusirmiut elder, Tugaq Tunraluk's comment when she stated: "I decided to wanting a big boat."[8] Through such change and accommodation – in essence, through "culturing" – the kayak has been replaced and its former role as an essential hunting tool is now part of Inuit memory culture.

Given this history, and at this late date the passing of knowledgeable elders, the kayak as museum object has become the information wellhead pertaining to the kayak complex and its function in traditional Inuit culture. The kayak as museum object, often supported by written narratives, represents the "expression of cultural phenomena"[9] and the object is now relied upon to provide the details of construction, shape, function and use.

The sample of known kayaks significantly increased in 1994 with the discovery of a kayak at the Marine Museum of Upper Canada in Toronto, Ontario. In September of that year, the author was invited by the Curator of this Marine Museum to view a kayak that had been retrieved from long-term storage. At the time there was no documentation for the kayak, but its overall shape and structure – namely its long and narrow bow, flat bottom, and full stern – indicated that it originated from the eastern Canadian Arctic and, more specifically, probably from the Hudson Strait.

Although the kayak clearly possesses eastern Arctic attributes, its physical characteristics represent only that part of the iceberg that floats above surface; the details of its much longer story – its original cultural context and subsequent history – remain below surface hidden with unknown dimensions. The one known piece of information that acted as a stepping off point in the search for provenance was the knowledge that the Marine Museum of Upper Canada had acquired the kayak from Dundurn Castle – the historic home of Sir Allan MacNab (1798-1862) – in Hamilton, Ontario. Further documentation pertaining to provenance and collection history was unknown, as was, at the time, a connection between eastern Arctic "explorations" and Hamilton. However, the hope lived that details bridging the chasm between an Arctic kayak and the home of a prominent lawyer, businessman, and politician, lingered in the records of Dundurn Castle. And it was not long before a telephone call that happens so very rarely in the museum world came through. The Curator of Dundurn Castle had located in the old Dundurn Castle ledger a single line entry stating that the kayak it received was collected from Hudson Strait in 1885 by J.W. Tyrrell.

With this one line, the kayak is elevated from being simply another example of an eastern Arctic style of kayak to being perhaps one of our most significant known examples. The line is pregnant with information. The kayak becomes soundly identified with the Inuit of Hudson Strait and therefore provides a foundation for determining Hudson Strait kayak characteristics. The kayak dates to at least 1885 when it was collected, making it – to the best of current knowledge – the oldest known extant kayak from the eastern Canadian Arctic in Canada if not all of North America. And very significantly, the collector, James Williams Tyrrell, author of *Across the Sub-Arctics of Canada: A Journey of 3,200 Miles by Canoe and Snowshoe Through the Hudson Bay Region* (1908) is known to have had extensive Subarctic and Arctic experiences.

Tyrrell is best known as the author of the above noted book, the account of the exploration, taken in 1893 with his brother Joseph Burr Tyrrell, to conduct an exploratory survey through the "Barren Lands" to

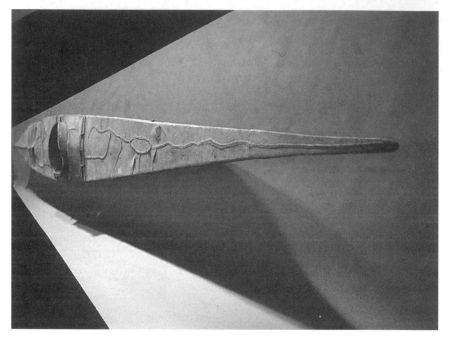

Two views of the Tyrell Kayak.

the northwest of Hudson Bay. This was a remarkable expedition, but it was only one in a long series of field work excursions that took Tyrell to Maine, northern Ontario, New Brunswick, Manitoba, Saskatchewan, the timberlands of the Rocky Mountains, the headwaters of the Mackenzie River, the Klondike, the east coast of Newfoundland, Hudson Bay, and – very significantly – Hudson Strait.[10] Tyrell's relationship to the Hudson Strait began in 1883 as Manitoba farmers confronted the shipping monopoly of the Canadian Pacific Railway. The farmers lobbied for the construction of a railway from Winnipeg to Churchill on Hudson Bay for the purpose of shipping their grain through Hudson Strait rather than via Montreal.[11] With such a railway and shipping route it was anticipated that the farmers would realize a saving of about $0.13 a bushel on freight costs. Additionally, it was felt that the opening up of the Hudson Bay shipping route would provide beneficial access to Hudson Bay mineral and fishery resources, as well as stimulate a northern advance of farmland. In short, in the political minds of the day:

The establishment of such a route would . . . be an incalculable boon to the North-West, would mark the beginning of an era in Canada, and would guarantee the development of a vast British Empire north-west of the great lakes that might one day become the Greater Britain.[12]

The longed for route presented a problem, however. As debates in the House of Commons brought to light in 1884, unknown ice conditions made the feasibility of commercial shipping through Hudson Strait uncertain:

Upon that question there is great diversity of opinion: some say that the immense icebergs and the peculiarity of the tides will be a permanent obstacle to the establishment of any permanent communication by sea between ports in the Hudson Bay and the seaports in Europe. On the other hand, it is asserted that from 1610, or during 274 years since the bay was discovered, ships have navigated it every year according to reports furnished by the Hudson [sic] Bay Company employees. This would tend to establish that there is at least a period in the year during which the waters of the bay are just as safe for navigation as the waters of the Gulf of St. Lawrence.[13]

After hearing numerous witnesses with both favourable and unfavourable opinions as to the viability of the route, the Canadian government approved the sum of $30,000.00 (in 1884) for the ". . . expenses of an Expedition (by water) to Hudson's Bay, to test the practicability of the route for commercial purposes."[14] The "Hudson's Bay Expedition" became the responsibility of the Department of Marine and Fisheries and it was given the mandate to test the waters of Hudson Strait and Hudson Bay and to set up Observation Stations in the Strait.[15] The Observation Stations were to be manned over the winter with the observers charged with recording the ice and meteorological conditions within their respec-

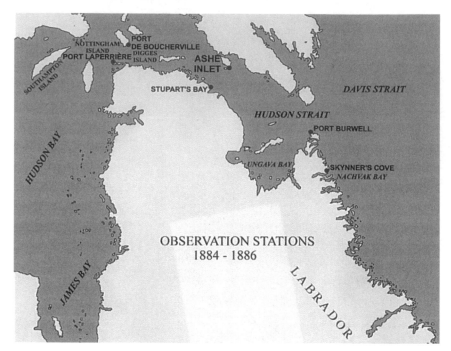

Map of Observation Stations, 1884-1886.

tive areas. In July 1884, the *S. S. Neptune* under the command of Lieut. A. R. Gordon steamed north and with its successful return, six Observation Stations in the Hudson Strait region had been established and staffed.

In May 1885, Lieut. A. R. Gordon – now commanding the *S. S. Alert* – again sailed north to test the ice conditions of the Strait, as well as to relieve the stationed men with new observers.[16] James W. Tyrrell was on board. Two years earlier, in 1883 at the age of fifteen, Tyrrell joined Dr. Robert Bell, Assistant Director of the Geological Survey of Canada, for a survey expedition of the Lake of the Woods area.[17] On the basis of this association, Tyrrell was well placed to be offered a position on the "Hudson's Bay Expedition" of 1885-1886 on which Robert Bell was the Geologist and Medical Officer.[18] Appointed as ". . . hydrographer, when moving in the open water, and meterological observer during the winter season,"[19] Tyrrell overwintered at the Ashe Inlet station on Big Island situated mid-length along the northern side of Hudson Strait.

The Observation Stations were closed at the end of the second winter season after which Tyrrell returned to Ontario.[20] In 1887, he established

James W. Tyrell at Hudson, Ontario, 1926.

himself in Hamilton, Ontario, as a Dominion Land Surveyor and well into his 60s, he conducted land surveys for both private and government concerns.[21]

For many years Tyrrell remained a strong advocate for opening up access to Hudson Bay and in 1905 he conducted a preliminary railway location survey from Prince Albert via the Saskatchewan, Nelson, and Churchill rivers to Fort Churchill.[22] In his own words:

. . . I am convinced that the sooner we provide ourselves with some adequate means of access and egress to this great realm of isolation the better it will be for the trade and commerce of our country, and for the thousands of those who may go up and possess themselves of 'Our Great Northern Heritage.'[23]

Finally, by 1929, harbour works, storehouses and grain elevators were in construction at Churchill[24] and, between August and October of 1932, the first shipments totalling 2,736,029-50 bushels of grain headed east out of Churchill harbour.[25]

During his posting at Ashe Inlet, Tyrrell became engaged in the Inuit culture and like many of his countrymen, through barter he was interested in acquiring Native articles. In a letter to his brother, Joseph, dated October 25, 1891, he makes reference to such a collection:

. . . I would be glad if you can bring along your little camera as I want to take photos of all the Eskimos' truck I have got.[26]

Tyrrell's interest, however, was not limited to collecting the exotic; he took an active interest in involving himself with the uses of Inuit technology. Although Tyrrell officially served as Hydrographer and Meterological Observer, while at Ashe Inlet he apparently adapted to Inuit ways and took great pride in his hunting prowess using Inuit technologies and techniques. His skill at throwing a harpoon is related in the following way:

I . . . had been diligently exercising myself in the art of harpoon throwing, and one day, having become quite an expert, was thus amusing myself when a party of natives came along. One of their number, doubtless supposing me to be a novice, stood up at what he thought a safe distance and said "Attay meloo-e-ak-took" (go ahead, throw). I, promptly accepting the challenge, hurled my harpoon, which made so straight for the astounded man's breast that he did not know which way to jump, and he barely got out of the way in time to save himself. As the shaft passed him and went crashing through a flour barrel, behind where he stood, his companions had a great laugh at his expense.[27]

This reference to Tyrrell's skill at handling the harpoon becomes quite significant in the context of the kayak and our attempt to ascertain the kayak's history. In the "Ashe Inlet Station Provision List" a "Kiak" is listed as part of the station's provisions.[28] It is, therefore, clear that, while stationed at Ashe Inlet, Tyrrell had access to a kayak. But the significance is greater, for in the following quotation Tyrrell relates his actual use of the kayak in concert with his newly learned harpooning skills:

. . . during the spring of 1886 when stationed at Big Island Hudson Strait, I fitted up my boat in proper shape with harpoons, lines, floats, and lances for hunting these creatures, and for a short time pursued the avocation of a

walrus hunter with success – using my rifle only to dispatch my victims after they had been secured by one or more harpoons with attached floats.[29]

At the completion of his posting on Ashe Inlet, the kayak accompanied Tyrrell south as is evident through reading the following 1891 citation again addressed to his brother Joseph:[30]

I will be very glad if you will bring up one of your cameras when you come and take or let me take pictures of my kyack (sic), *eskimo suits, hunting impliments* (sic) *etc.*

Eventually, the kayak was given to Dundurn Castle which in the earlier years of this century acted as Hamilton's museum. However, when Dundurn Castle was renovated to the period of Sir Allan MacNab, the kayak – out of place and context – was transferred to the Marine Museum of Upper Canada.

Tyrrell's attachment to the kayak was much more than simply a connection to a piece of used material culture; it created for him underpinnings of emotion and symbolized the essence of his Arctic experiences. Jean-Paul Sartre writes that the ". . . totality of my possessions reflects the totality of my being."[31] If this is valid, if what I am is what I have, then objects collected and possessed are an emanation of the self. In this light, the kayak and the other pieces Tyrrell collected were a soothing reminder and confirmation of his identity.

Tyrrell's reason to collect, however, was not solely to feed his sense of identification. The motivation to collect manifests itself in an additional interconnected layer identified here as "narrative support." Tyrrell possessed a clear notion that his collected artifacts held potential to illustrate papers and books, that is to say, as support for his written narratives.[32] The kayak also supported Tyrrell's unwritten narrative that was intended to be "read" by his surrounding public. And as we will learn in the following excerpt from an 1898 letter addressed to his brother, the unwritten narrative is troubling to current curatorial sensibilities:

I spent last Sunday at home and the old place was looking very pretty. I have my kyack (sic) *fixed up in the front yard and of course it is a great ornament to the place. I washed it out with a solution of corrosion-sublimate and William took the contract of painting it – and because of his peculiar touch was making a very fancy job; but Fannie thought it should be done plain and so went over his work.*[33]

With this rather unnerving image of a lawn ornament – although one that stroked Tyrrell's identity – the notion that artifacts possess many histories over time is clearly underlined. From Inuit manufacture to station provision, from Tyrrell's hunting equipment to artifact as memory aid, and from lawn ornament to museum object, the kayak has manifested different, or separate realities through time.

It is to the last reality – that is the museum context – that we now turn for it is in this context that the kayak reclaims its original ancestry. An anthropological perspective towards material culture illuminates objects within their cultural contexts. Objects and cultural contexts are subsumed within a system termed technology that is comprised of a web of materials, procedures, social representations and knowledge. In this light, if we can strip away the image of a lawn ornament, the notion that it supported a Euro-Canadian identity, and glaze over the chalked graffiti it bears on its skin cover, the kayak then rises like a phoenix from the ashes. It becomes the exquisitely crafted boat that it is and a piece of material culture constructed by Inuit men and women that is well adapted to function within Inuit sea mammal hunting technologies.

It is of interest to refer to Tyrrell's writing when giving consideration to kayak construction. The kayak frame is ". . . neatly made from all sorts of scraps of wood . . ." and ". . . the numerous pieces are all lashed together, especially with seal or deer skin, though sometimes, and preferably, with whalebone." Tyrrell continues:

The frame having been completed, it is then covered with green skins, either of seal or deer . . . with the hair removed. The skins are joined to each other as they are put on, by double water-tight seams, and are drawn tightly over the frame, so that when they dry they become very hard and as tight as a drum head.[34]

Tyrrell's description of kayak construction is quite accurate and it is particularly enlightening due to his reference to "whalebone" lashings. In this context, the term "whalebone" refers to the slats of baleen that end in the fine fringes that give baleen whales the ability to sieve plankton from the sea water. Significantly, in addition to sealskin lashings, Tyrrell's kayak includes lashings of baleen.

The kayak measures 656.5 cm. in length with a 63.5 cm. beam. At its greatest beam, aft of the cockpit coaming, the depth to sheer line measures 22.0 cm. (Table 1). With the kayak's greatest beam occurring aft of the cockpit, the kayak is given a full stern providing good stability and ample carrying capacity both below and above deck. The kayak exhibits a deep forefoot and a relatively flat bottom which at its widest beam begins to rise off the level to an upswept stern. This combination of deep forefoot and upswept stern are diagnostic attributes of the eastern Canadian Arctic kayak.[35] Well adapted for sea mammal hunting, the deep bow tends to grip the water while the stern, designed to generate lower frictional resistance, swings into line with the wind.[36] In winds and wave-torn seas, where the hunter waits for targeted animals to appear, the ability of the kayak to weathercock bow-to-stern naturally positions the kayaker in the most stable position.

Table 1. Maximum Dimensions (cm)

Length	656.5
Foreward Deck Length	338.1
After Deck Length	256.5
Beam	63.4
Depth to Sheer	22.0
Stem Height from Baseline	42.2
Stern Height from Baseline	18.8
Coaming Length	60.0
Coaming Breadth	49.3
Coaming Height from Baseline - Foreward End	38.8
Coaming Height from Baseline - Aft End	33.5

Dimensions of the Kayak.

In cross-section the kayak has a flattened bottom with flared sides that are slightly rounded rather than sharply chined. The flared sides and flat bottom will provide the kayak with excellent stability and the long narrow bow will gracefully cut the waves. The depth of the bow will provide excellent front buoyancy and the rise at the cockpit will be effective for shedding any water that may wash over the deck.

Equipped for the hunt, the kayak would have carried a harpoon resting with the point facing the stern along the starboard side of the coaming. At mid-coaming, the distal end of the harpoon shaft would have laid upon a harpoon rest which unfortunately is now missing. The two deck straps immediately in front of the coaming would have held a harpoon line rack upon which rested the coiled harpoon line. In addition, the straps may have held a furred skin to dampen the sound of water drips cascading off of the paddle. The harpoon line, attached to a toggling harpoon head and coiled on the harpoon rack, would have passed back along the starboard side of the coaming to a sealskin float positioned on the deck behind the paddler. Once the targeted animal was struck, the float attached by line to the harpoon head was thrown from the deck to act as both a drag and a marker. Finally, the last major hunting implement would have been a lance, held to the kayak by the aft deck strap, and used to deliver the final death blows once the animal had tired and the kayaker had positioned himself into striking distance.

The final implement to be discussed, and one that engenders great intrigue, is a narrow length of baleen fashioned to form a straight base with upright arms that was found in the kayak's hull. The current thought is this implement functioned as a rack attached in an upright position on the kayak's aft deck. This interpretation is based upon a drawing by Captain G. F. Lyon of a Hudson Strait kayak that illustrates the narrative of William Parry's Second Voyage of 1821 to discover the Northwest Passage.[37] In this drawing the artist illustrates such racks on both the fore and aft decks. If this interpretation is correct, this baleen example gives credence to the racks rendered in Lyon's drawing. It is thought that the upright arms of the rack would have prevented equipment and perhaps slain seals from sliding off of the deck. This implement would be especially useful if the weight of the seal in combination with heavy weather caused the aft deck to be awash.

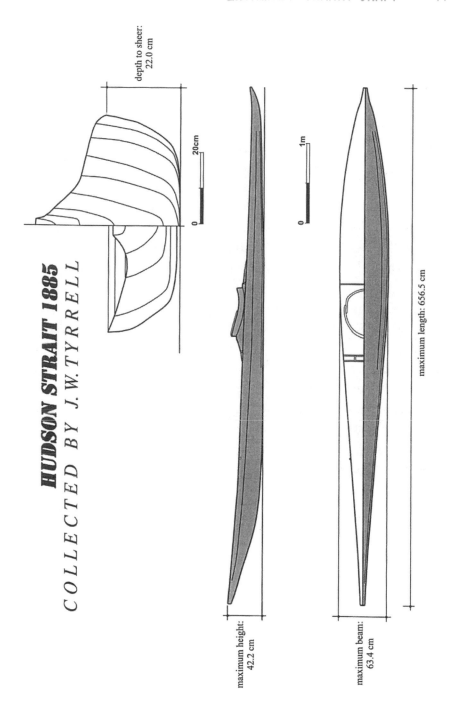

depth to sheer: 22.0 cm

20cm

1m

HUDSON STRAIT 1885

COLLECTED BY J.W.TYRRELL

maximum length: 656.5 cm

maximum height: 42.2 cm

maximum beam: 63.4 cm

Drawings of the Hudson Bay Kayak collected by James Tyrell, 1885.

The rediscovery of the Tyrrell kayak and its contexualization through written sources provides us with an early, documented specimen that can now act as a base-line piece to which other lesser known, or less understood, kayaks can be compared. Throughout its 112 year existence the kayak has moved through various histories and has miraculously survived numerous traumas to come full circle and rise again, to take on yet another history as a very rare representation of a cultural complex that has now been gone for many decades.

Tyrrell, who, we are led to believe, learned to become an accomplished kayak paddler and hunter, referred to kayaks as being "extremely cranky" in the hands of novices, but by experts they were commonly used "even in very rough water."[38] We can expect that Tyrrell considered himself to be an "expert," such that he viewed the possession of his "cranky craft" as an extension of himself and its collection as significant for the telling of his narratives. From our perch a century in passing, we are indebted to Tyrrell and to others like him who expended the energy and funds to collect so that we need not depend upon their narratives. Without the specimens, and without the museums that curate them, we would be left to ponder descriptions and artistic renderings that are potentially erroneous in nature. It is the specimen, and the task of contexualization, that grounds realities. Although in this one kayak the histories are diverse, it is this very diversity that characterizes history itself and, by looking through a wide-angle lens, the kayak comes to symbolize not only Tyrrell's, but our own identities.[39]

BARKLESS BARQUES

Eugene Arima

For recreational canoeing a sense of past development can add a wider, or longer, dimension to enrichen the already rewarding experience. At the most basic one might ask when man started canoeing, a simple enough question, yet not one we can answer with certainty, at least not today. Still, the matter of ultimate origin is worth considering and has been discussed before, for example, in the writing of James Hornell who begins with floats and rafts.[1]

About 40,000 to 50,000 years ago the Upper Palaeolithic begins, a florescence with better technology, art and expansion of the human geographical range into three new continents: Australia and the Americas. That the Bering Strait was dry for most of the recent ice age (Wisconsin, 90-10,000 Before Present) need not necessarily entail boats, though it was inundated twice at about 40-35,000 and 12-10,000 B.P. because, of course, the water could freeze too. The Torres Strait between New Guinea and Australia, however, calls for seaworthy boats since at the least extensive it was still about 100 km across and, of course, never froze. Jacques Cinq Mars, the archaeologist of early man at the Canadian Museum of Civilization, says that to populate a continent takes more than a chance castaway Adam and Eve couple. Rather he sees groups migrating by more than clumsy rafts and repeatedly moving back and forth across Torres Strait. Furthermore, if decent boats, perhaps dugout canoes, were around to enable the populating of Australia, they likely would already have been in existence for some time. But how much farther back in time is hard to say for lack of a prominent marker such as the arrival in Australia or the location of artifactual remains. The Neanderthals, who may be distinguished from around 200,000 years ago, did reach northern regions where watercraft seem essential for movement and subsistence, but whether they might have had more than simple creations for the occasion is hard to say. As for our Erectus ancestors, developed boats seem less likely. In the broad perspective, canoeing appears to be a relatively recent human experience.

Within the above overall framework, this essay will be mainly on northern skin-covered watercraft concentrating on design development, what little seems evident. Bark canoe design is covered well enough by many paddlers, makers and thinkers about the craft. Western carved canoes, the other major native watercraft category for Canada, are discussed rather sketchily due to the shallow time depth of available relevant data and still only nascent stage of developmental study. Although examined here alongside skin boats, these dugouts, for the most part, are not to be regarded as closely related.

The coracle is the ancestor of the umiak or open skin boat of the Arctic. It comes in a variety of sizes, materials, and shapes as has been excellently described by Hornell.[2] Occurring in the New World, notably as the Plains bull boat, as well as in Eurasia, the coracle is undoubtedly old, perhaps going back to at least the above mentioned circa 40,000 B.P. period of human global expansion. It is easy to make since the framework is of thin branches readily cut with a small knife blade, while a large skin for the cover of the typical small model would be available from hunting for a living. The gunwale, the main rigidity member, if need be is made of two or more branches bundled together or as repeated rings. The framework is similar to that for a wigwam type shelter but shallower, and indeed in Ireland is constructed upside down with the branches first planted in the ground in a circle then bent over allowing the frames, transverse and longitudinals, to be distinguished for a square latticework. Weighting with rocks flattens the bottom for stability.

Round coracles as in common conception do occur, for example the Plains bull boat, but more often they are elongated to some degree for better handling. Typically paddling is by draw strokes at the bow, often in figure 8 motion. When the power is off line, a circular coracle tends to swivel, even going round and round. In comparison, the Welsh coracle of our British-derived consciousness is a model of sophistication, its somewhat trapezoidal shape with a raked rounded bow, quite straight sides and stern and comparative deepness, being efficient for the river fishing purpose of the design. The small 1 x 1.3m size is set by the single horse or cow hide covering. It could be argued that the roundish wide shape of the coracle arose in part from being based on a single large skin. In other materials bigger coracles exist, like the 2-3m Iraqi *quffa* ferry for the Tigris, really a huge woven basket of close-set withes caulked with bitumen. Basketry coracles also occur sporadically in India and, as an isolated case, in Tonkin where it is an elongated egg shape. In Tibet are varied yak skin coracles, circular, oval, sub-rectangular and rectangular, again used for crossing rivers where bridges are few.

The Irish *curach* or curragh, often termed "canoe," is a sea-going super coracle. And there are traditions, true or not, of voyages across the sea to a paradise, the most famous being St. Brendan's of perhaps A.D. 519-24.[3] He probably visited Iceland, if not Canada, and since, supposedly, his three curraghs each carried 20 men, the design could have been quite big, possibly 10-12m long. Recent curraghs range from 3-6m, with pointed bow and square stern, but the hull framework preserves the coracle's latticework construction. The numerous stringers tied over U-shaped ribs are curved up at the stern to end at the straight top crosspiece. Incidentally, "coracle," "curragh" and "cwrwgl" (Welsh) are really the same word.

UMIAK

At the other end of Eurasia, the coracle takes to the Pacific in Kamchatka as the Koryak *gatwaat*,[5] keeping gunwales bent round at the ends but changing in bottom construction to that of the flat-bottomed, hard-chined *umiaq* (Inuit) or umiak in common spelling. Instead of the curragh's fine latticework, there is an internal keel, or principal centre longitudinal, which bends up into end posts for a strongly raked bow and more moderate stern and is flanked by a pair of chine stringers spread by crosspieces and fitted into the sides of the keel at the ends, thus defining the characteristic flat bottom.

Photograph of an Inuit umiak taken by A.P. Low of the Geological Survey of Canada at Wakeham Bay, Quebec, about 1880.

The Unangan or Aleut umiak, the *nigilax*, also has the gunwale curved round at the stern while the bow is pointed. A scale framework drawing fortunately is available of a circa 1805 example from the Alaska peninsula.[6] With the attestation of the Koryak and Aleut designs, also of the South Alaska-Kodiak ones not shown, the umiak's development from the typically round-ended coracle is clear, and there is no need to derive it from the rectangular Tibetan form shaped by four straight gunwale poles as does Hornell.[7] Where other umiaks often have the gunwales ending separately in hand-grip horns, development independent of Tibet seems likely. In southwest Alaska in the Kuskokwim-Nunivak Island region, there was an umiak with a pointed bow and a wide stern with two short gunwale horns,[8] a combination also occuring in a prehistoric Saint Lawrence Island kayak model of late Punuk Culture of A.D. 1100-1500.[9]

Large *gatwaat* and *nigilax* seem to have been about 9-10m long, the former proportionately broad at 2.5m beam while the latter is only half as wide. Used for whaling, they can be thought of as comparable in size to the fur trade canoe. Large umiaks from Chukotka to Greenland are commonly 11-12m. Very visible on the narrow *nigilax* is its "bifid bow" with a pointed top projection separated by a notch from a bigger convexly bulging cutwater blade below, a feature shared with the Kodiak Island and South Alaska umiaks. To a much less developed degree, the bulge sometimes occurs in Greenland where it is described as the "chin bow."[10] The latter seems an independent development for a sharper bow and shows how the pronounced form likely arose. In the bifid form, the separation of the wider top increases the hollow flam under the gunwales to throw off spray and ride waves. Since even the plain umiak ends, whether rounded or squared, are wider on top than below to form flam in the skin cover, the umiak appears the likely source of the Aleut bifid kayak bow to be discussed further below.

Umiaks appear to be influential in kayak design, which is natural since the same individuals built both. More constant in form over time, they may have provided stable reference points. Bering Sea kayak design in particular seems to owe a lot to umiak design. For example, the more or less upright stern likely comes from the umiak (see figure 1) in which it makes volumetric sense with the steersman *umialik* or captain right at the stern.

Figure 1: Sketch of umiak from East Cape.

Time of development is a difficult question with the umiak. Aleut authority, William Laughlin thinks the umiak and the kayak developed not in the Bering Strait region commonly associated with Eskimo origins but farther off in Asia, which brings to mind the Okhost Sea area again.[11] Laughlin links this Eskimoid skin boat development to the Eskimo-Aleut split circa 8-9,000 B.P., which he postulates on genetic, archaeological, and linguistic grounds – for example, after the last Valders ice advance of about 11-10,000 B.P. At the latest, the Aleuts must have had skin boats by around 4-5,000 B.P. when they crossed the wider, ice-free channels to populate their string of islands from Alaska. The Old Whaling Culture of 1800-1500 B.C. found at Cape Krusenstern, north of Kotzebue Sound, Alaska, must have had umiaks if not kayaks too.[12] As archaeological evidence accumulates, better guesses will become possible concerning the antiquity of skin boats as well as the dugouts and bark canoes whose beginnings seem vaguer still.

KAYAK

Kayaks and umiaks go together, complementary sister craft historically and prehistorically. The Greenland Inuit ("Karaallit") skin boat scholar, H.C. Petersen, cites an oral tradition that kayaks were first open on top, the same as small umiaks, becoming closed in later.[13] Indeed, little one-man umiaks only about 2.5-3m long are known, easily carried and gotten in and out of for game retrieval in floe edge hunting. Small kayaks for the purpose also exist, though more rarely because for all the trouble of building, one may as well have the more versatile full-size craft.

It is easy to think that the kayak developed out of the coracle as did the umiak. Aside from the flat-bottomed East Canadian Arctic design, kayak stringers are not usually brought in at their ends to join onto the sides of the keel in umiak fashion. If not for the decked-in top, the kayak is structurally closer to the coracle than is the umiak, with generally more numerous stringers laid over the many ribs in square latticework fashion. Although it is suppositional, one can conceive of the one-man coracle being built narrower and narrower for speed, handling and seaworthiness, until the cover was laced together, rather than to the framework after being brought down over the gunwale ring. The addition of the manhole ring or cockpit coaming would complete the transformation as exemplified by the Koryak kayak of around Kamchatka, Penshina Bay; it is short and wide with a very large cockpit hoop. The cross section is a V and the bow pointed, but sometimes the stern is rounded, perhaps continuing the oval coracle shape. Indeed, it is possible that the hull cross-section originally was rounded rather than V, since the earliest artifactual remains of kayaks indicate a rounded section with a flattening on the bottom for stability. The V would help for tracking and rougher conditions with the short wide shallow Koryak design, which we are fortunate to have in considering kayak development.

From southeast Disko Bay, West Greenland, at the Qeqertasussuk site comes, possibly, the earliest direct evidence to date for kayaks in what appears to be a light U-shaped rib 35cm across by 22cm high, a size which could fit in the bow or stern quarter depending on hull configuration.[12] If truly a kayak rib, this artifact of the Saqqaq Culture and dated to circa 2200 B.C., indicates an essentially flat bottom, perhaps slightly V, if the keel strip was deeper than the chine stringers, and rounding up to flat sides. While such inference may be tenuous, it does fit expectations for the early kayak cross-section, presuming a desire for stability.

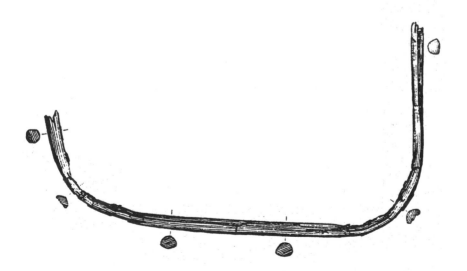

Figure 2: Sketch of a possible 4,000 year old kayak rib, Saqqaq Culture, West Greenland, c. 35 x 22 cm.

The earliest known complete kayak forms come much later. These are the finely made carved ivory models found in the Ekven site near Uelen on the Asian side of Bering Strait.[15] Of the Okvik-Old Bering Sea Culture continuum dated c. 300 B.C.-A.D. 500, the design is a complete surprise with horizontally forked ends (see figure 3). The bottom is a shallow arch rounding smoothly into flared sides. Above, the deck stringers are raised, perhaps being laid over deck beams fitted high at the top of the gunwale strips by shouldered ends in notches as one finds in the historical Inland Chukchi kayak, evidently a lineal descendant.[16] Whether the deck lathes were bare or skinned is unknown, but having them raised permits a level deck supported by crosspieces for the purpose of carrying loads. On the afterdeck of one of the models is a harpoon float of two sealskins. Such paired double floats were used until recently in East Greenland for hunting big sea mammals.[17] The cockpit hoop is egg-shaped, with a wider and flatter end aft as in the Punuk Culture model, discussed below, and also historical East Canadian Arctic kayaks. One should expect continuities in native watercraft design over two millenia, given the regard for tradition. But the surprising face in the cockpit of the carving is, to my mind, the nicest piece of continuity in design for it recurs in an ivory King Island kayak carving, collected by Edward Nelson on Saint Lawrence Island in the late nineteenth century. This carving is an amulet attached inside the real craft.[18] On a long paddle across the open sea one would be happy to have the kayak spirit along.

Saint Lawrence Island lies a good 200 km south of Bering Strait but only 65 km from the Asia mainland and has been culturally close to Chukotka for millenia. West Alaska is about 200 km away. From the big island's Northwest Cape come four important model kayaks from different periods of the Punuk Culture, which after a transitional century developing out of Old Bering Sea is dated A.D. 600-900 for Early Punuk, 900-1100 for full phase, and 1100-1500 for Late or even historic contact. Obtained in 1930-31 by Henry B. Collins,[19] they come from midden mounds left at different beach levels as the settlement, now Gambel, shifted over time to stay by the receding sea. The oldest model is an Early Punuk wooden kayak from the Miyowagh midden site with rising pointed ends and a round bottom.[20] The deck is flat and undetailed. The plain form contrasts with the rich Old Bering Sea model described above,

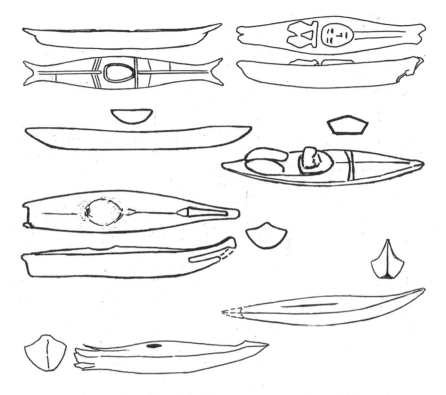

Figure 3: Prehistoric kayak models (diagrammatic not in scale) from the top and left to right. Old Bering Sea 300 B.C. – 500 A.D.; same with double float; Early Punuk A.D. 900-1100; Thule A.D. 1250-1450; Birnik A.D. 600-900.

yet could be related when considering overall cultural continuity. Curiously, one can see more of a connection to the historical Maritime Chukchi kayak with its multichine cross-section and similar ends.[21] The Chukchi acquired both kayaks and umiaks relatively recently from the Asiatic Eskimo.

The Miyowagh midden site also revealed a bark model double float kayak[22] and a bark model umiak like an elongated diamond when seen in plan view. This prismatic shape was, evidently, an Eskimo symbolic convention for boat and also can be seen in the kayak model. As well, two upright model wood busts wear peaked hats like recent Bering Sea kayakers.

The next full phase Punuk kayak model of ivory from the Ievoghiyoq site, with a kayaker figure, is of special interest to us in Canada because the design appears to be the source of the flat-bottomed hard-chined East Canadian Arctic kayaks and also the Greenland kayaks (both of which had similar cross-sections until the 1600s.) This ivory model has a flat bottom and is bordered by hard chines from a sudden turn up into the flared slab-like sides.[23] Though the hull deepens slightly forward, the bow stays low. The sharp ends are only moderately raked. While the model's bow is not yet high, the aftset cockpit hoop is deep and elongated with a straight back as in the historical East Canadian design. Then there is the double hunting float again to explain how it reached East Greenland. The linkage with these latter designs seems probable because, perhaps due to hostilities, some Punuk people migrated across the Bering Strait around the 10th century,[24] met with the Birnik Culture people in North Alaska and then formed part of the Thule Culture expansion eastward, as well as westward. In fact, Thule Culture is simply ancestral Inuit and, until lately, was thought by archaeologists to have spread in a fairly monolithic manner, but now varying migrating groups are becoming distinguished. From an ethnological perspective, Inuit groups cling strongly to their identity over generations so that a bunch of Punuk migrants could be expected to preserve their ways, including kayak design, through a sojourn among Birnik people who had a different multi-chine model.[25]

From Late Punuk is a strange ivory kayak model from the Seklowaghyaget site.[26] It has a square umiak-like stern with short gunwale horns and a rising pointed bow which is pierced for a length vertically and horizontally to show the keel and gunwale strips. Behind the aftset depression indicating the cockpit is a double float, the only form seen on these Punuk models and perhaps indicative of walrus hunting and whaling. The possible link to historical craft is even stranger in that the closest ethnographic piece, at least to our knowledge, is a nineteenth century model umiak from Nunivak Island or the Kuskokwim River in Southwest Alaska. With pointed bow and wide square stern, this umiak carries five hunters, has a seal aboard, and on the side, a painted *palraiyuk*, the Kuskokwim delta dragon. A logical development would be that the Southwest Alaska umiak lost the rounded stern of its South Alaska-Kodiak neighbours and influenced Bering Strait kayak design. The Seklowaghyaget model has the deeply ridged deck of the historic West Alaskan kayaks, a similar multichine lower hull section with round bottom turning smoothly into flaring bulged sides, and the skeg effect at the stern.

Last to be cited from Saint Lawrence Island is a two man ivory model kayak with two sets of double floats fore and aft. This was excavated from Old Gambel which was occupied into the nineteenth century.[27] Of the two cockpit depressions, the forward one is small suggesting that a boy sat there. Hence, the kayak may represent a trainer. The bottom cross section remains flat with hard chines and the low sharp ends are moderately raked exemplifying the continuity of kayak design from the classic full Punuk period. In the twentieth century, however, only the umiak continued on Saint Lawrence Island, no doubt due to its superiority for local hunting once modern American firearms became general.

Another archaeological model kayak specimen to be mentioned is a wooden Thule one from the A.D. 1250-1450 Clachan site in West Coronation Gulf.[28] Besides being flat-bottomed with hard chines and flared sides, it is deeper forward and has a high rising prow. The plan outline is prismatic following conventional abstraction. The deck is flat but lacks detail other than an aftset midline incision which might have been for the purpose of killing magically, whether to send the craft into the afterlife or to do someone in. Indeed, prehistoric kayak models may well have been more often made for ritualistic reasons than just for play. Most important in terms of design development is the fact that here we have the East Canadian Arctic/ previous Greenland kayak, seven centuries or so ago, over by Dolphin and Union Strait. It follows that the narrow multichines of the Copper, Nattilik, Caribou, and Igloolik (to the late nineteenth century) Inuit came later than the flat-bottom kayaks.

There is more prehistoric kayak design evidence like the Thule models and engraved images from the Canadian Arctic and Greenland; however, their coverage would be too time-and-space consuming. Also detailed discussion of the multitude of historical designs in developmental terms could be almost a book, one still to be written. As an example of the complex trends involved, as well as their often vague discernment, I have given a chart (Figure 4) of western skin boat forms, mainly Aleut and in aircraft spotter type silhouettes for simplicity of representation.

While the Aleut kayak designs have been partly ordered chronologically, developmental sequences did not happen uniformly throughout the

Figure 4: Some Aleut design relations.

very long island chain. Some more specific remarks may be offered for the chart figures, starting at the top left. The first is the already cited Jochelson illustration of a 105cm (41") Koryak umiak framework with the round gunwale rail ends and broad proportions recalling coracles. To its right, switching to the silhouettes, is a 3.2m x 71cm (10' 6" x 28") Koryak kayak with a rounded rather than pointed stern.[29] The hull section is one big V for tracking with the short wide craft. Next are the silhouettes of the 9.7m x 1.25m (32' x 49") Aleut umiak from Korukin's scale framework drawing in von Langsdorff.[30] Its stern is round at the gunwale as in the Koryak umiak, but the bow is pointed and the proportions much sleeker. The bottom is a V from the strong deep keel timber. Most eye-catching is the bow notch in profile with the big bulging cutwater below as already discussed. Beneath the bow end is a swift Aleut kayak from Akun Island at the east end of the Aleutian chain, collected in 1845 but preserving the open "Jaws" form of bifid bow.[31] It is 5.8m x 43.4cm (19' x 17"). Back on the left of the chart is a conjectural reconstruction based on a little carved wooden model from a burial cave of the breathtaking Islands of the Four Mountains, dating perhaps to the 1400s. Although inexact, it is included to show that the famous Aleut bifid kayak bow, for strong top flare, came later and that the wide-shouldered stern for extra stability and wave push from aft had had a very short blade projection. Below it is a model bow piece from Buldir/ Round Island in the Western Aleutians radiocarbon dated to around 1650.[32] The notch is present, open and with the bottom projection not level underneath, as in the 1799 James Shields' drawing from Unalaska shown below in silhouettes.[33] Shields' drawing seems stylized and not entirely trustworthy, but it is included partly due to the attention paid by baidarkaphiles today. His oddly dipped cockpit hoop has been replaced by the usual level form. He provides no cross-section, nor any scale and the size drawn is perhaps too large, though based on a guess for a reasonable beam.

To continue down the left side, we come to silhouettes of the 1805 Korukin framework drawing of an only slightly later Unalaska Aleut kayak.[34] It was 5.5m x 53.3cm (18' x 21"). Points of developmental interest are the closed "Loon's beak" bifid bow and the growth in stern blade projection. The closed bow form eliminated the need to tie a line or stick across the previous wide notch to keep out debris.

Returning to the right side of the chart we have below the 1845 Akun *iqyax*, a Kodiak Island bow piece given to Professor Laughlin as an archaeological specimen but, apparently, comparatively recent. It shows the likely source of the modern Aleut kayak bow with the bottom projection curved up over the top widened part. For the same reason a 4.3m x 65.6cm (14' 3" x 26") Kodiak kayak is shown underneath.[35] Then there is another prettier kind of raised bottom horn bow from the mid-nineteenth century or earlier, perhaps on an Aleut *iqyax* of 5.3m x 49.6cm (17' 4" x 19 1/2").[36] We end on the bottom right with silhouettes of a 1934 Aleut from Atka, 5.1m x 51.8cm (16' 9" x 20"), the well-known "Lowie Museum" specimen.³⁷ Obviously, however, much remains unsaid about kayak design development.

WESTERN CARVED CANOES

Unlike the skin boats which have substantial if sporadic prehistoric evidence enabling developmental interpretations from some fairly tangible starting points, even if conclusions go astray, the western carved canoes of the Northwest Coast and Plateau culture areas lack comparable archaeological information. The preservation of organic remains such as carved models is much poorer than in the Arctic area; indeed, the available models of past forms are very recent ones collected by Europeans only since the later eighteenth century. Archaeological study generally is much less developed than in the North. Consequently, interpretations of western dugout development become highly conjectural when extended past the brief period of European records. Nevertheless, a few remarks may be ventured to stimulate enquiry in this direction which will surely be taken farther by the next generation of watercraft students as regional archaeology finally flowers in the 21st century.³⁸

As with the skin boats, dugout development proceeds by a multitude of interactive factors such as available materials and tools, hydrodynamic considerations, applications, aesthetics, and other sociocultural aspects. The list can be extended easily by historical forces such as foreign influence, slow stylistic drift over time, and quicker mutation by accidental or idiosyncratic innovation – in other words, all the factors involved in analyzing sociocultural processes in general. If canoes, or other artifacts, are approached in such terms, the long neglected academic study of material culture will be brought into the mainstream of ethnological method and theory.

Trees, particularly Red cedar and Sitka spruce, obviously are the fundamental material for western dugouts. Since these trees grow tall and straight, material length is not too much of a problem except perhaps for big canoes (at times, say over 11m long) since the smaller end must have enough thickness. Width amidships is more often problematical since even for a moderate size canoe, say 6-10m long, a beam of at least 1.25m is often desirable at sea. There are narrower designs, of course, like the Westcoast (aka Nootka, Nuu-chah-nulth) 7m sealing canoes which were about 1m wide (traditional, not commercial fur sealing model). But for 1.25m beam amidships, the tree has to be a large one and while such were not uncommon, good accessible stands were not everywhere. When a 1.5m or better beam was wanted, as for a Westcoast whaling canoe of even moderate 8-10m length or the general use 12m moving canoe, the upper end of the tree range was approached.

For the now extinct super-size war canoe from 14 to 18m, the biggest tree was used. Thus, given the scarcity of this material and the need for great manpower in both the building process and operation, the extra large war canoes were a minority. Instead, smaller versions of the war canoe as well as ordinary big canoes were regularly pressed into service for hostilities. The manpower requirements of a big war canoe could be met given the comparatively large population concentrations possible on the Northwest Coast with its rich economic base of expertly exploited marine food resources. Through social organization the human resources could be marshalled for large undertakings by the Chiefs. Thus, the super canoe, wide as well as long, could and did develop. Ostentation was a prime motivating factor, too, in the prestige ridden social system.

Even in just canoe-making terms, pride is high, and individuals strive for excellence, which sometimes furthers design. For example, trying to outdo another for size, a Barkley Sound builder joined two cedars side by side to get about 3m beam.[39] More often, width is increased by heat spreading the hull. The greatest development of the technique is toward the north end of the area where trees are not so large. There, the Tlingit tribes hollow the log through a narrow top opening to keep an extra amount of wood for the sides along the main length. Before spreading, the hull has a strange appearance with the sides curving over on top to a slot-like opening wider toward the ends, since the sides have to be freed.

Another more readily remarked technique for gaining width is to build up the sides with added pieces. West Coasters do so integrally,[40] but the Tlingit attach a gunwale plank on the outside the length of the main hull body: "Get every inch you can," as Qwi:stox, my canoe carving teacher, would say. Freeboard is gained as well. This Tlingit addition modifies shape and becomes a stylistic feature, even carved integrally into smaller one piece hulls, a case of practical form turning aesthetic for more than expected design influence. As a plank it also adds strength with its straight grain. A weak point in dugout hulls is where the sides narrow into the sharp ends because the grain runs out. Consequently, with readily split wood like the red cedar commonly used, the sides cannot be turned in too abruptly because less of the grain will be in the thinned-down hull wall. A more oblique approach allows for greater grain length within the wall, encouraging hull design which narrows gradually to the ends with finer lines. The other solution of a thicker hull wall makes for a heavy canoe, of course, but can be found in a few blunt ended river designs in which the extra weight is more tolerable than at sea, for example, by poling. It is worth noting that in skin boat construction, fine lines develop from the wood material used as well, but in a different way from its gradual bending properties.

The Northwest Coast war canoes draw special attention with their impressive size, exotic appearance and the romance of Indian wars at sea.[41] The first European historical records of the later 18th century, as well as native oral traditions, note two major kinds: the Manka (Kwakiutl term) of the Westcoasters and Kwakiutl (now Kwakwaka'wakw) and the so-called "Head" canoe of the peoples to the north, for example, Haida, Tsimshian and Tlingit. They appear to be designed from different base models for different fighting tactics. The Manka seems to be a variation on the so-called "Nootka" or "Southern" canoe of the Westcoasters of Vancouver Island and Washington State, its ends being brought up high. The bow, especially, is altered by widening into a shield against arrows, pierced for shooting as shown in Paul Kane's mid-19th century illustrations, which likely rely on models and recollections. The stern is strongly raked rather than near vertical, which would have aided manoeuverability by decreasing submerged length in an extra large canoe and by enabling the canoe to go backward better, as might be done after landing bow first when attacking a village, again as pictured by Kane.[42] Whether the raked stern recalls an earlier West Coast form cannot be said, at least not at present. There is always the possibility that relevant prehistoric evidence will surface on this as, indeed, for other design features. Since the upright stern is an extreme form, it may be expected that a raked form preceded it, though this is not to say the other Nootka models developed from the Manka.

Another comparison with the Head canoe is possible in that the Nootka stern resembles the former's bow in profile. Whether or not the two are related, the Nootka stern was used for ramming, an action which would nicely account for the Head canoe bow form. But the Head canoe is readily derived from the so-called Sitka or Spruce canoe of the same northern sector, both lacking flam or hollowing at the ends since they remain narrow blades on top. It is logical that for ramming, the upright cutwater edge extends down into the water because if the blade is raised, as in Lieut. Blondela's sketch of a big Tlingit canoe when la Perouse visited Lituya Bay in 1786,[43] it can precariously override the other canoe. Ramming was done broadside to break the comparatively eggshell-thin hull. The extra immersed bow length impeded turning, but the raised stern helped swing the back around. Windage was doubtless adjusted fore and aft, and the 1786 Tlingit canoe, discussed above, has a couple of holes in each big blade presumably relieving side pressure. It remains to be confirmed whether, with the leading bow edge down to the water, the extra immersion added speed via a longer waterline. No doubt speed was sought, the wide tipped model Head canoe paddles noted by Holm obviously being for driving power, not hunting silence.[44]

Both the Head canoe and Manka disappeared early in the 19th century, made obsolete by firearms. Only models remain of them, albeit with the ends exaggerated half as large as in reality. Variation is evident for the Head canoes at least, with the Tlingit ends being more pointed at the top corner than the Haida from greater rake and top slope. But the 1786 Tlingit canoe has squared ends in profile, perhaps an older form and indicating stylistic drift. An end design trend is better documented in regular Southern canoes starting with the low extended bows in John Webber's 1778 drawings for Captain James Cook at "Nootka" and, oddly, no higher head at the stern.[45] Duff's favoured early model has an extra high stern together with the only moderately rising low bow.[46] Photographs from the 1860s show the bow still low. In later 19th century photos bows become higher. Both higher and shorter bowed, the fine Cape Flattery canoes take the trend to its logical conclusion in the rough sea conditions there.

Since the early 19th century, Northern and Southern canoe ends widen on top for the flam which throws off waves and can even plane on them when plunging. This hollowing which is carried smoothly to amidships where it becomes slight, is considered very important for proper performance and not just visual style.

As remarked in the skin boats section, the umiak ends with their wide tops develop a nice hollow in the upper sides and the Aleut kayak ends are deliberately designed to be similar. Wilson Duff related the Nootka canoe to the umiak, even supposing that one of the latter voyaged south to start both whaling and the flat-bottomed canoe form.[47] A model in the British Columbia Provincial Museum was particularly influential for his inference because the inner sides had a wavy line painted on which looked like the umiak skin lashing.[48] Since Nootkan whaling is only attested for the past thousand years[49] (while Eskimos have whaled several times longer) Duff's conjecture should not be dismissed out of hand even though chances for such an umiak voyage seem remote. For the moment, however, it seems safer to regard the well-developed coastal designs as adaptations to the sea of simpler forms such as the river dugouts.

Two main riverine kinds, the broad-ended "shovel nose" and the sharp-ended, may have developed longer and higher cutwaters with a wide top and flam from the first and without from the second, as in the Manka and Head canoes respectively. When the extended cutwater is a narrow blade on top, the convexly spread hull sides coming in to meet it naturally curve concavely the other way for horizontally hollow ends. With the ends wide on top, the hull sides tend to stay wider below for no waterline hollowing as in the Nootka canoes where it is consciously avoided. Such is the expectation, but, as usual, exceptions occur as with those Coast Salish canoes which have moderately wide end tops for flam and also waterline hollowing, more readily achieved with their rounded bottoms. The broad-ended river dugouts extend from northern California, where the Yurok and Karok make particularly blunt canoes, to the Salish region up to the Fraser and Bella Coola rivers. They are good for poling, standing in or on the roomy ends which sometimes have a flat lip as in the square-ended "punt" canoes. Heading into current, blunt ends do not veer off to the side as readily as sharp ones and yet resistance to progress can be lessened by raking them well. The Yurok-Karok design with near vertical bow is deceptive in that the flat face is above surface and the rockered hull has a very easy entry underneath. Squared off end construction is possible with that northern California dugout since the redwood used splits less readily than red cedar, again the material factor in design. Shorter length for the carrying capacity is handy for the use situation. Although the peaked end shape seems visible again in well inclined form in the long Bella Coola oolachen canoe, any resemblance seems an accident of the latter's construction. Why sharp-ended river canoes take over to the north is not clear, but they accord nicely with the former flamless extended blade ends of the northern coastal canoes. Lastly, it might be noted that while the White man's attention is drawn by the visible topside forms, from the native perspective the bottom is of special concern as those learning from living tradition come to know. Of course, by the mid-20th century western dugout traditions became very attenuated, indeed broken in most places, so that many modern reconstructors, both Indian and White, carve inadequately but are blinded by the enthusiasts' pride. Things should improve in the next century.

THE DAO OF PADDLING

Bert Horwood

I grew from infancy to young manhood cradled and nurtured by the great valley of the Ottawa River. It took from 1932 until 1949. During that time, recovery from a major economic depression and the turmoil of a World War swirled around, almost unnoticed by me in any important way. The world of the valley, as we called it, was in many respects quintessentially Canadian. There was an embracing landscape, the rolling purple black hills of the Laurentians. There was the perpetual smell of bark, sawdust and lumber mills. Whistles of the great transcontinental trains wailed in the distance. Our piece of the mosaic was itself a mosaic of cultural origins – Celtic and English, French, German, and Polish – while quietly waiting in the background were the Algonquin People, hemmed in to their patch of land at Golden Lake. And running through it all, driving it and washing it, actually creating it, was the great Ottawa River and its tributaries, running then more freely than they do today.

For me then, and for many years afterwards, the canoe was the craft that went with the river. It is true that we Pembroke lads loved to watch the pointers for the lumber drives being built in Cockburn's boat yard. And canoes were scarce in the valley compared to rowboats with motors. But it was the canoe that carried the history of the river from Aboriginal times, through exploration and trade right into the present, and taught me how to match those journeys beyond the horizon. Just as the river was the single critical presence in that piece of Canadian life, the canoe was the most important instrument for knowing it.

Years later, in other places, my vision expanded, but the real and abstract notion of river and canoe seemed still to be a thing of Native invention and European exploitation. I carried that bias with me into my contribution to the first Canexus Conference held at Queen's University in 1988 to celebrate the canoe in Canadian culture. I suspect that my fellow planners felt much the same. Certainly, the relatively limited cultural scope of the published conference proceedings support this view.[1] Since then, much has changed. Native voices are actually present, for one thing. And the existence of a rich Asian element in the Canadian mosaic is another. It is a subtle but significant change that the title of the second Canexus Conference pluralized "culture" and became "The Canoe in Canadian Cultures." Because of the centrality of the river and the canoe in my formative years, and because of the rich stimulus provided by later encounters with Chinese philosophy, I now see how these two, apparently isolated domains create a wonderful synergy that is entirely in keeping with Canadian culture.[2] It is ironic that the gold of the orient desired by the old explorers who sought the northwest passage may well have come to us in the form of Daoist philosophy.

In [paddling] . . . there is a line called a sacred line – the slalom – a line of moving, dynamic balance with the flows of energy in the place. There, for a few moments, one can get close to the streamings of energy that are our universe.[3]

To consider the Dao[4] of paddling is to consider the connections between paddling and the "streamings of energy that are our universe." Here, the substance of reflection is not so much technical, or narrative, as it is numinous. The canoe, a useful object in trade, travel, education and recreation, is being treated differently, as a way of meditation and an entry into mystery. Even though this numinous aspect of canoeing is specifically mentioned only occasionally in the popular canoeing literature, I believe it is an aspect commonly experienced by paddlers.

Eastern thought has been steadily entering the Euro-Canadian culture during the last half of the 20th Century. People who once approached paddling in purely European terms, filtered by the North American landscape and opportunities, now have attitudes enriched by various ideas derived from sources such as Buddhism, and Daoism. One of the reasons is that much eastern thought emphasizes the relationships among things which build wholes rather than dwelling on the distinctions and dualism which dominates Western thought. Eastern thought provides insights and explanations for our experiences which are not readily available to European Canadians. In this essay, I will use the explanatory power of Daoist thought to explore the Canadian experience of canoes and canoeing.

Daoist thought has two branches: one is philosophical and spiritual without a structured religious component, and the other is formally religious. The philosophical branch appeals to me because of its explanatory power and because of the way it places human activity into the natural world of which it is a part. Alan Watts, one of those who made Daoist ideas accessible in North America, summed it up:

Certain Chinese philosophers . . . explained ideas and a way of life that have become known as Taoism – the way of [human] *cooperation with the course or trend of the natural world, whose principles we discover in the flow patterns of water, gas and fire, which are subsequently memorialized or sculpted in those of stone and wood, and later, in many forms of human art. What they had to say was of immense importance for our own time when in the +20th century, we are realizing that our efforts to rule nature by technical force and "straighten it out" may have the most disastrous results.*[5]

Figure 1: The tai ji diagram shows the dynamic interplay of polarities to form a whole.

Three Daoist notions, all flowing from the central idea of harmony with nature, are particularly useful. One is the idea of emptiness, the second is natural or effortless action, closely related to "flow," and the third is the union of polarities characterized by the term "tai ji."[6] These three ideas can be applied in a kind of dialogue with four aspects of canoeing: the form of the canoe, the act of paddling itself, the nature of rivers and, that quintessential union of them all, the canoe trip. The dialogue will serve to simultaneously illuminate inner dimensions of paddling and reveal the richness of Daoist ideas.

The familiar tai ji diagram (see figure 1) provides an essential reference for this discussion. The large circle boldly represents a global or universal whole. The curved halves represent polarities each of which defines, limits, and enhances the other. One part is called yin (soft, for example) and the other yang (hard, to complete the example). If the white portion is a valley, then the black portion is a mountain. Neither can exist without the other. Thus, bannock, as extolled by Bob Henderson as a leading metaphor for harmonious relations with place,[7] has a crisp chewy crust which defines the soft flaky interior. But that example is static and the tai ji diagram is a dynamic symbol. If the white portion is winter, then the dark portion is summer. And by tracing the curving lines one can feel the beautiful way in which one season merges into the other. In fact, in the deepest part of "winter" there is a dark spot which symbolizes the essential presence of the other pole. This matches our experience at the winter solstice: even though the full, hard, cold of the winter has not yet come, we know that the nights are growing shorter and the long traverse into summer has already begun. The reciprocal relationship is found in the "summer" segment. Again, Bob Henderson's claim that stillness is a critical complement to travel is a working example of this fundamental polarity in canoeing. It is important to note that the segments of the diagram are not dualistic or absolute opposites and that there is some risk in applying the diagram to independent or unrelated extremes.

Much Daoist instruction is indirect and parabolic. The story is told of a student of a Daoist martial art who was struggling. The notion of "emptiness" eluded her. The master's instructions to stand "with the four empties: empty arches, empty hands, empty chest, and empty mind" was meaningless to her. She was impatient and frustrated with the emphasis on getting the form of the art correct. One day, at tea break, when she returned to the master with the steaming tea pot, she saw that he had broken the tea cups. His answer to her puzzled look was to say, "You see? Form is also emptiness." The story would be more dramatic if it had been a paddling instructor who had smashed a canoe. But the point would have been the same. The form of the canoe is a manifestation of that emptiness without which the object could not possibly be what it is. The open canoe is a particularly apt illustration, because it is the emptiness and openness that make the craft useful and easy for loading. And thus we get names like "vessel" which express the receptive and load-bearing property of water craft.

On the other hand, or rather, from the other side of the tai ji diagram, a canoe's form is hard and thrusting. The bow can cut through the water, parting it to right and left, just as it can buoyantly rise to a wave. If you trace the lines of the tai ji diagram several times and then trace the lines of a canoe (see figure 2), it is possible to feel the way the way in which the two sets of curves are related. The form of a canoe is also an expression of cooperation with the flow of nature. The genius of the Eastern North American Native people illustrated this cooperation with the hidden capability of the grain of bark and wood. That capability is precisely the flow patterns memorialized in wood referred to by Alan Watts quoted earlier. None of this is surprising to anyone who, in bending cedar canoe ribs, has felt the sweet compliance as the wood stretches and settles into its curved form.

In this volume, Kirk Wipper and Eugene Arima show how canoe form

Figure 2: Canoe contours form a variation on the tai ji diagram.

relates both to function afloat and to the properties of the available materials. Bruce Hodgins adds that the canoes of central Canada were made to be carried. Portaging, says Bruce, in effect, is the polar complement of paddling. The mutuality of tai ji is expressed in Bruce's notion that the canoe (or the land) which carries us is an entity which, in turn, we must carry.

The act of paddling is an embodiment of Daoist ideals. From the point of view of the human paddler, the movements are fluid and curved, much like the lines of the canoe and the tai ji diagram itself. Jim Raffan caught this spirit when he wrote, "The recovery of our paddle tips is a sine wave pattern I never noticed before: first close to the canoe as the power phase of the stroke is completed and then swung out like a pendulum, and back to the gunwale again."[8] Free form paddling is much like a floating, upper body version of a Chinese martial art. Simply paddling across a still body of water in perfect accord with a partner evokes the same relationship. A few lines from a Rikyu poem:

Garden path, tea-room!
The guest and with him her host
together at tea:
their action is harmony
and nothing stands between them,

prompted Daniel Vokey to write: "The lines bring to mind memories of smooth evening water, droplets from two blades in perfect rhythm."[9]

Jim Raffan shows his sensitivities to the Dao while paddling in another lyrical passage which illustrates the Daoist principle of effortless or natural action:

The paddling rhythm allows us to focus on the here-and-now. Senses are tuned and aware, but not focusing on anything in particular. I'm aware of bodies falling easily into the monotony of the motion. The magic of paddling for hours is the efficiency of the action. For every action there is a resting phase – the yin (sic) of exertion, the yang (sic) of rest. For every expenditure of energy, there is renewal of breath and power from the motion of the boat. Resting phase: hands fall forward, shoulders tilt, the blade drops into the water and every part of the body evenly flexes to the task. Exertion: I look down and see my bare toes flex against the sand in the bottom of the boat as the stroke begins. The thigh follows, left more than the right. The demand of the right side of my torso is smooth and even. The demand on the left side – the side I'm paddling on – is wave-like. I look down as the power of the stroke peaks: chest and upper arm flex together as the paddle swings forward again. Gail's back shows the other side of the effort. Sheets of muscle in her back are a series of delicately shadowed triangles that focus their force towards her spine. Her shoulders glisten in the light and drop slightly as she tips forward and begins a new stroke. Watching the sequence of motion played out through the smooth muscles in Gail's back makes me aware of a high-frequency tingling in the nape of my neck. I daren't tip forward for fear of springing a wire. It seems odd that the paddle is the object being powered and the spine is the place from which the power is being dispatched. Our paddles enter the water on opposite sides of the boat, but I'm conscious right now that the power is centralized. It comes from the core. It's motion derived of the soul and of the land whose energy flows through in every sense.[10]

Effortless action sounds like an oxymoron, but that is more a flaw in expressing the Daoist concept than a real contradiction. The feeling described above might better be called natural action, or acting with easy efficiency. Skilled, rhythmic paddling, like many other activities, can be performed with little conscious effort, no self-consciousness at all, and no strain. The passage of time is perceived differently when we are acting without self-conscious effort. This is closely related to the so-called flow experience described by Csikszentmihalyi.[11] Acting, as it were without trying, is far from carelessness and it is far from being confined to gentle flatwater paddling. The exact same, easy application of just the required force at just the right time and place to do the job can be seen and felt in any expert whitewater run. I suspect that this is one of the subtle factors which makes Bill Mason's "Path of the Paddle" films a joy to watch, even for arm-chair canoeists. It is the ultimate in relaxed performance, the art which conceals art.

Natural or effortless action can be interpreted as a meditative state. In the passage above, Jim Raffan refers to "senses being tuned and aware" while falling, unfocussed into the "monotony of the motion." This is a reasonable, unsophisticated account of entry into a form of meditation and is entirely compatible with yogic readings of the ancient Daoist texts. Jim's reference to the central role of the spine in generating the motion of paddling adds support for linking effortless action with some form of meditation.

Of course, paddling is not just a matter of moving the paddle, gripping one's toes and propelling the canoe. Forces of current, waves and wind all work their actions naturally and unself-consciously on the hull and on the paddle blade, too. For me this is where the most beautiful interactions of the paddler and the "flows of energy in the place" occur. To angle the canoe so that paddle, wind and waves allow for safe if slow progress, to angle and move the canoe so that current, pressing differentially on the curves of the hull moves it across the stream, to find and use the fluid lines at the edges of eddies, these are manoeuvres in which gravity and the fluids of the place naturally meet the paddler's skill and generate new expressions of harmony. Sometimes, when the wind is too great, or the angle does not get set correctly, or a shallow rock intervenes, the paddler's intentions are not harmonized with the natural forces. Nature almost always wins, and the wise paddler knows how and when to yield with good grace and recover balance. This is the same wisdom which the ancient Daoist texts ascribe both to sages and to rivers. In the words of Grey Owl:

. . . as we penetrate deeper and ever deeper into this enchanted land, The River marches with us. More and more to us a living thing, it sometimes seems as if it was watching us, like some huge half-sleeping serpent that observes us dreamily, lying there secure in his consciousness of power while we . . . play perilously on his back.[12]

River is a favourite metaphor in modern and ancient Daoist literature. Dao itself, being ineffable and quite beyond verbal description or definition, can only be spoken of metaphorically and poetically. Dao is like a river flowing through time and the universe. Water is yielding, always occupying the lowest position and always stopping or moving as obstacles allow. It is opportunistic. Rivers teach Daoist lessons such as humility (a river always takes up the inferior position, but is nevertheless able to wash away mountains) and effortless action (water is soft and biddable, but in motion it can wear away the hardest rock without effort). Rivers also offer a typically Daoist paradox. It is a famous truism that one can not paddle in the same river twice. Rivers provide us with direct experience of the mystery of instantaneous change within long-term constancy. Rivers, like Dao itself, are continually renewed even as they pursue their natural course. Paddling provides an excellent opportunity to reflect on ideas like these as one watches the character of a river unfold. There is something utterly primeval about it, as though, paddling along, looking around, one was living beyond the limits of time, being swept along on a great universal stream.

The canoeing literature shows that paddlers are sensitive to the different personalities which rivers present. The commonest accounts of rivers emphasize their danger, challenge and "wildness" in the sense of being remote and free-flowing. That is the yang aspect of a river. Because it is more rare to give equal emphasis to the yin aspect of rivers, I want to show what such an account might look like. I've chosen the Horton River because it would be hard to make into a raging monster which had to be tamed by great feats of derring-do. It is not a river about which heroic deeds are done and tales told. The Horton, in the Northwest Territories, runs northwards to the sea between the great Mackenzie to the west and the picturesque Coppermine to the east. For me, the Horton is a gentle and nurturing river, although in Daoist fashion, I rejoice in its sometimes forceful nature. And of course, it is important to recognize that the character of a river, especially an Arctic river, changes dramatically with the time of year and the weather.

It is almost impossible to describe a river without also describing the experience of learning to know it. In other words, I find objectivity out of the question in this case. It is also impossible to isolate one component of the experience from another. To explore a river by canoe is to bring together all the ingredients, the craft, the act of paddling, the nature of the river and their several interactions with human beings.

Like most rivers, the Horton displays on a small scale the same features it has on a large one. The clear water from Horton Lake flows north in sinusoidal flow around gravel bars, repeating the way the valley winds back and forth in grander loops. Despite being north of the Arctic Circle, and well north of the standard tree line, the Horton Valley has trees along its banks to within a few day's travel from the mouth. The river is bounded by rolling hills most of its length, but there is a short section with higher rocky walls and towers, the so-called canyon. Even here the river is benign. The sky is easily visible; the rapids are the natural and easy consequence of the water acting, as someone has said, "in perfect accord with the situation." Portages, lining and shooting the water, all fall into place with relative ease.

In the lower third of the river, one of the dilemmas offered to paddlers is which of several passages of water among the gravel beds to choose. I had an interesting experience there, paddling in a luminous thick mist which the northern sun at the horizon had set to glowing like the interior of a pearl. It was impossible to see far enough ahead to tell which channel had the most water. Instead, my partner and I learned to rely on the tell-tale movement of the flecks of foam around the canoe. We had better success following the foam than we did in choosing a channel by eye when there was greater visibility. To "go with the flow" in this case was invariably the right, natural thing to do. But we had to surrender our distance vision to learn where the flow was. Being fully and attentively in the present, right here, right now (and not over there, later on), is be fully tuned to the harmonies of the place.

Jim Raffan provides a vivid description of the consequences of failing to be fully resonant with the harmonies of the place.[13] A herd of caribou were starting to swim across a river. One canoe slipped downstream across the path of the oncoming animals to secure a better angle for photographs. The leading caribou, alarmed, turned about and swam back into the herd with ensuing mayhem that left everyone, especially the caribou, in a devastated condition. It is well, when remembering the deep satisfaction of harmony, to be equally aware of the pain of disharmony.

In its northern stretches, the Horton becomes turbid with a yellow flocculent material that smells reminiscent of a chemistry lab. This comes as a shock because it is exactly like some sort of industrial pollution, not the kind of thing one expects from a pristine Arctic river. The cause is the presence of a form of coal along the banks which spontaneously ignites. This is the source of the Burning Hills along the coast where the Horton empties. The ash of the burning is a new form of earth. Higher up, the river is washing away earth, tearing down the hills and baring the rocks; here it is carrying newly formed products to be deposited in its delta and to form who knows what earthy layers in the future of the planet. At the same time, my initial distaste for the murky water and the sulphurous fumes was rapidly giving way to a respect for this generative aspect of the earth's crust. The air and the water cannot be so bad, not when you go for a stroll and, over a rise, see the next hills covered with thousands of slowly moving caribou. Animals act naturally and effortlessly, just as we do when we catch the tide of Dao.

Canoe trips have been likened to a heroic quest[14] but they also resemble a tai ji diagram. Trace the sinuous curved line across the tai ji diagram and notice the narrow space to begin. Beginnings are difficult. But soon one is into the swing of it. Ever so subtly, at some surprising mid-point, canoe trippers realize that the trip has passed a turning point, they are on the other side of starting. And the cycle is completed with return, but not quite to the same place because the universe has shifted during the time.

I have tried to show that in the fabric and form of canoes, in the act of plying paddle or even pole, in the nature of rivers and travelling upon them by canoe, there is a strong presence of the mystery which the Chinese have taught us to call Dao. It has been there all along as evidenced by sensitive hints in writing about canoeing. Its healing numinosity has been expressed by writers. Ned Franks wrote of a trip on the Bonnet Plume ". . . we weren't looking for difficulty and adventure . . . [but] a chance to get body mind and soul together in the healing canoe country."[15] And in another way, Martha Craig, in 1905, wrote:

When the rivers are freed from their icy chains, the innermost depths of my being respond to the calls of the wilderness. Tell me where anything comes from, and I will tell you whither it is going. Things animate and inanimate move in circles. In their course they change their identity from time to time, but each change is only a step on the journey back. I go back to nature because that is where I came from, that is where we all came from. We are all on the way back, but at different stages on the journey.[16]

But it's more than getting back to nature, or making "crooked nerves straight."[17] There is a temptation in Daoism, as in all philosophies, to pontificate and to draw morals to guide, if not rule, human behaviour. Daoist writers caution against any such thing. Thomas Merton summarizes the cautionary lessons about making any virtue become a thing to be obtained.[18] Any such virtue turns into its polar vice, say the ancient texts. The making of rules, for example, is also the making of rule-breakers. It's

Figure 3: The logo from the first Canexus Conference held in 1988 illustrates the unity of paddler and landscape.

more a matter of "acting within the framework of circumstances." And, ". . . as long as one's deeds are in accord with the time and one leaves no sloppy traces, then the action is correct."[19] To seek the Dao in paddling is to engage the incredibly difficult business of simply being there, appreciatively and receptively. It's about being available to be touched by awe and to learn to know one's path as easily as one knows to swing the paddle. Thus the canoe is a means of meditation at least as much as it is of transport, trade, and recreation.

The logo used for the first Canexus Conference (see figure 3) is a graphic portrayal of the unity of a paddler's inner and outer worlds. It would be equally accurate to have drawn a female paddler incorporated organically into the land. To simply be in a canoe with meditative awareness, suspended, as it were, between earth and sky is to become, for a time, fully in touch with Dao.

There is something inconsequential and futile in writing about Dao. The key is in that word "about." One can only write around Dao. It slips out of the grasp and, like a shadowy presence in the night, can only be seen when not looked at. Thomas Merton wrote to the effect that a person who can say what Dao is, does not know, and a person who knows Dao, can not say.[20] To find out, let's go paddling.

Traditional Longboats of Asia Pacific

Adrian Lee

Canexus Pacifica Canadensis: Paddling Cultures of Pacific Canada

As the next millennium looms just ahead of us, Canada's paddling heritage and culture are being enhanced and transformed by the infusion of several other equally compelling paddled watercraft cultures, all of which have their roots in the Pacific hemisphere. The nation's post industrial romance with the canoe and canoeing is being animated and enriched from Victoria to Halifax, Edmonton to Stratford. These trans-Pacific waves have come to be regarded by many as beautiful and stirring, impressive and engaging; the impacts on the quality of life, the arts and Canada's multi-cultural society, welcome and lasting.

Ultimately, Canada's traditional "heritage and romance of the canoe" must come to be redimensioned to take into account recent permeations and stimulations of other great canoe cultures: the Asian *long zhou* – dragon boat, the Polynesian *va'a* – outrigger canoe and the Pacific Northwest ocean-going dugout canoe, all "longboats" when compared to even the larger varieties of bark fur trade canoes. Also, the Arctic ocean kayak (which of course does not fall into the "longboat" category) deserves mention here due to the profound impact it has had upon both the Canadian and world paddling scene since its introduction into temperate Canadian waters by a pioneering New Zealander who settled on the Pacific coast.

Dragon Boat race in Hong Kong.

And who among us cannot help but be awe struck by the monumental artistic achievement and spiritual genius of the late Bill Reid, whose bronze mythological dugout canoe cum ark, *Spirit of Haida Gwai*, stands as a superlative gift to the world from one of Pacific Canada's premier canoe cultures.

DIFFERENT STROKES

Throughout the 1990s, tens of thousands of urban, information age "blade runners" – vast numbers of whom are not descendants of Canada's historical founding nations – have been taking up paddling with a passion, crossing cultures and connecting spiritually with the ways of the *huli pau* (an outrigger canoe capsizing where the outrigged pontoon arcs overhead through a complete 180 degree rotation), *Ch'ü Yüan* (a revered, patriotic Chinese historical and literary figure who lived circa 300 B.C.E.; alt. *Qu Yuan*) and *baidarka* (an Aleutian variety of sea kayak).1 And all the while most of them have remained oblivious to the ways of the *portage* (overland canoe transport), *j-stroke* (technique to prevent a canoe from heading zig zag) and *bannock* (bread-like staple food of the fur trade era).

And then there are the *pullers*, what today's paddlers of the great carved cedar trees of the northwest coast prefer to be called. Their generation coincides with the watershed reached in terms of the rebirth and revival of the great maritime heritage of the Hawaiians, the Maori (of New Zealand) and the indigenous peoples of the north westcoast (who are thought to have descended from the ice age Asians who trekked across the Bering Strait land bridge.) Today, the making and paddling of large traditional canoes by descendants of these sea-faring paddling cultures have served to empower them towards reaffirming their historical societal values, some of which have suffered grievous diminishment and extinction over the previous three centuries following contact.

The Canadian paddled watercraft scene, traditionally speaking, has long been dominated by Olympic style sprint canoe shells and kayaks, marathon racing boats, tripping and wild water canoes, war and fur trade canoes and white water kayaks. At the close of the twentieth century, the new waves and faces of contemporary paddling culture have come to be based upon watercraft traditions respected for more than two thousand years outside of Canada, traditions that are surely to endure alongside and enrich the Canadian canoe and paddled watercraft experience for all time.

RENDEZ-VOUS WITH THE DRAGON

The first reference to Asia's longboats ever to appear in Canada was in October of 1945.[2] World War II finally was coming to an end and the following year was to be the Diamond Jubilee of the City of Vancouver. One way to celebrate this sixtieth anniversary was suggested by the Consul General for China to the city's mayor at that time, namely, organizing a traditional Chinese dragon boat race festival. While it still remains to be researched whether such a suggestion actually ever was implemented, a commemorative statue of a dragon with a plaque engraved in both English and Chinese characters was presented with ceremony to mark the occasion of the proposed dragon boat races. This obscure statue eventually found its way to the Museum of Anthropology in Vancouver where it remained unnoticed for decades.

It wasn't until forty years later, when Vancouver celebrated her centennial via Expo 86, that annual dragon boat races came to be established in Canada. By 1989, races also had begun in Toronto, the same year that the new Canadian Museum of Civilization (CMC), located in the capital region, presented an exhibit on the experiences of pioneering immigrant Chinese in Canada. In 1990, without any prior knowledge of the Chinese exhibit, I paid a visit to the CMC for a completely unrelated purpose – in quest of the replica sister craft to Bill Reid's original Haida canoe, *Luu Tas* – and chanced upon the historic 1945 dragon boat statue which was on display, lent by the Museum in Vancouver. Through subsequent research and aid from the staff of both museums, I was able to establish the context for Canada's first links with Asian longboat lore and customs.

What is so remarkable about the prescient Consul General's obscure boat race proposal – made four years before China's 1949 revolution – can be gleaned from an account of the 1945 presentation that appeared in the *Vancouver Sun:* "Vancouver's dragon [boat] festival, if inaugurated, could be[come] one of [North] America's most attractive celebrations and con-tribute greatly to the interchange of culture and custom, as well as com-merce between Canada and China."[3] Indeed, this is precisely how organizers of the annual dragon boat races in Vancouver and Toronto, Canada's two principal festivals, positioned their events by the early 1990s, namely as a way of promoting the positive interaction beween the Chinese and other Canadian cultures through the vehicle of traditional paddled longboat races.

FALSE CREEK SALT CHUCK

While the central and eastern portion of Vancouver's False Creek water-way played host to Expo 86 and the country's first dragon boat races, further down the creek at its western entrance off English Bay, *Ecomarine Ocean Kayak Centre* was being established by leading sea kayak and ocean touring small boat touring expert, John Dowd. Originally from New Zealand, Dowd can be credited with being the earliest pioneer to popu-larize commercially the use of sea kayaks in Canada as a form of paddling recreation, beginning around 1980 – at a time when putting out to sea in small paddled craft was considered to be highly unusual, eccentric or worse. His definitive book on the subject, today in its third edition, has sold on the order of fifty thousand copies.[4] Kayak touring has an immense following that has echoed right across the country and is on par with traditional canoe tripping in terms of offering a complete wilderness travel experience by hand propelled small craft.

Yet another False Creek institution which started up during the same period in the 1980s is the False Creek Racing Canoe Club, Canada's largest club of active paddlers (some 600 during peak season) of multiple disciplines, ranging from surf ski to downriver canoe to outrigger to marathon to flatwater to fur trade canoe. Started by Canadian Olympian, Dr. Hugh Fisher (kayak medalist, Los Angeles 1984), the FCRCC has attracted not only devoted paddlers but also thousands of newcomers to competitive paddle sport. Besides being the technical development locus for the dragon boating phenomenon that descended upon Vancouver, the club went on to build the country's first program for outrigger canoe racing, which consisted of an outrigger boat fleet, specialized technical instruction, training and competition at meets in California, Hawaii and Fiji. This pioneering activity helped to spawn other outrigger clubs and training programs.

Paddlers from "the Creek" went on to initiate both the Canadian Outrigger Racing Association and the Dragon Boat Racing Council of Canada, two national status organizations to facilitate competition between paddling crews from Canada and the rest of the world. Members also founded Canada's first and North America's pre-eminent manufacturer of fibreglass dragon boats, which has enabled thousands more participants to be introduced to this form of paddling. Club members have been flown to Oregon, New York, California, England and Germany to contribute paddling expertise to local enthusiasts who are hungry to learn more about the secrets for making dragons speedy. The pivotal role that this organization and its members have played during a short 12 years in exploding the paddling horizons for thousands of west coast Canadians is unmatched.

PADDLE TO THE SEA: DAY OF THE LONGBOAT

Every year since 1987 the University of British Columbia Department of Intramural Sports and Recreation hosts what can best be described as the fur trade canoe version of the Oxford – Cambridge collegiate boat race.

In honour of the original inhabitants of the area, the event is publicized as Day of the Longboat. More than 275 ten-person crews of university students, faculty and the community-at-large take part in practice drills and an autumn weekend of racing, which is conducted on tide-affected sea water. Not infrequently, novice crews have to be plucked from the frigid waters of October. The race takes the form of a Lemans style start where the steerspersons, at the sound of a gun, must rush down the beach to their awaiting and all-loaded-but-for-one fur trade canoes; head the canoes out perpendicularly from shore towards a turning mark buoy, turn ninety degrees to race parallel to the sandy shore for about 500 metres; at a second mark, head directly back to the shore and upon reaching the beach, the bowmen /women exit and run up the beach to collect a baton, returning with it back to the awaiting canoe; once embarked, the crew has to double back to the starting shore. In order to finish, upon arrival at shore the bowmen / women must rush up the beach to deliver their individual batons to the finish area and signal their finish by striking a gong. This is probably the best attended event in the world involving fur trade canoes (in ways that were never contemplated for this type of craft) and certainly the most remarkable in terms of originality for ocean canoeing.

But what is most significant from a Canadian canoe culture perspective is that a large proportion of the Day of the Longboat participants hail from landlocked places where they ordinarily never would have experienced the ocean with its salt water (nor would they ordinarily ever have set out to seek same) let alone tried to learn canoeing. The event provides a compact, if not unconventional, introduction to Canada's fur trade canoe heritage to university-aged people who probably never would have considered gaining such a perspective on their own. It is done in a fun filled, exciting, social and safe way, complete with hot tubs, crew gag costumes, salmon barbeque and wrap up dance and awards ceremony. As a race official at this annual saltwater canoe fest, perennially I am intrigued by the reactions and responses to this uniquely west coast experience on the part of students attending UBC from far off countries – such a far cry from gunwale bobbing on Ontario's Lake Muskoka or ice canoe racing on the St. Lawrence River at Quebec City's Winter Carnival.

PACIFIC FIRST NATIONS PERSPECTIVE

This overview of Canada's Pacific region paddling would not be complete without a brief mention of the resurgence of canoe culture among the first peoples to have inhabited this area of the world. In the mid 1980s when the late Bill Reid fashioned *Luu Tas*, the first traditional longboat to be done in many decades, he reversed a trend that might otherwise have resulted in the complete demise of the sea-going heritage of his ancestors.[5] Today, more and more people within the mainstream community are growing in awareness of the modern revival of ancient indigenous canoe traditions and culture and of the central role that the ocean-going dugout canoe has come to play in that rebirth. A similar Aboriginal cultural renaissance through the restoration of great canoe lore has been ongoing by native populations in several other locations throughout the Pacific Rim. Hence, Canada's Pacific First Nations canoe reawakening also can be viewed within the larger context of a larger world wide longboat revival movement of the late twentieth century.

West coast Canadians over the last 20 years have been exposed to imported forms of paddling and, more importantly, attitudes and perspectives about paddling which are significantly different from the usual views and concepts commonly held among canoeists of Central Canada, be they marathon, whitewater, sprint racing or tripping enthusiasts. I was born, raised and taught to paddle in Central Canada and grew to appreciate this rich heritage by mastering the lean turn landing and the running pry, by carving solo paddles of maple and refurbishing classic Peterborough canvas and cedar strip canoes, by being attentive to Wipper, Stringer and Mason, and by studying material culture contained in such collections as the Kanawa International Museum of Canoes and Kayaks (now incorporated into the Canadian Canoe Museum situated in Peterborough), the Canadian Museum of Civilization and the Royal Ontario Museum.

At the same time, like many other dragon boating Canadians of Chinese descent, I have been able to explore my Asian ethnic roots through the medium of the path of the paddle. This has been accompanied by concurrent interest in the paddling culture of Oceania, with visits to both the Hawaii Maritime Museum located in Honolulu and the Te Papa Tongarewa Museum recently opened in Wellington, New Zealand, as well as the Royal Barges Museum in Bangkok, Thailand and the Museum of Anthropology in Vancouver. All of these institutions feature substantial materials on long canoes.

For many paddlers of the west coast, there is a strong non-Canadian cultural component inherent in the songs their particular paddles sing. This diversity, as expressed through different paddling cultures, is perhaps a useful metaphor for affirming Canada's diverse cultural makeup and present day social realities. What makes all of the various forms of paddling worthwhile is that while their common theme of 'free movement over water in response to the blade' exhilarates, at the same time the different boats and different ways and waterways for their use continuously lead to creativity, rejuvenation and growth as one learns to adapt to and adopt new perspectives: action and reaction.

A DISTINCT FIELD OF ENQUIRY: PADDLING CULTURES OF THE PACIFIC BASIN FROM 2000 B.C.E. TO 2000 C.E.

This likely serves as among the first, if not the first piece of writing, to recognize and examine the vast richness and diversity of various longboat cultures, traditions and technologies as a collectivity on a circum-Pacific, pan-Asian basis. Furthermore, it suggests that as a field of enquiry, the study of Asia Pacific longboats is an important but so far neglected area of specialization on par with the studies of paddled watercraft indigenous to other regions of the world.

The plank-built canoes, dugouts, outriggers and kayaks of Oceania, the Arctic regions and the Americas have long received the attention of ethnologists, scholars, museum curatorial staff and others. However, the focus on Asian paddled watercraft, up until now, has remained only at the level of single hull types within a specific region or geo-ethnic scope, viewed in relative isolation from the vast totality of a now more recognizable, larger and distinctive family of watercraft and hull forms. The reasons for this neglect are many: the barriers of language, great distances combined with remote or closed access to rural areas, high travel costs hindering wider access and penetration, decades of civil, military and political unrest during modern times (for example, the Sino-Japanese War, World War II, Communist Revolution, French and American wars in South East

Asia, Khmer Rouge Regime) a general low interest in or disregard for traditional boat culture within the Asian academic community and, finally, the lack of any unifying or organizing principle(s) for in depth study.

This brief overview develops a seminal point of departure for examining and discussing the phenomenon of Asia Pacific longboats as a thematically cohesive whole, within the greater context of the world's families of paddled watercraft.

ESSENTIAL CHARACTERISTICS OF ASIA PACIFIC LONGBOATS

Ten distinguishing features and generalized characteristics of the traditional long watercraft of Asia shall be identified for purposes of study, as follows:

(i) exceedingly narrow of beam while extremely long of length, making for a characteristically very slender, open, undecked boat;

(ii) minimal or low freeboard, with shallow draft and depth;

(iii) paddler capacities ranging from 20 to 100 or more; paddlers positioned in pairs, paddling from a sitting, stooping or standing position;

(iv) stylized craft uses and functions: ceremonial, festive, ritualistic, religious, symbolic, competitive racing and contest;

(v) impressive overhanging, projecting or soaring prows and or sterns; upswept sheer lines towards one or both extremities; stem and or stern often narrowing to nearly a point;

(vi) magnificent symbolic markings, carvings or other colourful regalia and ceremonial rigging and decorative adornments;

(vii) an elaborate associated folk symbolism, mythology, and folkloric customs, meanings and significances;

(viii) specialized means for co-ordinating paddle stroke cadence, synchronicity, changes of tempo and direction and signalling manoeuvres;

(ix) the unique problem of maintaining, along the longitudinal axis of the hull, horizontal and torsional structural rigidity (for instance, preventing hull hogging, sagging and corkscrew-like twisting); as well as maintaining hull symmetry over such a long yet narrow hull;

(x) aft stationed helm control using one or more specialized steering sweep oars or paddles.

As with most generalizations, some types of longboats deviate from these generalized features, the Royal Barges of Thailand being an exemplary exception. Wider of beam, some of these designs bear ceremonial, pavilion-like shelters.

PREHISTORIC, ARCHEOLOGICAL AND HISTORICAL ORIGINS

The earliest depictions of watercraft exhibiting the aforementioned characteristic features have been carbon dated at more than two thousand years of age and are associated with the regions comprised of southwestern China and northern-most Viet Nam.[6] These images of manned longboats are inscribed in profile on ancient religious ceremonial bronze drums and suggest craft of elaborate use and design.

An ancient Chinese paddle almost identical in design to that still in use today has been dated at more than 5000 years of age. Thus, longboats are known to have been paddled by some of the earliest civilizations of East Asia. Chinese historical classics and works of literature and fine art throughout the classical and pre-modern periods also depict the role that these craft played throughout ancient times. For example, thousand year old silk scroll paintings held in the Palace Museum collection in Beijing show a variety of different types of paddled longboats, in particular, both *long zhou* and *long chuan* varieties of dragon-headed watercraft (respectively, *lung jiau* and *lung syhun* in the Cantonese dialect pronunciation).[7]

HULL FORM EVOLUTION AND CLASSICAL CONSTRUCTION

The subset of craft about which we have come to know the most today appears to have been derived from both the dugout log (particularly the multiple lashed log or *catamaran* style of hull) and the bamboo raft, based on Hornell's classical scheme of watercraft archeology and evolutionary development.[8] In fact, the invention of watertight bulkheads, now a universal practice in marine hull design and construction throughout the world, is regarded as being Chinese in origin and is thought to be based on a botanical structure that occurs in nature: the septums (cross membranes) found within bamboo stalks at the nodal sections. (A piece of bamboo, when split in half longitudinally, resembles the bluff bow and stern classic lines of traditional Chinese oared, transom-sculled and paddled small vessels.)

In southern China, where the use of dragon boats is mostly centred, the earliest, crude, lashed dugout log forms of construction eventually gave way to fine carvel-style wood hull construction in the coastal boat building centres. However, even today, the Miao ethnic minority still fashion hollowed, lashed log boats and race them in the rural Qing Shui River valley of Guizhou province. Vessels built throughout the current century in the estuary region of the Zhu River mouth (the coastal Pearl River delta adjacent to Hong Kong) exhibit some of the carvel construction features and classic lines of junks and sampans, suggesting the influence that dragon boats have had on these two kinds of distinctly Asian vessels and vice versa.

WATERWAYS

Local terrain features and waterway conditions have been influential factors in long-boat evolution, as is usually the case with respect to the origin and evolution of most small vessels. Longboat culture has survived even to this day and thrived throughout contemporary Asia, particularly in the following riverine and lacustrine regions, as follows:

– along Asia's great river systems: Chang (or Yangtze), Zhu (or Pearl), Lancang (a.k.a. Mekong), Chao Phraya

– on principal inland lakes: Dongting (China), Inle (Burma a.k.a Myanmar)

– around coastal inshore waterways and archipelagoes: eg. Malabar (i.e. Kerala State of India) Indonesia and Malaysia.

DRAGON BOATS OF CHINA

Perhaps the best known form of longboat in the world outside of Asia, dragon boats are also the most numerous type of longboat in use today. Dragon boat racing has spread to places as diverse as Rome, London,

Two teams preparing for a dragon boat race in Taipei.

Berlin, Stockholm, Capetown, New York, San Francisco, Toronto, Vancouver and Sydney. These craft always have a projecting prow in the shape of a carved dragon's head and are found not just in China, but wherever large concentrations of ethnic Chinese can be found in South East Asia, for example, Singapore, Malaysia, the Philippines and Viet Nam.

The racing of dragon boats is part of a millenniums-old observance of ancient folk customs. These are closely connected to the annual summer solstice, the harvest, sacrifices, shamanistic religious beliefs and the dragon deity which, in Asia, reigns over the waters and throughout the celestial realm, therefore holding ultimate sway over both flood and drought and, thus by extension, famine and well being.9 Unlike the dragon, the griffon and other medieval, fantastic beastiary of European, Judeo-Christian and Middle Eastern civilizations, the dragon symbolizes for Asians, beneficence and propitiousness.[10] Put more simply, dragons are regarded as good and positive rather than demonic, evil and something to be slain. Typically, the Asian version of dragon does not breathe fire nor does it have wings, as depicted in Western folk culture.[11]

DRAGON BOAT FESTIVAL: A EUROPEAN MISNOMER

This mid-summer ritual is known as *duan wu* or *duan yang* (here tran-
scribed into the nationally standardized Mandarin Chinese dialect pronunciation whereas the majority of Chinese living in Canada speak the
Cantonese dialect and thus would pronounce the identical Chinese
written form characters something like *dyeun ing* and *dyeun yang*). *Duan
wu jie* (jie = festival) is observed according to the timing of the traditional
Chinese calendar, which is based partly on 29 and 30 day lunar cyclical
periods and partly based on 15 day solar intervals or "joints," and occurs
on the fifth day of the fifth Chinese lunar month. This reckoning is very
roughly analogous to the modern, western Gregorian calendar dates
around the Summer Solstice, June 20, 21 and 22. The date of 'double fifth,'
therefore, moves around on today's calendar, the same way that the observance of Easter varies every year.

When European visitors to China first became aware of the annual
many-handed boat races more than one hundred years ago, they dubbed
the event the Dragon Boat Festival (literally, *long zhou jie*), even though
this corruption is not at all an accurate translation of the name for the
annual festival. But it is this misnomer that has stuck today in the English
language when referring to the tradition of racing dragon boats. Besides
boat racing, there are many other rituals and customary practices for
marking the occasion.

MODERN DRAGON BOAT RACE FESTIVALS

In the mid 1970s, the Hong Kong Tourist Association began promoting an
annual international dragon boat race event, inviting participants from
around the world to take part. Eventually, they helped to arrange for boats
to be exported to many cities throughout the world and races came to be
organized beyond Asia. By the mid-to-late 1980s, Canada joined the ever-
growing number of countries enthusiastic for the excitement, challenge
and fun of having 20 paddlers, a drummer and a steerer work as a co-
ordinated whole to challenge other craft over a straight line course of a
distance of around 650 meters or 2,100 feet.

In Japan, there is a variant of the Chinese dragon boat that is called a

Dragon boat crew practising at Toronto Island.

peiron boat, likely a corruption of the chinese *bai long/ pah luhng*, which translates as white dragon.

OTHER TRADITIONAL LONG BOATS OF SOUTH EAST ASIA

Less well known to Westerners are Asian craft which are very similar to dragon boats: long, slender, low of freeboard, paired paddlers, but generally without the elaborate markings and dragon headed prows. These vessels are to be found throughout Indonesia (including Borneo), Malaysia, Cambodia, Laos, Bangladesh, Burma (Myanmar), Singapore, Thailand, India and Viet Nam. They are not variants or derivatives of dragon boats but rather indigenous longboat designs. In all cases, their only function nowadays is ceremonial; they are not designed for general passenger water transport, agricultural support, fishing nor for waging war. All are magnificent to behold, fully manned and underway with dozens of paddles flashing and water aspray.

CHANDUN SERPENT BOATS OF INDIA

These craft exhibit stupendous flying sterns that rise nearly vertically some six metres above the water surface. The overhanging slender bows project like giant horns, gently rising forward from water level for about four metres.[12] Male paddlers maintain their paddling positions from these lofty mid air perches by straddling their legs around the fore and aft projections, hugging on to the boat with their thighs. Midships, fore and aft, the rest of the crew are in seated positions. *Chandun* are raced annually as part of the Onam festivities observed in the coastal state of Kerala.

LEG PADDLED CANOES OF MYANMAR (BURMA)

The most astounding feature of these craft is that, not only are all of the crew standing to paddle, the method of paddling is to hold the top end of the shaft with one hand while wrapping the outboard leg around the blade shaft in such a way as to propel the boat forward, empowered by means of the muscles of the hip and leg, not both arms.[13] These boats are used ceremoniously to transport double man-height sacred artifacts to a lakeside temple site. Several such boats travel in a procession as the flotilla makes it way to and from the principal temples on a major Burmese lake, as part of the Bhuddist observance of Lent.

ROYAL BARGES OF THAILAND (FORMERLY SIAM)

Without a doubt, the Royal Barges of the Imperial Navy of Thailand have to be the most astounding and breath-taking of all paddled watercraft to be found anywhere in the world past or present. The hulls of these traditional craft are finished in gold leaf and the prows consist of magnificent carved mythical figures, for example *naga, hongse* and *garuda*. This fleet of state ceremonial boats is part of the military and is manned by recruits uniformed in red tunics of the Thai Royal Navy. There are capital ships, processional outrider boats and craft of various size, sophistication and status for various members of the royal family, ministers and officials. Chanters provide cadence, while paddlers execute an elaborate stylized stroke called bird wing paddling. In this manner, all the blades in unison are lifted deftly and dramatically with a rhythmic swaying motion of the paddlers' torsos, swung gently overhead and held aloft momentarily before being dropped back into the water for the next stroke pull. The effect is as stately and majestic as it is mesmerizing and lyrical. State waterborne ceremonial processions occur today only rarely and the entire flotilla stretches out along the Chao Phraya for more than one kilometer.

MAORI *WAKA TAUA* OF NEW ZEALAND

Though not of direct Asian heritage, the *waka taua* vessels of the Maori people are the most dramatic and most elaborately finished large complement paddle craft of Oceania/Australasia. It is theorized that a land bridge once connected the southeast Asian mainland mass to what are now the outlying islands of Oceania during the last ice age. The Maori long have had a tradition of ornate and profoundly symbolic stylized wood carving and design. This is reflected especially on the waka prow board and the vertical stern projection which can shoot skyward for several metres. Paralleling other Pacific First Peoples of the canoe and the sea, the use of *waka taua* today is an integral part of sustaining strong, vibrant connections with ancient indigenous values and beliefs during modern times.[14]

VA'A OUTRIGGER CANOES OF POLYNESIA

Made famous by the opening sequence of the *Hawaii Five-O* televison series of the 1970s, outrigger canoe racing is a burgeoning sport throughout the Pacific Rim areas of North America, New Zealand, Australia and the various island groups from the Hawaiian to Polynesia.[15] An intriguing aspect of the long distance marathon races is the water crew changes. For the six person outrigger canoe, there is a crew of nine paddlers. Periodically throughout the races, paddlers will exchange with one another without losing stroke or headway. This is accomplished by the fresh crew being deposited from a motorized support craft into the ocean ahead of and in the pathway of the oncoming canoe, to tread water in line with the intended course of the approaching craft. As the canoe races by, sometimes pitching in heavy seas, in pre-arranged sequence an active paddler swiftly ships his blade and tumbles overboard frogman backflip style, to tread water and await pickup by the support boat. Meanwhile, the craft hurtles forward and the treading crew person must avoid being struck in the head by the on rushing outrigger float and the boat itself: the fresh crew ducks beneath the horizontal strut as it passes overhead under speed then bobs up to reach and grasp the gunwale in order to haul him or herself into the canoe and into the position recently vacated by the exiting change-out crew. The new crew unships the blade and resumes paddling. The most accomplished teams are able to execute these changeovers with minimal loss of strokes and speed to the boat.

OCEAN-GOING CEDAR DUGOUT CANOES OF PACIFIC NORTHWEST AMERICA

Located on the shores of the northeastern sector of the Pacific, south of Alaska, are great rain forests of giant cedars. From felled trees hundreds of years old, the indigenous peoples fashioned enormous canoes suitable for putting to sea in the quest for whales, among many different functions. The design of these craft with their distinctive flaring, cutwater bow and harpoon notch is further enhanced by artistic renderings along the hull and ornate paddles that can function not only for propulsion, but also as weapons.

While this hull design is, of course, not to be found anywhere outside of the Pacific Northwest region, it is known that during an ice age long past a land bridge once joined eastern Siberia with Alaska, allowing for ancient nomadic Asians to pursue migrating animal populations into the western Arctic, thus leading to the inhabiting of the northwestern portion of North America.

The combined result of exquisite watercraft form, function and style is not confined to just actual operational watercraft, but also has been captured permanently in time, in the form of two greater than life-size bronze sculptures by the late world renowned Haida artist, Bill Reid. The *Black Canoe* and the *Jade Canoe*, displayed in the eastern United States and in western Canada, respectively, portray a stirring aboriginal vision of a society of great ocean-going canoemen.

CONCLUDING OBSERVATIONS

While each of the aforementioned craft can certainly be examined in isolation of all of the others and stand in its own right, it is only when all of the various traditions are viewed as part of a unified collectivity that the remarkableness and ingenuity of these kinds of craft as a distinct class can be appreciated. The construction of such outsize hand-propelled vessels implies the need for a co-operative group undertaking, typically a village or clan unit, as does fulfilling the many-handed manning requirements. That such large boats are essentially and largely ceremonial rather than economically or militarily functional (exceptions: Thai, Maori and Pacific Northwest) speaks to the important status and role that are associated with their manufacture and long historical period of use. The fact that so many different cultures, throughout Asia in particular, are all engaged in comparable activity – practising stylized rituals involving long slender boats full of pairs of men – is cause for investigation and reflection.

An article such as this can begin only to scratch the surface of the subject matter. With so little information available for many of the regional craft, more in-depth study of this class of boats is bound to be in order. If this review can stimulate more awareness and interest in the study of Asia Pacific longboats, then we are moving closer to rounding out our global understanding of this under-represented and little-known realm of great canoe cultures and traditions of our shrinking world.

THE CANOT DU MAÎTRE — MASTER OF THE INLAND SEAS

Peter Labor

We swung sideways in the swift current and for the first time in more than 8,000 km I felt vulnerable. This shell of painted fiberglass and wood had faithfully carried us across a country, and now, in a shallow stretch of the Peace River in northern Alberta, it was threatened — not by tumultuous storms or raging rapids but by a moment of hesitation and shallow swift running water. The avant (bow paddler) was the first to lose steerage as we headed upstream, and with the bow lost, the massive hull of our canoe turned broadside to accept the full force of the current along its 12 m length. Bumping over submerged boulders, and helpless to correct the errant course of our craft, I prepared for the worst, imagining nine paddlers and hundreds of pounds of gear dumped into the silty waters. Perhaps it was a mistake to take this grand craft away from the inland seas of lakes Huron and Superior for which it was designed. Perhaps, like a fish out of water, we had taken the canoe out of its element and expected too much of it and ourselves.

Along the north shores of Lake Superior, the songs of the voyageurs echoed off the towering cliffs for hundreds of years. Brigades of canoes laden with trade goods headed west from Montreal Island to Grand Portage[1] at the head of the greatest of the Great Lakes. Leaving at first thaw from Lachine, above the mighty rapids on the St. Lawrence River, the canoes made their way up the Ottawa and Mattawa rivers, across Lake Nippissing and down the French River to the clear waters of Georgian Bay before reaching Lake Superior at Sault Ste. Marie. After a rendezvous of a couple weeks at Grand Portage for trade and meeting with old friends, the brigades headed back to Montreal carrying furs from the northwest, bound for the heads of English gentlemen as beaver-felt hats.

Built by hand from the thick bark of birch trees, and designed for speed and carrying capacity along this route, the Montreal canoe or "canot du maître" was, an ideal craft. Under the power of up to a dozen voyageurs, stroking 45-60 times per minute and carrying four tons of trade goods or furs, it was possible to average speeds of five knots.[2] Due to its size and stability the canot du maître paddled well in winds that left smaller boats on shore, but it could still be landed and pulled up on nearly any beach or sloping headland. The canoes even sailed well, alone or rafted with others, and with a stiff following breeze, kicked up a wake to rival the best tuned sailing ship. In addition to these admirable "sea-going" characteristics, the canot du maître shared the heritage of its smaller cousins and, when faced with an impassable rapid or height of land, became cargo, riding on the strong backs of those who were passengers just moments before.

The canot du maître, however, represents much more than a functional latter-century 18-wheeler. Captured in art and spirit, it symbolizes a vast land of rock and water and an era of adventure and growth. More importantly, the canot du maître exemplifies one of the most culturally defining periods in Canadian history. The canoe was developed by Aboriginal builders to meet the needs of geography, adapted by French, Scottish and British entrepreneurs to meet the demands of the economy and animated by mostly French-Canadian and Métis voyageurs who made a shell of bark, roots, sinew and wood dance and fly like a living creature.

The canot du maître likely arose from the finely crafted bark canoes created by the eastern Algonkians and, though the name translates appropriately to "Master Canoe," it actually refers to the Le Maître family of Trois-Rivières "who built canoes which carried 12 to 20 men apart from baggage and mechandize."[3] Of particular note in the design of the canot du maître was the traditional upswept bow and stern, often decorated with brightly colored designs showing animals or decorative symbols, accompanied by the insignia of the fur trading company under which the canoe was employed.

Bow of a fur-trade canoe from a Francis Anne Hopkins painting, showing the distinctive bow decoration.

Though a liability in a strong cross-wind, these high ends provided additional protection from deep swells on the open lakes and contributed a point of security for the *avant* and *gouvernail* who often stood in the ends of the canoe to steer. Most importantly, the ends served as resting points for the overturned canoe, such that with the addition of a canvas tarp the voyageurs had a roomy shelter to pass the short night.

Perhaps the most recognizable end-decoration is that of four comma-like shapes joined in a circle, reproduced by Frances Anne Hopkins in her various paintings of the Montreal canoe. The origin of this captivating symbol remains a mystery, but is traced to both early Micmac art and a European source as the four-headed Basque "luburu." It may be that one culture copied the symbol from the other, or both found it elsewhere, but despite the cultural differences, the symbol seems a universal representation of good luck which readily is identified with the canot du maître.[4]

The canoe also allowed efficient passenger travel, with the additional burden of a passenger making little difference to the speed and ease of motion. Along with its smaller cousin the canot du nord or North canoe,[5] this canoe, possessing the ability to accommodate an additional passenger, likely contributed to the increasingly successful mapping and exploration of the continental interior by allowing the attending bourgeois the opportunity to make careful notes, diary entries and cartographic measurements without stopping.

The exceptional size of these craft not only set them apart in terms of their utility in carrying furs, but also in their relationship to the sense of time and space in a vast land. Hugh MacLennan, in his classic book *Seven Rivers of Canada*, noted that space in our daily lives can only be measured by the time and expenditure of effort it takes people to cover it.[6] If such is the case, than the canot du maître, with its ability to cover large distances in a relatively short time, began the shrinking of a country which was later followed by the impact of the railway, the Trans-Canada highway and continental air travel.

To hear or read about the canot du maître is to imagine the possibilities. To see and touch a reconstructed full-size craft is to understand the reality. But to paddle a canot du maître with a full crew on the waters for which it was constructed, as I did some years ago, is to know much more.[7] What was once function and beauty is now power and song. While there are very few birchbark canots du maître around, and even less opportunity to paddle them, fiberglass and wood reconstructions allow an authentic experience in Montreal canoe culture.

On the command of *"En Avant!"* from the gouvernail, twelve paddlers reach for the water, pulling first without effect. Then the canoe surges forward as each paddler slowly joins the stroke of the *avant*, until at a cadence of 45-55 strokes a minute, it settles into a groove, carrying forward as happily as it sat still moments before.

Running a straight-line course between headlands on a great interior lake, the canoe becomes an island – a part of the changing landscape – but at the same time an entity unto itself. Conversation groups form within the boat (since it is nearly impossible to carry on a conversation between the bow and stern) and the island inhabitants fall into a rhythmic trance, maintaining the momentum and carrying the canoe forward. Unlike paddling smaller tandem craft, where each paddler plays an active and obvious role in steering, balancing and propelling, in the canot du maître it is entirely possible to pass two hours completely within oneself without the slightest connection to time, space or surroundings. On several occasions I have even seen paddlers fall asleep in mid-stroke, only to awake in

Members of the 1993 Alexander Mackenzie voyage to commemorate the three hundredth anniversary of the first crossing of the continent by canoe.

time to recover and plant the blade once more without disturbing the momentum.

The experience is about rhythm and momentum and paddling together is everything. It is useless for any one individual to pull really hard. All the power is generated by "hitting" the stroke in perfect timing and synchronization. While many people marvel at the reported historical stroke rates of 45 or more strokes a minute, such a cadence seems natural when adapting to the short, choppy stroke emphasizing a "body drop" over the paddle. The speed and ease of movement then comes through a smooth combined effort rather than individual feats of strength and, when everyone is stroking exactly together, the boat flies with a will of its own. It is not difficult to imagine where the stories of "La Chasse Galerie"[8] arose, once one has paddled a canot du maître on the calm waters of a moonlit night.

It is interesting to compare some of the reports of the voyageurs' typical activities when paddling big canoes to modern realities when tripping in such boats. Is it mere coincidence, for example, that the voyageurs' hourly break to fill their pipes with tobacco and take a five minute breather coincides with the need to stop regularly to relive a bladder compressed by the rocking and swaying motion of paddling. Pipe break, perhaps, has a better ring to it in the journals of history than pee break, and thus it was recorded by many noted travellers and historians.

The voyageurs were also well-known for their early morning starts and for paddling several hours before stopping for breakfast. Such an effort not only loosens up sore muscles and cramped hands from the night before, but also gives an opportunity to make some distance before a morning breeze rises, while avoiding the early crop of mosquitoes and blackflies. Breakfast in the boat means breakfast away from the flying pests.

Though I doubt even the most light-hearted voyageur sang in this early morning period, there is no doubt that the culture of the canot du maître includes a culture of song. A voyageur with a strong lead voice often even drew more pay from the company for such a skill, and took much pride in leading the canoe in song. The melodies of many familiar French-Canadian tunes naturally meet the heartbeat-rhythm of the stroke, accenting the effort while easing the strain. The melodic strains of "A La Claire Fontaine" are equally matched by the rolling chorus of "En

Re-enactment Voyageurs sharing the Peace River with the local mosquitoes.

Roulant Ma Boule" or "En Voyans de l'Avant," and with short verses and memorable refrains, it is simple to sing along. I wonder sometimes, however, at the often reported fact of the *avant* being the strong singer, as it is nearly impossible to hear the *avant* (who sits facing forward) from the stern of the canoe. A much more practical position for a song leader is near the stern where the voice carries forward over the other paddlers. Near the stern is also the most practical place for the guide, who can better survey the condition of the winds and waves, and then communicate easily with the gouvernail for appropriate navigation.

So it was from the stern that I yelled for everyone to lean downstream. We bounced and bobbled sideways down the swift, shallow current of the Peace River, periodically striking a slightly larger boulder and teetering to the side before slipping over it and continuing our uncertain descent. Though it seemed longer, it was likely less than a minute before the avant was able to catch enough water to pull the bow back up into the current, and the whole boat regained its vertical upstream position in the river as we collectively breathed a sigh of relief. Once again the canot du maître had proven itself stable and worthy, even here in this shallow river far from the deep waters and open skylines of the inland sea of Superior. We gathered on shore to consider our situation, and taking lines in hand continued upstream tracking the boat from the shore until we reached deeper water.

The days of the voyageur and the fur trade brigades of Montreal canoes are gone, but the spirit of the craft lives on. The canot du maître met the challenges of the Canadian landscape and imagination and remains an iconic wonder of design, utility and art. Best of all, the heritage of the canoe is not lost, in that much of the experience can be relived by simply taking a paddle in hand, joining a group of paddlers and listening for the gouvernail's command…En Avant! – a signal to go forward into the past.

MANUFACTURE OF BIRCHBARK CANOES FOR THE FUR TRADE IN THE ST. LAWRENCE

Timothy Kent

During the first century or more of French settlement in the St. Lawrence Valley, the voyaging canoes used by the French who resided in the valley were manufactured primarily by native builders. The French travellers who needed canoes for trading, exploratory, military or missionary expeditions usually acquired their craft either directly from the Indian builders or from French middlemen. This was pointed out in the narrative of the missionaries Dollier and Galinée. In 1669-1670, they made a voyage into the interior which encompassed the St. Lawrence River, lakes Ontario, Erie and Huron, and the French, Mattawa and Ottawa rivers. La Salle and his small party, en route to the Ohio Country, also accompanied them on the first portion of the journey. The priests' journal reads:

Our fleet, consisting of seven canoes, each with three men, left Montreal on the 6th of July, 1669... These canoes cost Frenchmen who buy them from Indians nine or ten crowns in clothes, but from Frenchmen to Frenchmen they are much dearer. Mine cost me eighty livres. It is only the Algonkin-speaking tribes that build these canoes well.[1]

In 1696 the King issued a proclamation which closed most of the posts and forts in the interior and halted the issuance of trading licenses. All voyages into the interior were forbidden, except those which were required to maintain the four select forts in the Great Lakes region which were not closed. With a minimal market to supply, canoe production on the St. Lawrence virtually ceased. Louis Callières, the Governor General of New France, noted in a letter to the King in 1702, six years after the proclamation: "We lack bark canoes of which the Colony is entirely deprived since we no longer go to the Ottawa country."[2]

The merchant, Denis Riverin, sent a memoir to the King's minister, Pontchartrain, in 1705, in which he described in great detail the procedures of the fur trade as it had been carried out before the 1696 proclamation. In the description of the voyaging canoes which were used by trading parties, the author noted:

The Indians and especially their women excel in the art of making these canoes, but few Frenchmen succeed in it. These canoes used to cost only twenty ecus, but since [the French began] *to roam the woods their value has risen as high as four hundred livres.*[3]

Beginning in about 1715, the interior trade resumed and the posts and forts in the interior were gradually re-established. This caused a major resurgence of canoe building in the St. Lawrence Valley. In addition, numbers of canoes were purchased by the government for the 1715 campaign against the Fox Indians west of Lake Michigan. After the initial flourish of canoe construction, business levelled off. Beauharnois and Daigremont, officials of New France, observed in a letter of October 1, 1728: "The number of canoes has greatly diminished in Canada."[4]

As noted in the 1705 memoir, a few French craftsmen were building canoes in the St. Lawrence settlements by the turn of the century or before. As the trade expanded, this production increased considerably over the 18th century, primarily in the area of Trois-Rivières and along both shores of the St. Lawrence just upriver from there. The river widens in this stretch, for a span of about 28 miles; this section of the St. Lawrence is called Lac St. Pierre.

Howard Chapelle wrote in 1964 that the supply of voyaging canoes that was produced by native craftsmen in the St. Lawrence region in time became insufficient for French needs, and that the native builders were unreliable and uncertain as a source of canoes. He asserted that the canoe factory that was established by the French at Trois-Rivières (as if there were only one) was "the only possible solution."[5]

A wide study of original reference materials of the period disproves Chapelle's ethnocentric assertions and assumptions. In fact, I have found numerous period references which prove that native builders provided a great many of the expedition canoes that were built in the St. Lawrence and Ottawa valleys over a span of more than two centuries. In addition, the evidence clearly indicates that some of the most prominent "French" factories employed Indian workers, for at least some phases of production. It is also clear that nearly all of the major "French" canoe yards on the St. Lawrence were located at or near substantial native communities, presumably to draw from the skilled craftspeople who lived in those communities.

To gain an understanding of the locations on the St. Lawrence at which voyaging canoes were built, as well as the individuals who constructed them, one must examine the Indian settlements along the river (see page 103). The native communities were strategically positioned to serve as guard posts for each of the three main French towns on the St. Lawrence. They were located in these areas to protect the settlements against incursions by the Iroquois and other native allies of the British, as well as attacks by British forces.[6]

Two mission villages flanked the French settlements on Montreal Island. The village called La Prairie de la Madeleine, Sault St. Louis or Kahnawake was positioned on the southern shore of the St. Lawrence, opposite Lachine and southwest of Montreal. The mission of Lac des Deux Montagnes, Kanesatake, or Oka was placed on the northern shore of the Ottawa River at its junction with the St. Lawrence, northwest of Montreal. In addition, native settlements were located at Trois-Rivières and close by, to the west, at Pointe du Lac. On the opposite side of the St. Lawrence, the mission communities of St. François du Lac and Beçancour protected the southern shore of the Trois-Rivières area. Near Quebec, the native settlement of Lorette was located a little northwest of the city. These native communities provided warriors and expedition canoes for most of the major military campaigns that were carried out by the French. In addition, these same warriors served as home guard units for their own settlements as well as those of their French neighbors.

The importance of these native settlements for the protection of the French on the St. Lawrence was underscored in the closing months of the French and Indian War. After the fall of Quebec to the British in September

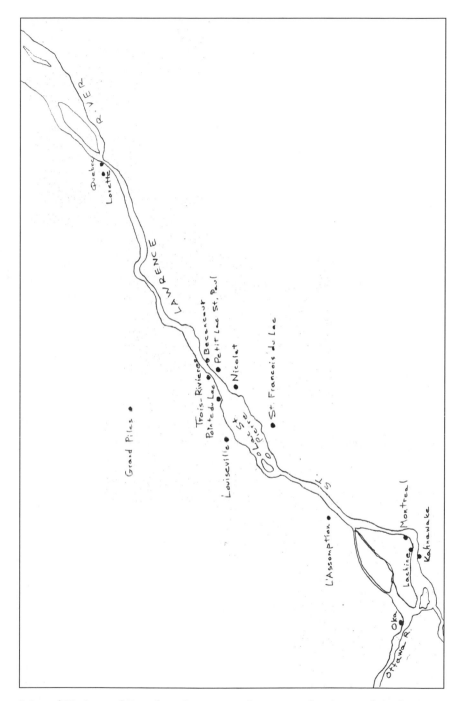

Map of Native and French settlements and canoe production yards in the St. Lawrence Valley. Edwin Tappan Adney located a half-size craft at Grand Piles.

of 1759, the French officials and the army retreated to Montreal for the winter. Sir William Johnson, the Superintendent of the Affairs of the Northern Indians for the British, sent a message to the various native groups at their settlements on the St. Lawrence: "Keep out of the way when the English army approaches."[7] During the summer of 1760, delegates from all of the native settlements in the valley met as a group with Johnson, to establish a pact of neutrality. Shortly thereafter, the British finished surrounding the French officials at Montreal; the French surrendered there on September 8th.[8] The manner in which the British dealt with the native allies of the French who had settled on the St. Lawrence testifies to the long-term relationship of these settlements with the French.

By 1640, sizeable groups of Indians had settled the first of these native communities at Quebec and Trois-Rivières. They were composed of mostly Algonkins, with some Hurons and Montagnais.[9] Parties from these two native settlements began trading in the 1640s in the interior regions north of the St. Lawrence, in Montagnais territory. Travelling in their own voyaging canoes, some of them travelled north of Trois-Rivières up the St. Maurice River system and beyond, while others paddled down the St. Lawrence to trade up the Saguenay River.[10]

This trade began during the first half-century of French commerce on the upper St. Lawrence, when the general pattern consisted of brigades of interior Indians paddling out to the French settlements to trade. At this early date, the native communities at Quebec and Trois-Rivières were constructing and using voyaging canoes in the St. Lawrence Valley. Over the following decades, this manufacture gradually expanded as the native population on the St. Lawrence grew and the need for canoes by the French expanded. These native-built craft provided transport for trading and military voyages of both the Indians and the French.

A typical example of the native villages on the St. Lawrence providing canoes and warriors for a combined French/Indian military expedition is the Denonville campaign of 1687. That summer, 200 native canoes and 300 warriors from the various communities on the river joined the French militia and regular troops and 200 *bateaux* (wooden boats) for a campaign against the Senecas south of Lake Ontario. The warriors who joined the expedition included 160 Iroquois from the two villages that flanked Montreal, a few Algonkins (from Oka near Montreal or from Trois-

Rivières), 60 Abenakis from the two villages across the St. Lawrence from Trois-Rivières and 40 Hurons from Lorette near Quebec.[11] Fully half of the watercraft which transported the combined military forces of this expedition were native canoes from the St. Lawrence Valley.

The following text provides a capsule history of each of the native communities on the St. Lawrence as well as a sampling of references to the use of voyaging canoes from these communities.

LORETTE AND QUEBEC

The Indian settlement near Quebec grew in 1650, with the arrival of large numbers of refugee Hurons fleeing from the destruction, by the Iroquois, of their home villages near Lake Huron. At first, they settled on nearby Ile d'Orléans, but they soon moved to Quebec to avoid further Iroquois attacks. In 1668, the community moved to nearby Beauport, and the following year to Ste. Foy, on the opposite side of Quebec. There, they were joined by a number of Iroquois converts. In 1673, the Huron/Iroquois settlement moved a short distance to Ancienne-Lorette and, in 1697, to the nearby location of Jeune-Lorette, about nine miles northwest of Quebec.[12]

The village counted about 30 warriors in 1710[13] and about 60 warriors in 1736.[14] In the first decade of the 1800s, the community consisted of about 200 people living in about fifty wood and stone houses.[15] A letter from 1709/1710 describes the industrious villagers of Lorette:

*They cultivate corn like the other Indians in the colony but are better workers. The work they do in selling fish, game, **canoes, and gum** [my emphasis] and the good use they make of the money received means they make a living and are not a charge on His Majesty.[16]*

The villagers produced canoes in a full range of sizes, from small ones for a single hunter to the largest freight canoes. In 1738, Claude LeBeau travelled with two Huron men, probably from Lorette, on the rivers of eastern Canada. In his description of the canoes produced by the Quebec Hurons, he noted: "They are of different sizes of two, four, and up to ten places, distinguished by the crosspieces. Each place [of the large canoes] must accommodate easily two paddlers, except the ends, which can only accommodate one."[17] Each "place" to which LeBeau referred is the space between two thwarts.

By the early 1800s, the Lorette community relied even more on its production of native items for sale. An 1832 document indicates that they sold the following items at the Quebec market and at the entrance to their village: ". . . moccasins, snow-shoes, sashes, Indian sleighs, fur caps and mittens, collars of porcupine quills, purses, bows, arrows, and *paddles*."[18] (my emphasis) Although birchbark canoes were not listed in this particular document with the paddles, it is highly likely that they were still being produced for sale by the Lorette Hurons at that time.

In 1756, four years after Louis Franquet penned his report on the principal canoe yard at Trois-Rivières, another French officer described the construction of voyaging canoes in the St. Lawrence Valley. Capitaine Leduchat observed such craft being built at Quebec City.[19] In his *Relation*, he indicated that those which he saw under construction measured 30 feet long by 2 feet deep and cost the government 400 livres. These measurements of French feet (*pieds*) convert to 32 feet by 2 feet 2 inches in modern English measure. He noted that ". . . the largest bark canoes are 30 [French] feet long, can contain 20 men easily, and when they are loaded 4 men suffice to navigate them." It is not known whether the canoe production yard which was observed by Leduchat was that of the Hurons or whether it was a different yard at or near Quebec.

KAHNAWAKE

The mission settlement of Kahnawake, which stood on the southern shore of the St. Lawrence southwest of Montreal, was first established for Iroquois converts in 1667. Over a span of 49 years, its location was moved slightly westward four times, in 1676, 1690, 1696 and 1716. Various Iroquois groups lived in the community, but the majority of the inhabitants were Mohawks. The village was called La Prairie de la Madeleine, Sault St. Louis, or Kahnawake because of its location beside the Sault St. Louis (the present Lachine Rapids). The people who lived there were often referred to as the Iroquois of the Sault.[20] A letter from 1709/1710 indicates that "They number about 190 warriors. There is always a garrison of soldiers there with a commanding officer."[21] The estimated count of warriors living in the community numbered 200 in 1716, 300 in 1736 and 300 in 1763.[22] By the first decade of the 1800s, the village was made up of about 800 people living in about 150 houses of stone.[23]

The traditional homelands (in the present state of New York), from which the Iroquois settlers had emigrated, lay south and southeast of Lake Ontario. White birch did not grow in much of this territory. In the western and central Iroquois lands, there were four rather small, isolated areas of white birch growth, as well as two larger areas which projected northward from the major birch region of Pennsylvania. In the eastern Iroquois lands, the northern portion of Oneida territory and much of the northern and eastern portions of Mohawk territory sustained considerable white birch growth.[24] Due to the availability or lack of various types of trees, elm bark canoes were much more common in Iroquois culture than birchbark canoes. However, the Iroquois acquired many birchbark craft in their raids on the St. Lawrence settlements.[25]

Those Iroquois who emigrated northeastward to live among the French quickly adopted the birchbark canoes of their French and Indian neighbors. The missionary priest, Fr. Claude Chauchetière, served the Iroquois community of Kahnawake within a decade of its founding. In 1686, he authored a report on the nineteen-year history of the mission village, illustrating it with his own finely detailed ink drawings. In one of the illustrations, entitled *The Indians Settle at La Prairie de la Magdeleine Alongside the French*, the artist/priest depicted the Iroquois paddling, poling, and portaging birchbark canoes.[26]

In the same year of 1686, a military expedition of 107 Frenchmen travelled northward via the Ottawa and Abitibi rivers to capture the three trading posts of the Hudson's Bay Company on James Bay. The forces included 70 voyageurs led by six Canadian officers. Chevalier de Troyes, the commandant, recorded in his account these notes about the expedition canoes, some of which were acquired at Kahnawake:

The men were well equipped, and had acquired so many canoes en route [to Montreal] that I was able to push on directly to the end of the island [Montreal Island]. Following my instructions, the men had assembled a number of sleds there. These were to be used for hauling over the ice the canoes, supplies, and munitions necessary for such a long journey. In north-

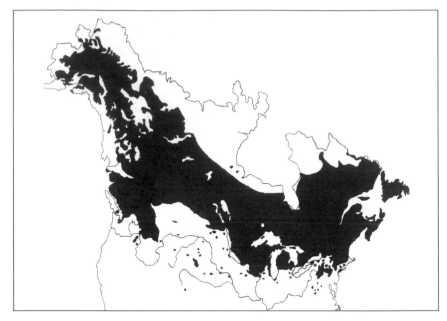

Natural range of the white birch tree.

*ern countries, this method of travel is quite common. . . . On the thirtieth of March, I distributed thirty-five canoes – as many large ones as small ones – among my men and set off again. With the exception of the Reverend Father Silvie, I was followed by the entire detachment and all of the gear. Father Silvie remained on the island to await the return of some men **who were coming from Prairie de Magdaleine [Kahnawake] where they had gone for some additional canoes.**[27]* (my emphasis)

A watercolour of Kahnawake, done in the early 1700s, shows a village composed of 54 Iroquois longhouses aligned in two rows parallel to the St. Lawrence and an adjacent complex of Jesuit buildings.[28] The latter includes a chapel connected by an enclosed corridor to the priest's house, plus a stable and a small dwelling. The Jesuit complex is enclosed by a low fence of upright posts. Seven canoes appear in the foreground; all have high upswept ends similar to those which were drawn in 1686 by the missionary artist Chauchetière at the village. Three of the craft are pulled up on the riverbank, while four are in use. All are of medium size, with three or four persons in each of the canoes which are afloat. Two have masts

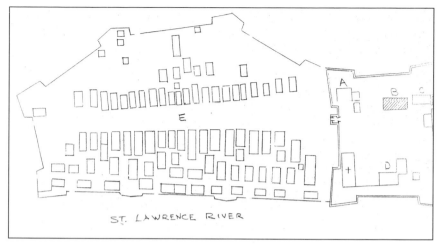

Kahnawake in 1752: A merchant's house and buildings; B. canoe shed; C. soldiers' quarters; D. priests' house; E. Iroquois village.

rigged for sailing. The scene indicates a village very much attuned to the use of birchbark canoes.

A detailed map of the settlement was drawn in 1752 by the engineer Louis Franquet, entitled *Plan of the Fort of Sault St. Louis, with the Iroquois Indian village.*[29] He estimated the population of the community to be 1,000 to 1,100, with about 200 warriors. In the intervening decades between the previously described painting and Franquet's map, the village had grown considerably; about 35 longhouses had been added, mostly between the riverbank and the first row of longhouses. In addition, a second priest's house had been built, connected to the original one.

Of significance to the present study is a series of structures which had been built just inland from the Jesuit complex. At the right on the map is a house for the soldiers that were garrisoned at the village (*corps du garde*) and a barn (*écurie*). At the left are two attached structures and a separate adjacent building. This latter complex is labeled "the house of the French merchants named Desonier." The Trottier/Desonier family was one of the most prominent families in the fur trade of the French regime, as it had been since the trading expedition of 1660-1663 to Lake Superior.

In the center lies a large structure which is labeled as a *hangard* – a canoe shed. According to the scale of the map, the building measured about 5 *toises* by 12 *toises*, which equals about 32 feet by 76 feet.[30] The canoe shed was positioned between the soldiers' quarters and the traders' buildings, adjacent to the Jesuit complex and the Iroquois village which could (and did) field 200 to 300 warriors in the service of the French. Its location reflects the various kinds of voyages on which the canoes were used, as well as the personnel who travelled in them. No indication was given by Franquet as to whether canoes were built and/or repaired in the *hangard*, or whether they were only stored there between expeditions, as was done in the *hangard du Roi* (King's canoe shed) across the St. Lawrence in Montreal.

As protection against possible attack by British forces and their native allies, the Iroquois village was encircled by a palisade of upright posts, while the adjacent French complex was enclosed by a stone fort. The engineer indicated that at the time of his survey the two interior stone walls of the French complex ". . . are hardly done, nor is the part of the enclosure around the village which faces the river."

OKA OR KANESATAKE

In 1676, the Sulpicians established a mission community of Iroquois converts at Mont Royal, a little inland from Montreal. The settlers became known as the Iroquois of the Mountain, due to the location of the mission. By 1694, the community consisted of 50 longhouses, 15 French-style houses and a church, surrounded by a palisade; four years later, a stone fort was added. Thus, the settlement had a similar appearance to that of Kahnawake, as mapped by Franquet. In 1704, this village site was abandoned, having been re-established on the Rivière des Prairies near Sault au Recollet (Recollet Falls) north of Montreal. At its new location, the village was rebuilt in the same format, with the natives living in a palisaded village and the missionaries in a stone fort. By 1709/1710, the community had both an Iroquois and an Algonkin populace, with the larger Iroquois segment having forty warriors compared to the thirty warriors of the Algonkins. In 1721, the village moved a final time, to the north shore of the Ottawa River at its junction with the St. Lawrence, northwest of Montreal. This segment of the Ottawa River is called Lac des Deux Montagnes. Here at Oka or Kanesatake, the Iroquois and Algonkins were soon joined by Algonkins from Ste. Anne at the western end of Montreal Island and Nipissings from nearby Ile aux Tourtes.[31]

The community was constructed in two distinct segments, as shown by a detailed map drawn in 1743.[32] On a point of land projecting into the Ottawa River stood the church, home and stable of the missionaries, surrounded by a stockade with four bastions. This French complex was flanked on one side by the Iroquois and Huron village and, on the opposite side, by the villages of the Nipissings and the Algonkins. In 1736, the community counted the following warriors: 60 Iroquois, 50 Nipissings, and 20 Algonkins. By the first decade of the 1800s, the total population of the settlement numbered about 2,000.[33]

The two main segments of the community, Iroquois and Algonkin, remained distinctly separate; they even had separate church services, in their respective languages, in the single mission church.[34] However, Mohawk eventually became the language spoken by each of the groups in the settlement.[35] Perhaps that is the reason that some French maps, such as one from 1750, indicate Village *des Iroquois* for the Oka settlement.[36]

References in period journals of the fur trade era reveal that the native community at Oka supplied voyaging canoes and canoe repair materials to the trade. In 1783, Jean Baptiste Perrault travelled from Montreal to Cahokia in the Illinois Country, to work as a clerk there for a Mackinac trader. The brigade of two canoes departed from Lachine on May 28, 1783. Perrault's journal records the purchase of an additional canoe at Oka, shortly after departing from Lachine:

We set out the next day . . . and Encamped at the Lac des deux montagnes. Our canoes Being overloaded, our Bourgeois (a term which all the voyageurs in general use) *was compelled to obtain a third Canoe in order to Relieve us. . . . The water was still so high as to compel our Bourgeois To engage Two more men.*[37]

(The source of the first two canoes of this brigade is discussed in a later portion of this chapter.) A decade later, in 1793, John Macdonnel signed on with the NWC as a clerk. At Oka, his brigade purchased canoe repair materials and probably a canoe as well. Macdonnel's journal reads:

May 27th Monday . . . proceeded to Pointe au gravois opposite the Indian village of Lake of two Mountains where we put up for the night. Next morning the guide & I went accross (sic) to the Indian Village for a supply of bark, gum, and wattap, to mend our canoe in case of need.

30th. Walked up the Long-sault . . . we slept two nights at the head of the third of three portages. . . . The reason of our staying two nights at this place was to wait the arrival of our associate brigade conducted by an old guide named Denis who we find broke one of his Canoes and is gone back to the village of Lake of the two mountains, either to get another or materials to repair the broken one.[38]

In 1761, Alexander Henry the Elder travelled to Michilimackinac; he was one of the very first of the British and American traders who entered the interior fur trade after the conquest of New France. With the resumption of the trade after the war, virtually all aspects of the former French trade were revived, utilizing the same canoe sources, voyageurs, interpreters, clerks and customs. When Henry left Lachine in his brigade of canoes with his French trading associate, the party proceeded from Ste. Anne across Lac des Deux Montagnes. His account indicates: "At noon, we reached the Indian Mission of the Seminary of Saint-Sulpice [Oka]. . . . Here, we received a hospitable reception, and remained during two hours."[39] Henry does not indicate the purpose of their two-hour stopover at the village. It is highly likely that his French Canadian trading partner was purchasing canoe repair materials and/or making arrangements for the resumption of the building of freight canoes by the villagers.

Fur trade canoes which were built in the region of the Ottawa River and its tributaries became known as *Nadowe chiman* or *Adowe chiman*, which means "Iroquois canoes" in the Algonqian languages.[40] This naming custom certainly must relate to the long-term manufacture of voyaging canoes at the two Iroquois communities of Kahnawake and Kanesatake (Oka) which flanked Montreal Island.

The involvement of these two Iroquois settlements in the trade was not limited to canoe building. During the French regime, Kahnawake became the headquarters for the illegal trade with Albany. Furs were transported from there southward via the Richelieu and Hudson rivers to Albany, to be exchanged for British goods, which the Indians often preferred to French items. The Algonkins living at Kanesatake also participated actively in this illicit trade.[41]

By the 1780s or earlier, the independent Montreal trader, Beaubien Des Rivières, had established several posts on the upper Ottawa River and in the Lake Abitibi region to the north. The village of Oka provided most of the men, as well as the provisions, for his interior operations. In the spring of 1788, the village provided him with about 150 bushels of corn and sufficient flour for the sustenance of his brigades and post personnel during the coming year.[42] It is also highly probable that Oka supplied the fur trade canoes for his brigades as well.

The two Iroquois settlements flanking Montreal, plus the offshoot community of St. Regis further up the St. Lawrence, provided a great many voyageurs to the trade in the latter years.[43] Between 1790 and 1815, approximately 350 men from these three communities were hired by the Montreal fur companies. They paddled the routes to the upper Ottawa River and to Moose Fort on James Bay, as well as to Grand Portage, Rainy Lake and the far northwest. The greatest single concentration of Iroquois hirings took place between 1800 and 1804, when the NWC and its rival the XY Co. were expanding their territories and needed great numbers of men. After the coalition of these two companies in 1804, the hirings slackened. Between 1815 and 1821, the HBC hired both Canadians and Iroquois voyageurs at Montreal, as the company expanded its territory into the Athabasca region. Colin Robertson, who headed this expansion, wrote in 1819:

I have frequently heard the Canadian and Irroquois voyagers (sic) disputed as regards their merits, perhaps the former may be more hardy or undergo more fatigue, but in either a rapid or traverse, give me the latter, from their calmness and prescence (sic) of mind which never forsakes them in the greatest danger.[44]

After the amalgamation of the HBC and NWC in 1821, the HBC continued to hire Iroquois voyageurs from the mission settlements. Correspondence of the company from the 1840s and 1850s indicates that the majority of the voyageurs who paddled in the brigades on the St. Maurice River system from Trois-Rivières in that period were hired from Kahnawake and Oka.[45] Philip Burns, the HBC agent at Trois-Rivières, wrote to Edward Hopkins, assistant to Governor Simpson of the HBC and husband of the artist Frances Anne Hopkins, at Hudson's Bay House in

Lachine concerning the paddlers that Hopkins hired for him. Burns wrote on August 19, 1848: "I also received the list of the names of the Eighteen Iroquois under engagement for the second trip to the Saint Maurice they all appeared and behaved well."[46]

Simpson drew from the same supply of Iroquois voyageurs at the mission settlements to make up the crew for his own canoe, as well as for the crews needed for occasional local usage in the Montreal area. A fellow traveller on one of the Governor's voyages wrote: "He had a picked crew of Iroquois canoemen from Caughanawaga, above Montreal, than whom there are no better in the world."

When the Prince of Wales made his royal visit to Canada in 1860, Governor Simpson arranged a canoe regatta for the Prince near Lachine, which took place on the first day of August. The *Illustrated London News* reported to its readership in Britain:

A flotilla of nine large birch-bark canoes was drawn up in a line close to the head of the island . . . their crew, composed of 100 Iriquois (sic) Indians, from Caughnawaga and the Lake of Two Mountains, being costumed en sauvage, gay with feathers, scarlet cloth, and paint.[47]

TROIS-RIVIÈRES AND POINTE DU LAC

The Trois-Rivières region and the St. Maurice River system formed the traditional boundary on the north side of the St. Lawrence between the Algonkins and the Montagnais. The Algonkin territory lay upriver, to the west of the St. Maurice. As early as the 1620s, a mixed group of Algonkins and Montagnais settled at Trois-Rivières and planted crops. Numbers of Algonkins continued to reside there after the French community was established in 1634. After the decimation and dispersal of the Algonkins in the Ottawa River region by the Iroquois in the 1640s and 1650s, many refugees settled at Trois-Rivières and at the Algonkin community of Pointe du Lac, about seven miles up the St. Lawrence on the northern shore. In 1736, the Algonkins of the area counted 15 warriors and, in 1757, a similar number. The last fourteen families moved from these two communities to the mission at Oka in 1830.[48]

In considering the native canoe builders of Trois-Rivières, one must look to the writings of Louis Franquet, whose map of Kahnawake has been discussed. He was sent by the French court in 1752 to assess the state of defense of the military posts of New France. In his report, entitled *Voyages et Mémoires sur le Canada*, Franquet included a description of his visit to the most productive canoe yard in Canada at the time, at Trois-Rivières.[49] This yard is presumed to be that of Louis Le Maître.[50] Franquet's full report on the canoe yard is presented later; here are only certain passages which pertain to the native builders:

> *It is in this city where they make the best bark canoes; I have been to a [canoe] yard. . . . The craftsman who makes them did not want to divulge his secret, that is, the way he determines the curvature of the two ends. There is another one here who makes them also, but he is not so successful. The first makes such a large quantity that he draws on the king every year for more than 6,000 livres.* **Women and girls work on them.** (my emphasis)

Numerous period references have been cited in this study which clearly portray the traditional division of labour by gender in native construction of birchbark canoes. The same custom appears to have been widespread across much of the birchbark canoe country: if men, women, and children were available to assist in the canoe building process, the men performed the woodworking and overall assembly tasks, while the women and children sewed the canoes with roots and sealed the seams with gum. Even at the major fur trade canoe yards in the interior, such as at Fort William, where French-Canadian craftsmen were often brought in, the traditional division of labour was often upheld, with native women sewing and gumming the craft. It is abundantly clear from Franquet's description that the Le Maître canoe yard at Trois-Rivières likewise followed the traditional division of labour: "*Women and girls work on them.*" There is little doubt that the women and girls whom he employed were natives, practising a traditional craft that had been handed down for centuries through many generations of their ancestors. The craftwomen were presumably Algonkins who lived in Trois-Rivières or in their nearby settlement of Pointe du Lac. Franquet refers to the French-Canadian craftsman who operated the yard (presumably Le Maître), but he does not indicate whether other men, French or Indian, were employed in the production.

Quebec Canoe, built before 1860 in the St. Lawrence or Ottawa Valley regions.

The report by Louis Franquet is one of the most detailed of the descriptions of canoe building in the St. Lawrence settlements. Virtually none of the other observers mentioned a division of labour by gender, or implied that native workers were employed. If the practice of employing native women and girls was carried out at the canoe yard which was the most prominent one during the French regime and later, it is highly likely that such a practice was also carried out at other "French" canoe yards on the St. Lawrence as well. Proof of this assertion is found in an account written by Isaac Weld in 1796. He observed:

Nearly all the birch bark canoes in use on the St. Lawrence and Utawa Rivers, and on the nearer lakes, are manufactured at Three Rivers [Trois-Rivières], *and in the neighborhood,* **by Indians** *(my emphasis) The birch tree is found in great plenty near the town; but it is from the more northern part of the country, where the tree attains a very large size, that the principal part of the bark is procured that canoes are made with.*[51]

The Algonkin community of Pointe du Lac was located about seven miles up the St. Lawrence from Trois-Rivières and its canoe yards. About eleven miles further upriver from Pointe du Lac lay Rivière du Loup (later named Louiseville). Here, Charles Le Maître dit Auger ("called Auger") settled and established a canoe yard, in about 1698 to 1704. He was a paternal uncle of the builder, Louis Le Maître. Charles dropped the Le Maître portion of his name, using only the name Auger. In the 1700s, his sons Charles, Étienne, Michel and François assisted their father in the canoe production.[52] The proximity of the Auger canoe yard to the Algonkin settlement at Pointe du Lac suggests the probability that native workers were employed in the yard, for at least some phases of production, as they were at Louis Le Maître's yard in Trois-Rivières. The Auger canoe business is examined in detail later.

ST. FRANÇOIS DU LAC AND BEÇANCOUR

The consideration of the native work force in the building of expedition canoes in the St. Lawrence Valley leads to the two remaining native communities that were established among the French. Abenakis from New England began emigrating to the areas of Montreal and Trois-Rivières some time before 1662. Some of the men married Algonkin and Nipissing women from the mission settlements. Through these associations, they engaged in fur trade voyages to Lake Huron, where they were seen by Father Nouvel in 1675. One group of Abenakis accompanied La Salle on his 1682 expedition to the mouth of the Mississippi. By 1690, a large group had established the village of Odanak or St. François du Lac on the St. François River near its junction with the St. Lawrence.[53] The usefulness of this native settlement as a defensive post for the French settlements was made clear by Governor Denonville, who wrote of this community in 1690:

It will be necessary to carefully maintain and fortify that village for, doubtless, the English will be able to send some Iroquois to attack it. This mission protects Quebec which will not be attacked until the former be taken.[54]

In 1704, a large group of Abenakis emigrated from New England to settle about 25 miles further down the St. Lawrence from St. François, on the Beçancour seigneury. In 1736, the two Abenaki communities counted

180 warriors at St. François and 60 warriors at Beçancour.[55] In 1759, the village of St. François was destroyed by the Rogers Rangers in an overland surprise raid from New England; the Abenakis rebuilt it in 1767.[56]

A number of Abenakis were employed in the fur trade; one example is found in the ledger books of the merchant, Monière of Montreal. In the fall of 1734, François Ménard, the interpreter at Michilimackinac, was about to travel from Montreal to his post at the Straits. He hired an Abenaki to make the trip with him. On September 24, Monière billed Ménard for the following items, which were delivered to the Abenaki: one 2-point blanket, two pounds of tobacco, and one bundle of wattap (lashing roots).[57]

Several links connect the settlement of St. François du Lac to the Le Maître canoe yard at Trois-Rivières and the Auger yard at Louiseville. (Trois-Rivières and St. François lie about 25 miles apart, on opposite sides of the wide St. Lawrence.) The first known connection of the two canoe builders to St. François dates from Charles Auger's marriage to Madeleine Crevier in 1689. Madeleine's uncle, Jean Crevier, a fur merchant of Trois-Rivières, had purchased the seigneury of St. François in August of 1676, fourteen years before the Abenaki settled there. Jean was captured by the Iroquois in 1693; he was traded to the Dutch at Albany in August of that year, but he died shortly thereafter. His wife died at St. François in December of 1711.[58]

A second link is that of Louis Le Maître's son, Joseph. He married a young woman from St. François whose parents had been settled there since at least 1699, and he established a canoe production yard there in the second quarter of the 1700s.[59] In addition, Louis Le Maître's cousin, Charles Auger Jr., one of the canoe-builder sons of Charles Auger, also married a young woman from St. François.[60] The final connection is that of Antoine Du Guay, a descendant of one of the Du Guay familial connections to Louis Le Maître and his brother, Pierre Le Maître dit Lottinville; Antoine also operated a canoe yard at St. François, from at least 1816 to 1849. Documentation exists in a fur trade journal for the use of two of the canoes which were produced in the yard of Joseph Le Maître at St. François du Lac. (Joseph had died in 1750, but the yard was kept in operation by other Le Maître family members.) In 1783, the NWC clerk, Jean Baptiste Perrault, travelled from Trois-Rivières to Montreal in preparation for his departure for the Illinois Country. His father, who had married Louis Le Maître's daughter, Marie, at Trois-Rivières in 1757, was involved in the fur trade at Louiseville. Through his friendship with a Michilimackinac merchant named Marchesseaux, the father had arranged for his son, Jean Baptiste (Louis Le Maître's grandson), ". . . to go to Illes-y-noir in the capacity of clerk," according to the son's 1783 journal. His entries continue:

The tenth of may, in eighty-three. M. Marchesseaux ordered me to bring together at montreal the men whom he had engaged. [He lists nine names.] I was to conduct them to St. francois Des wabannakes [Abenakis], and to procure and bring along two canoes from the home of Mr. LeMaitre. The twelfth of may at eleven o'clock in the morning I was ready to set forth. My mother entreated me to have something to eat, but my Heart did not permit it . . . then I betook myself to Ste. Francois to procure the canoes. I arrived at montreal the fifteenth of may, at noon.[61]

As has been previously discussed, it was this brigade of two canoes that was found to be overloaded, and its trader needed to purchase a third canoe at Oka shortly after departing from Lachine.

The employment of native women and girls in Louis Le Maître's manufactory at Trois-Rivières has been pointed out, as well as the comment of Isaac Weld concerning the building of fur trade canoes in the Trois-Rivières area by Indians. It is highly likely that the canoe yards which were established at the large Abenaki community of St. Francois by Le Maître's son and other builders related to him drew considerably from the native work force there.

Two other canoe yards were also operated in the latter 1700s in the area where the Abenakis lived. One was located in the community of Nicolet, which lay at about the halfway point in the 25 mile span between the two Abenaki communities of St. François and Beçancour.[62] This yard was run by Antoine Leclerc, a descendant of Louis Le Maître or his brother, Pierre Le Maître dit Lottinville. Again, the location suggests the probable employment of Abenaki workers in the canoe production.

One example of the manufacture at Leclerc's yard at Nicolet is represented by a notary contract of November 2, 1785. In this agreement, Leclerc contracted to build a canoe for Mr. Frobisher (one of the NWC supply partners in Montreal). No description or size specifications are given, but the price of 350 livres indicates that it was the largest size of craft.[63]

In the same era, Jacques Lottinville Jr. (a descendant of Louis Le Maître's brother Pierre) operated a yard at Petit Lac St. Paul, about four miles upriver from the Abenaki settlement of Beçancour. On April 9, 1792, he agreed to supply a number of "8 place canoes to be built on the large building frame" to the following series of NWC supply agents at Montreal: McTavish, Frobisher & Co.; Todd and McGill; Forsyth, Richardson & Co.; and William Grant, Campion & Co.[64]

Franquet indicated, in his 1752 report on the Trois-Rivières canoe yard which he visited, that voyaging canoes were also built at other locations in the St. Lawrence settlements: "It is in this city where they make the **best** bark canoes." (my emphasis) He also noted that there were two major canoe yards at or near Trois-Rivières: "There is another one there who makes them also but he is not so successful. The first makes such a large quantity that he draws on the king every year for more than 6,000 livres."

Documentation has been found for two major canoe yards in the Trois-Rivières/Lac St. Pierre area in the period of 1752. It is clear that the most productive yard, the one observed by Franquet, was that of Louis Le Maître. His son Louis Jr., assisted in the operation of the yard until the death of Louis, Jr. in 1755.[65] The "less successful" manufactory was apparently the yard founded by Louis' uncle, Charles Le Maître dit Auger. The latter yard, located 18 miles up the St. Lawrence from Trois-Rivières at Louiseville, built canoes and did considerable repair of canoes for Montreal merchants. By the time of Franquet's visit in 1752, Charles was deceased; the yard was then run by his sons, Charles Jr., Étienne, Michel, and François.[66]

There is also a possibility that the "less successful" yard may have been that of Jacques Leclair dit Blondin, which also was located at Trois-Rivières. Leclair (or Leclerc) was descended from Louis Le Maître or his brother, Pierre. An example of his output is reflected in a notary contract of November 19, 1765. Leclair contracted to build for the merchant, Aaron Hart of Trois-Rivières, an 8-place canoe " . . . entirely from new materials."[67] This clause in the contract implies that old, unrepairable canoes were sometimes stripped of their intact wooden elements, for reuse in new craft. This procedure has also been suggested in relation to the large stock of "unrepairable" canoes listed in the 1816 inventory of Fort William.

The complete text of Franquet's 1752 report is presented herewith, followed by a selection of references which indicate the activities which took place at the Le Maître and Auger canoe yards in and near Trois-Rivières.

It is in this city where they make the best bark canoes; I have been to see a [canoe] yard. They were building an 8-place one; it was 33 feet long, five wide, two and onehalf deep and cost 300 livres. [These measurements, made in the 18th century French unit of a pied, convert in modern English measurements to 35' 2" length, 5' 4" beam, and 2' 8" depth.].[68] *When they are done, they send them to Montreal; they are destined for the upper country, to carry troops as well as provisions and merchandise. The craftsman who makes them did not want to divulge his secret; that is, the way he determines the curvature of the two ends. There is another one there who makes them also but he is not so successful. The first makes such a large quantity that he draws on the king every year for more than 6,000 livres. Women and girls work on them. They are made wholly of birchbark with rounded ribs that are used in place of knees. They are of cedar or pine wood, two lignes [each 1/12 inch] thick at most, and three pouces [inches] wide, and the seams, covered with pine gum, are watertight, but one must also beware of rocks.*[69]

If all or nearly all of the craft which the Le Maître yard produced for the state each year were of the largest size (costing 300 livres apiece), Louis Le Maître's annual production for the state would have been approximately twenty canoes. This annual production figure does not take into account the canoes that his yard produced for private traders.

In 1741, Louis Le Maître provided two canoes to Mr. Gaucher dit Gamelin, the trader at the Rainy Lake post at that time. The sale was handled by the Montreal merchant, Alexis Monière, who was Gaucher dit Gamelin's trade associate. Monière's ledger reads: "1741, May 20. Paid to Mr. Lemaitre of Trois-Rivieres for two canoes which he sold to Mr. Gauche (sic)."[70] In the same summer of 1741, the prominent Montreal merchant, Ignace Gamelin, made an agreement ". . . with the named Le Maître, living at Trois-Rivières, to furnish to him all of the bark canoes that the said Le Maitre and his son will make on the large building frame, to begin the said delivery with the first canoe that they will make in the spring of the present year 1742 . . . with the exception, however, of the two canoes that they must furnish to Sieur Hery, merchant of this town." No notary contract was drawn up at the time of this agreement, but it was recorded the following year in a "declaration" by Gamelin on May 30, 1742, in Montreal.[71]

In the fall of 1745, Louis Le Maître hired Charles Du Puis to supply the canoe yard with bark for a period of two years. Louis agreed to pay him five *livres* per roll for the heavier bark for the bottoms of canoes, and fifty *sols* (2 1/2 *livres*) per roll for bark to be used for canoe side panels. The pieces of bark of both qualities were to be three French fathoms long (totalling about 16 English feet). The two men signed a contract of their agreement before the notary, Caron, at Trois-Rivières on September 27, 1745.[72]

Louis signed his name on documents as Lemaistre; others frequently wrote Le Maistre or Le Maître.[73] During the 19th century, a doctor in St. François du Lac named Joseph Lemaître claimed that he owned the stamp that his great-grandfather had used to mark his voyaging canoes.[74] The present location of the stamp is unknown.

The ledger books of the Montreal merchant, Alexis Monière, contain numerous entries reflecting the activities at the canoe yard of Charles Le Maître dit Auger and his four sons at Louiseville (at that time called Rivière du Loup). In 1735, Charles sold a canoe through Monière to La Vérendrye, presumably for one of the latter's voyages beyond Lake Superior. From this sale, Charles applied 40 livres credit toward the account of the missionary at Rivière du Loup/ Louiseville. Monière's ledger entry for June 20, 1735, reads: "Credit to Mr. Matisse, at the present time missionary at Rivière du Loup, per Mr. Auge, on a canoe he sold to Mr. de La Vérendrye, 40 livres."[75]

A year later, Monière sold another of Auger's freight canoes, to two prominent Montreal fur trade merchants. He recorded in his ledger; "1736, July 17. Credit to Mr. Auge, to delivery of 1 bark canoe which I formerly sold to Messrs. Gamelin and Lamarque. (80 livres)."[76]

The reputation of the canoes which were produced in the Auger yard at Louiseville apparently extended to the Indians of the upper Great Lakes region and beyond. In about 1770-1775, an unidentified French trader and interpreter of the upper country assembled a French-Indian vocabulary of some 200 words and expressions, and sent it to François Trinque of

Montreal.[77] Most of the terms are closely related to the Algonkin and Ojibwa terms listed in John Long's 1791 account entitled *Voyages and Travels of an Indian Interpreter and Trader*.[78] Of the following extracts, the final one is the most significant for the present study of the canoes produced in the Auger yard:

(translated from French)	(original manuscript)
The French	*Mistigouche*
The English	*Agnache*
The Grand Portage	*Quechionigam*
A kettle	*Asqueque*
An awl	*Oscatcie*
A paddle	*Apoiye*
Canoes	*Canots Oge [Auger Canoes]*

Alexis Monière often hired the Auger family to repair and refurbish fur trade canoes. The following are samples of the many entries in Monière's books pertaining to these transactions:

"*1735, June. Debit Mr. Marin. To repairs [by Mr. Auger] on his large canoe, 9 1ivres. Paid to watch over his 2 canoes, 10 livres.*

Debit Mr. LaMadeleine. Paid to Mr. Auger toward repairs on his canoe, including 3-1/2 fathoms [brasses] of bark and all the wattap required for same, plus watch over the canoe, 55 livres.[79] [The 18 1/2 feet of repair bark which was required and the high price indicate that the required repairs must have been rather extensive.]

1736, January 24 Debit Mr Auge senior of Rivière du Loup as requested in his note; delivered to his son Charles:

9 bundles of wattap @ 20 s., 9 1ivres
1 small caribou hide, 5 livres"[80]

Apparently Charles Auger, Jr. travelled from the yard at Louiseville to Montreal or Lachine during that winter. There, he made canoe repairs, for which he needed the supply of lashing roots and caribou hide.

In 1777, the trader, John Long, wrote about his departure for the Lake Superior country:

The residents in Trois-Rivières live by their commerce with the savages, and the manufacturing of birch canoes. . . . On the fourth of May, 1777, I left Montreal with two large birch canoes, called by the French, maître canots, having ten Canadians in each. . . . The canoes are made at Trois-Rivières; they are, in general, eight fathoms long, and one and a half wide . . . of this size they will carry four tons weight each.[81]

Mr. Long apparently thought that all of the canoe yards were at Trois-Rivières, rather than at several locations along both shores of the Lac St. Pierre segment of the St. Lawrence.

The HBC trader, William Tomison, wrote to the home office in London from York Factory on Hudson Bay in 1786. Regarding the canoe production at Trois-Rivières, which supplied the rival St. Lawrence traders, he noted: "For many years back [there] has been a sort of monopoly from father to son. I am informed that they build about 100 canoes every year."[82] Tomison was on the mark in his assessment of the close relationships of the various builders in the Lac St. Pierre area. Some of them were related by birth in the Le Maître family, while others married into the Le Maître clan.

Mention has already been made of the nephew/uncle relationship of Louis Le Maître and Charles Le Maître dit Auger. Sons of each of these families mastered the craft of their fathers: Louis Le Maître Jr. worked with his father until his own death in 1755, while son Joseph eventually established his own yard across the St. Lawrence at St. François du Lac. Charles Auger's sons, Charles Jr, Étienne, Michel, and François assisted in the Auger yard at Louiseville. The continuation of the canoe-building tradition in the following generations of the various related families is reflected in notary contracts of the 1790s. The builders, Jacques Lottinville Sr. and Pierre Lottinville, (descendants of Louis Le Maître's brother Pierre) and Joseph Jutras (who had married into the Le Maître family), operated a production yard at Trois-Rivières. On January 2, 1795, they contracted with McTavish, Frobisher & Co. (the NWC supply partners) to furnish a number of ". . . 8 place canoes to be built on the large building frame."[83]

Various "French" canoe yards in the region of Trois-Rivières and Lac St. Pierre have been detailed, as well as the native yards at Lorette/Quebec, Kahnawake and Oka. In addition to these locales, other sources of voyaging canoes in the St. Lawrence Valley are sometimes revealed in period documents. One such record is found in the 1799 ledger books of the North West Company. Entries in the ledger indicate that two additional sources of canoes were utilized that year, in addition to the usual yards discussed above. The notary in the seigneury of L'Assomption, about 22 miles downriver (northeast) from Montreal, apparently served as a middleman for various craftworkers in his area at that time. In 1799, he supplied the NWC with 15 North canoes, 21 canoe sails, and a number of paddles. In addition, Jacques Giasson was paid 280 francs that year for providing two North canoes.[84]

THE LATE YEARS

The need for fur trade canoes in the St. Lawrence settlements rose considerably during the period of about 1799 to 1804, during the five years of stiff competition between the XY Co. and the NWC. Increased numbers of voyageurs also were hired in Montreal during this period. Canoe production again rose during the years 1814 to 1821, when the HBC expanded its field of operations into the Athabasca country, in direct and fierce competition with the NWC.

To lay the groundwork for the acquisition of canoes, crews, and supplies to begin the HBC Athabasca campaign, Colin Robertson travelled to Montreal in 1814. He did not open an HBC office directly, but, after considerable searching, found a company of Montreal agents who would represent the HBC. The firm, Maitland, Garden & Auldjo Co., then worked in direct competition against the agents of the NWC who had been headquartered in Montreal for more than three decades.[85]

By 1819, the HBC had opened its own office in Montreal, at 79 Rue St. Paul.[86] No HBC agents appear to have operated in any other towns on the St. Lawrence until after the amalgamation of the HBC and the NWC in 1821.[87] The Montreal firm of Maitland et al arranged for the construction of voyaging canoes for the HBC's Athabasca campaign, as did the HBC agents in Montreal from 1819 on. One of the builders contracted by the company was Antoine Du Guay, a descendant of one of the Du Guay familial connections of Louis Le Maître. By the first decade of the 19th century, he operated a canoe yard at St. François du Lac. In 1816, Du Guay agreed to build canoes for the Hudson's Bay Company; on May 30 of that year, he signed a notary contract to construct *canots du nord* (North canoes) for the firm. The contract specified that the craft would have interior measurements (within the area bounded by the gunwale caps) of four fathoms (about 24 feet in English fathoms) in length by one-half fathom (about 36 inches) in width.[88] Four years later, on January 5, 1820, he again contracted to build canoes of the same dimensions for the "Honourable Company."[89]

After the coalition of the NWC and the HBC in 1821, a dramatic reorganization of the fur trade transport system took place. York Factory on Hudson Bay was made the primary point of import and export for all of Canada, rather than Quebec and Montreal. In addition, wooden boats manned by semi-skilled boatmen were substituted for canoes manned by skilled paddlers wherever the conditions of the waterways permitted the substitution. These two changes drastically reduced the number of voyaging canoes and voyageurs that were needed, on both the Montreal-to-Fort William route and on the many interior routes.

However, certain waterways were impossible or very impractical for boat travel; on these routes, canoes and voyageurs continued to handle the cargo transport. In addition, the supplies of Canadian provisions and other items which were shipped to the posts of the upper Ottawa River from the St. Lawrence region still were transported by canoe from Montreal. Finally, Governor George Simpson, the head of the HBC for all of North America, established his headquarters at Lachine in 1826. This created a continual need for canoe transport of the Governor and other passengers on official business trips between Lachine and the major inland posts and those on Hudson Bay, as well as the transport of mail between these locales.

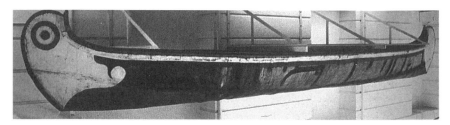

Royal Canoe, built in the second half of the 19th century, in the St. Lawrence or Ottawa Valley regions.

An example of such mail delivery is mentioned in a letter from Simpson to the HBC office in London, written on July 18, 1831. Simpson was in the interior, attending to summer business, when he wrote: "We were rejoiced to learn by the receipt of Chief Factor James Keith's Despatch of 12 May, forwarded by Express Canoe from Lachine . . ."[90]

Canoe traffic on the Ottawa River was reduced after a winter sleigh road was built in 1839 from Montreal to Mattawa, for the transport of heavy and bulky cargo during the frozen winter months.[91] The road was extended further up the Ottawa to Lake Temiscamingue in the mid-1860s; this led to the elimination of large-scale canoe transport on the lower Ottawa River.[92] Another major reduction in canoe traffic from Lachine took place after the death of George Simpson in 1860. Virtually all canoe transport from Lachine finally ended in 1880, when the Canadian Pactfic Railway extended westward from Montreal to Mattawa.[93]

The extension of railway lines to many locales in the upper Great Lakes region and further northwest in this same era also ended canoe transport in those areas as well. However, the transporting of goods by large birchbark canoes continued for several decades longer in many areas of the region which extended northward to Hudson Bay from the upper Ottawa River and lakes Huron and Superior. These canoes finally were replaced early in the 20th century by canvas and wooden canoes, wooden boats, mechanized boats and railways.

Against this backdrop of the latter years of voyaging canoes, the story returns to Trois-Rivières and the Lac St. Pierre area after 1821. An inside view of events which took place there is revealed in the correspondence of Philip Burns. Burns was stationed at Trois-Rivières in 1821 as the agent in charge of the newly opened HBC office, which served as the depot for the St. Maurice district. His letters to his superior, George Simpson, at Lachine report the minute events of the fur trade in the region. They span the period from the 1821 amalgamation of the two great fur trade companies until Burns' death in 1856, toward the closing years of bark canoe transport in the St. Lawrence Valley.

At the time of the coalition of the two huge companies in 1821, each firm had amassed a considerable number of canoes. With the drastic cutbacks in the canoe transport of trade goods, furs, and food supplies after 1821, the combined inventory of fur trade canoes was sufficient to supply the needed craft for many years. In this era, many of the canoe yards on the St. Lawrence closed, since the production of new craft was so little needed. The stock of existing canoes in the St. Lawrence Valley canoe sheds only required periodic repairs and refurbishing to satisfy the transportation needs of the HBC.

The company still used canoe brigades on the St. Maurice River system, with Trois-Rivières serving as the depot. In addition, brigades from Lachine still made cargo runs to the posts on the upper Ottawa, as well as mail and business passenger voyages to the distant interior posts.

It may be more than coincidental that the canoe yard of Antoine Du Guay at St. François du Lac remained in business during the era when many yards were closing, as he continued to do work for the HBC. This may very well be related to the fact that the Du Guay yard built canoes for the company in 1816 and 1820. That period had been the peak of competition between the HBC and the NWC, and Du Guay's yard in the St. Lawrence settlements was deep in "NWC territory." Governor Simpson, headquartered at Lachine, may have directed the company business to Du Guay after the amalgamation of the two companies, as a reward for his services to the HBC in 1816 and 1820.

At any rate, Du Guay (he spelled it Dugue) supplied new canoes as needed for Lachine and Trois-Rivières and, as well, repaired the existing stock of canoes at both of these locations. In 1837, an additional request was made of him, to provide canoe bark to the posts down below (*postes d'en bas*). These posts were probably those of the "King's Domain" on the lower St. Lawrence, which the HBC leased from the government from 1831 on.[94] Du Guay wrote to Philip Burns at the Trois-Rivières office:

2 March, 1837. St. Francois.
I cannot send a reply as . . . I did not receive the bark. As the weather contin-
ues to be bad in the woods, it is not possible to try to get it. I cannot promise
to furnish this bark. I will write you if I can procure it [translation]. *Notre*
serviteur, Antoine Dugue.[95]

Through 1848, no other individual besides Du Guay is ever mentioned in Burns' letters to Simpson in connection with the building or repairing of canoes for the HBC. It appears that Antoine Du Guay supplied all of the company's needs in these categories, at both the Lachine and Trois-

Rivières depots. Burns was the sole agent for the HBC in the Trois-Rivières region, which had long been famous for the construction of voyaging canoes. Had other craftsmen in the area been involved with the company, they certainly would have merited some mention over the years in the reports which Burns sent to Simpson concerning company business in the Trois-Rivières district.

In addition, Burns made statements in his letters concerning the delivery to Du Guay of all of the bark which would be brought down by the brigades on the St. Maurice River. This lends further support to the premise that Du Guay was the only builder in the Trois-Rivières region who supplied canoes to the company in this era. Rolls of birchbark were procured by the traders from native suppliers at the interior posts of the St. Maurice River system. They then were shipped with the down-bound brigades to Burns at Trois-Rivières, who, in turn, sold the bark to Du Guay for the construction of canoes for the HBC. This system of providing bark to the canoe yards of the Lac St. Pierre area probably was initiated during the French regime of the previous century, as bark sources in the St. Lawrence Valley became depleted. As previously mentioned, the St. Maurice source of canoe bark was noted by Isaac Weld in 17[96].

The following note from Antoine Du Guay to Philip Burns and the excerpts from Burns' letters to Simpson present an inside view of canoe construction and repair in the 1840s and 1850s in the St. Lawrence Valley. The Du Guay canoe yard may have been the last substantial production yard in the Trois-Rivières / Lac St. Pierre area that built voyaging craft.

In late October of 1843, Du Guay had finished an order of canoes for the depot at Lachine. He had hoped to deliver them in the usual manner via the St. Lawrence, but the weather so far had made the upriver trip of some sixty miles between St. François and Lachine impossible. He wrote to Burns at Trois-Rivières:

10 Nov. 1843, Saint Francois
I am writing you to request your kind assistance in telling M. McKenzie that the canoes for Lachine have been ready for 14 days and have been taken to the channel for departure, but the Ice and the cold prevent this, and we await good weather, which we are hoping for, to take them. [translation][96]

The following spring, Du Guay notified Burns on April 7, 1844 that he and his son would be at Lachine three days later, on April 10. Burns wrote Simpson on April 8: "I beg leave to say that I have delayed answering your letter of the 25 ult. [March] until I should have received an answer from Antoine Dugay (sic) which I received yesterday wherein he says that he will be at Lachine with his son on the Tenth Instant [April]."[97] Six days later, on April 13, he wrote: "I hope that Dugay (sic) has reached Lachine according to his promise."[98]

Du Guay indicated a specific arrival date, brought along his son, and apparently stayed for at least several days at Lachine or Montreal. No mention was made in the letters of the delivery of any canoes. Thus, it appears likely that the two Du Guays made the trip to Lachine or Montreal to carry out repairs on some older canoes, to prepare them for the upcoming season of travel.

Before considering Du Guay's canoe production further, a synopsis should be made of the brigades for which he supplied the canoes. The brigades that departed from Lachine are well known, but those travelling on the St. Maurice River system seldom have been described. The correspondence of Burns indicates that the brigade from Trois-Rivières made two round trips each year up the St. Maurice and back. The group of three to five canoes usually departed from Trois-Rivières early in the summer, and again in late August or early September. The canoes returned to Trois-Rivières singly, rather than in a brigade, often spaced at intervals of a week or more. The final canoe normally returned to the St. Lawrence between the end of September and the middle of October.

The voyaging craft which were used by the brigades were of North canoe size, normally manned by six paddlers. Burns wrote to Edward Hopkins at Montreal on August 19, 1848 concerning the voyageurs that Hopkins had hired for the St. Maurice at Montreal: "I also received the list of the names of the Eighteen Iroquois under engagement for the second trip to the Saint Maurice they all appeared and behaved well."[99] He mentioned later in the letter that there were bills of lading included for the three canoes which were manned by these voyageurs. Nearly all of the references to the voyageurs in the letters refer to Iroquois.

When the second brigade of the summer of 1855 ascended the St. Maurice from Trois-Rivières, the usual crew of six men paddled in each of the two canoes that were travelling together. But illness thinned the ranks, as indicated in a letter which the trader, Richard Hardesty, wrote to Burns on August 31 from La Tuque, while he and the canoes were en route:

Another of our men an Iroquois has been sick since we passed the Grand Mere on the 26th inst. and no chance of his getting better. I find that I am obliged to leave him here to get a passage down by the first canoe that will be leaving here. Joseph Marie has also been idle since yesterday moming, or rather pretends to be ill and refuses to go any farther, he also remains here, and we are now obliged to proceed on with only five men in each canoe and I expect that I shall have to leave pieces out of each canoe at one of the [word illegible] *or the others will not go beyond this.*[100]

These large canoes were not the only size of birchbark canoes which were used by the St. Maurice voyageurs, especially when the large craft were damaged. Burns wrote to Simpson on September 19, 1855:

I have received a letter from Mr. Hardesty by four Gowers (sic) *and comers* [voyageurs]. *They came down in two Small Canoes, one of the Large Canoes being useless and unfit to send back again.*[101]

It is not known whether Antoine Du Guay supplied the HBC with these two-man sized craft. The excerpt underscores the damage which was often incurred by the cargo canoes en route.

The list of equipment and food supplies which accompanied the canoes from Trois-Rivières is set forth in a letter from Burns to Simpson of August 19, 1854:

I herewith annex a list of supplies required for the four canoes to be sent up the Saint Maurice.
I Canoe Line for Each canoe, the same as last sent
2 new oilcloths, and the two that I delivered to Mr. Hardesty to repair the same
2 Kettle baskets
1 Carry strap for each man
1 Bag Pork
1 Bag Pease (sic)
3 Bags Biscuits[102]

The diet of the St. Maurice voyageurs may have been altered a little the following year. On August 9, 1855, Burns reported to Simpson: "I received this morning thirty bags flour and fourteen Bags Corn shipped by Mr. Louis Boyer."[103]

The correspondence of Burns to Simpson in the fall of 1848 furnishes considerable information on the production at Antoine Du Guay's canoe yard at St. François du Lac. On September 6, Burns wrote:

The Canoe No. 5 arrived this afternoon [from the St. Maurice]. . . . *The Iroquois delivered* [to] *me two rolls of Canoe Bark. I will deliver the Bark that may come down to Antoine DuGay (sic) the Canoe builder.*[104]

He reported two weeks later, on September 18: "The Iroquois of the 4th. Canoe arrived last night. They brought down three rolls of Canoe Bark. . . . They have not delivered [to] me their Portage Straps."[105]

In his letter of October 16, 1848, Burns discussed the St. Maurice canoes which were built in 1847 and repaired in the summer of 1848. He also referred to those that were constructed in the spring of 1848, which would need only minor repairs and gumming in the spring of 1849 to be ready for the first voyage of 1849. His letter reads:

One of the Saint Maurice Canoes built in 1847 as [has] *not been used since it was repaired last summer. the other built at the same time made a Trip as the 4th. Canoe, and it came down in good order. and with little repairs to this canoe both can make a second Trip in Summer without some damage. . . . Those built last Spring 1848 are in excellent order. those last will only require but little repairs and gumming in the spring. I am in consequence of oppinion (sic) that no new Saint Maurice Canoes will be required for the ensueing spring. . . . What will I charge Dugay (sic) for the canoe Bark that came down from the Saint Maurice?*[106]

Burns' missive of November 1, 1848 reveals his anxiety about the damage that could occur to his stock of canoes over the coming winter; but he does not specify what protections he expected Du Guay to apply. The letter also appears to indicate that Du Guay had another order of canoes finished and ready to deliver to Lachine via the St. Lawrence, as he did five years earlier in November of 1843. Burns wrote:

I think it would be well that Dugay (sic) should come here to fix the Saint Maurice Canoes for the winter, at present their having no protection against injury by the frost during the ensueing winter. If he goes to Lachine before the closing of navigation, he could come down here on his return, and then go to Saint Francis (sic) from hence, after having done to the canoes what is necessary.[107]

These references in Philip Burns' letters extend through the end of 1848. They indicate that Antoine Du Guay's canoe yard was still producing new voyaging canoes for both the Trois-Rivières and Lachine supply depots at that time. The letters also show that Du Guay still was actively engaged in delivering those canoes by river, as well as making repairs to older canoes at both of the towns.

The references to Du Guay in the letters of Burns suddenly cease at the end of 1848. His name does not appear again in the correspondence of Burns to Simpson, which continued until Burns' death early in 1856. The unbroken series of French-Canadian builders of voyaging canoes in the Trois-Rivières / Lac St. Pierre area appears to have ended with Antoine Du Guay. No information has come to light yet concerning any further manufacture of canoes for the HBC in that region. In fact, letters from Burns to Simpson offer evidence to the contrary: they indicate that HBC canoes were shipped by steamboat from Montreal to Trois-Rivières in 1852 and 1854. This procedure appears to indicate that voyaging canoes no longer were being built by that time in the Trois-Rivières region and that the stock of such canoes there was no longer sufficient. The supply of canoes in the HBC canoe sheds at Lachine or Montreal was apparently sufficient to supply the needs of the St. Maurice brigades as well as those departing from Lachine.

On February 8, 1853, Burns wrote:

I beg leave to enclose you my account up to 30 Dec. 1852, I got a deduction of 20/ made by Tait for the Freight of the four North Canoes.[108]

His letter of November 11, 1854 reads:

I refer you to my letters of the 15th. and 23rd June 1854 and that of Mr. Finlayson of the 20th June of the same month stating to an overcharge for freight of two canoes from Montreal to three rivers. I wish to be informed if the owners of the Steamer have made any deviations in that case as I am now settling the freight and Boarding accounts of the outfit of 1854.[109]

Even if the production of fur trade canoes had ceased in the St. Lawrence Valley, the existing canoes of the company at Trois-Rivières and Lachine still needed periodic repairs and refurbishing, to keep them in operating condition. Within 2-1/2 years of the last mention of Antoine Du Guay in Burns' letters from Trois-Rivières, Pierre Marois was carrying out such repairs on the HBC canoes at both Lachine and Trois-Rivières, as Du Guay had done before him.

In 1851, Burns was making preparations to send off the St. Maurice brigade for the second trip of the summer. He wrote Simpson on August 2: "I have only one Saint Maurice Canoe repaired for the next trip up the Saint Maurice. The others that are in store still require repairs for the next voyage."[110] At the time, Pierre Marois was at Lachine, repairing the canoes there. On August 6, Burns urged Simpson to send Marois down to Trois-Rivières soon, so that he could make the needed repairs there:

The sooner Marois is sent down to repair the Canoes the better, in order that I may have them ready when you will order them to be sent up [the St. Maurice]. *I will thank you to send me by him some stationary* [sic].[111]

Burns had canoes in storage at that time which were considered not repairable for company usage. In anticipation of liquidating these craft, he sought Simpson's advice on April 15, 1851: "I will thank you to inform me in your next letter, in the event of my finding a chance to dispose of some of the unservisable (sic) Saint Maurice Canoes, what will I sell them at."[112] By late September, he had found a buyer for one of these canoes. On September 26, he reported:

I sold a Saint Maurice Canoe which was unservisable (sic) for the company.

I sold it for 25$ and on condition that they should take up the four Bales of Indian Presents as far up as the Vermilion; the canoe left at 1 p.m. with the 4 Bales.[113] (The Vermilion River is in the St. Maurice River system.)

No letters from Burns to Simpson for the year 1852 are preserved in the Hudson's Bay Company archives; thus, the study advances to 1853. That year, the traders up the St. Maurice continued to trade for canoe bark in the interior and send it down to Burns at Trois-Rivières. Some of the bark may have been used for repairs on St. Maurice craft, but Burns also shipped out two lots of bark.

Apparently Burns had received a request for certain canoe materials that year. On September 19, he wrote to Simpson: "I beg leave to enclose Bill [of] Lading of five packs of Made Skins brought down by the Iroquois & Eleven Rolls of Bark. . . . I have received the Canoe Ribbs (sic) for Mr. Price in good order."[114] On October 8, he reported that he had shipped to Montreal to Mssrs. Wm. Price & Co: "6 Dozen Canoe Ribbs (sic) – 5 s [shillings] per Doz. 8-1/2 Fathoms Bottom Bark – 7/1 [7shillings 1 pence per fathom]."[115] The ribs and the 51 foot supply of bottom bark probably were used for the renovation of several damaged canoes.

His final shipment of bark that year departed on October 17: "I have shipped this night by the Steamer John Munn three Rolls of Canoe Bark to the care of Mr. Louis Boyer as ordered."[116] Louis Boyer and the firm of Boyer and Hawley acted as agents for the HBC in Montreal, purchasing flour and corn for the brigades and selling such items as seal oil, salted salmon, and buffalo robes which were collected by the HBC.[117] The firm had apparently received a request in Montreal for canoe bark.

On September 13, 1853, Simpson asked Burns whether he had received any further requests for canoes or canoe materials. Burns reported on February 21, 1854 that he had received no more such requests.[118]

Pierre Marois continued his repair work on the HBC canoes at Trois-Rivières and Lachine in 1854. On August 19 of that year, Burns wrote:

I beg leave to inform you that four canoes will be repaired on Monday next, in the course of the day. I will retain Marois to repair the fifth one that I have in those of the Large Sized ones, in case of any accidents to those intended to send up there. Waters are very low now in the Saint Maurice.[119]

Nine days later, on August 28, he wrote: "Marois having completed the repairs to the canoes, I send him back & I enclose you the account of Sophie Poliquin which states that he as [has] been at work Eighteen days."[120] A series of letters by Burns from Trois-Rivières in August of 1855 report on the progress of Marois' repair work that year. He spent seventeen days at Trois-Rivières, repairing the two canoes that were to ascend the St. Maurice that August, plus a third one which would be ready for use the following spring. After completing his work at Trois-Rivières, Marois apparently travelled by steamer up to Lachine, to do the required repairs on the canoes there. Burns wrote:

7 August 1855
I am in receipt of yours by Telegraph. with respect to the State of the Canoes, they will require some repairs. the Timbers of two of them, the maitre [gunwales], *are weak but I believe can be repaired. I am of oppinion* (sic) *that three of them can make a summer passage. I have had them examined by two voyageurs and that is their oppinions* (sic), *they will require some small repairs to the bottoms and head.*[121]

9 August 1855
I beg leave to inform you that Pierre Marois made his appearance this morning, and he is now at work repairing the Canoes. He told me that two Canoes are required. he selected the two best ones, and he says that he cannot have them ready before Saturday the 18th.[122]

19 August 1855
The two canoes will be ready tomorrow, to a certainty. will I retain Marois to repair a third Canoe or will I send him up by the first steamer [to Lachine to repair canoes there]? *please answer by telegraph. Last year he was kept here to repair one over the number required at the time, which was found ready this spring.*[123]

25 August 1855
I beg leave to inform you that Pierre Marois as [has] *repaired the third canoe. 1 advanced him 5 shillings. I enclose you his account for board and lodging. he commenced to come on the 9th instant* [August].[124]

In his references to Pierre Marois, Philip Burns never indicated where the canoe repairman lived. He may have resided in or near St. François du Lac, the home of his predecessor, Antoine Du Guay; but there is no direct evidence for this in Burns' correspondence. Nor did Burns indicate whether Pierre was French or Métis (mixed-blood). Families of French Canadians named Marois had lived in the St. Lawrence settlements since at least 1687.[125]

The returning St. Maurice canoes brought down to Trois-Rivières in 1855 the usual supply of canoe bark. On September 19, Burns reported:

Four Gowers (sic) and Comers [voyageurs]. . . *came down in two Small Canoes, one of the Large Canoes being Useless and unfit to send back again. I received by them five Rolls* [of] *Bottom Bark said to Contain Twenty one fathoms.*[126]

He wrote on September 28:

Pierre Towasconton the Guide arrived this afternoon from the Saint Maurice, and as [has] *brought down Twelve Rolls of Canoe Bark d,*[127]

These comments in September of 1855 are the final references to fur trade canoes and canoe materials in the letters of Philip Burns to George Simpson; Burns passed away six months later. His business letters from Trois-Rivières contain an invaluable record; they document the waning years of the production of birchbark voyaging canoes in the area of Trois-Rivières and the Lac St. Pierre portion of the St. Lawrence.

A NEW PHASE

The supply of canoe bark, which was harvested in the upper reaches of the St. Maurice River system from the 1850s on, may may have been shipped to various posts for the repair of canoes; it also may have been carried by brigades for emergency repairs en route. It might even have been used for the production of new voyaging canoes on a limited scale in certain locales. But much of the bark was probably utilized locally, by the Abenaki canoe builders at St. François du Lac.

The use of and market for large fur trade canoes waned in the St.

Lawrence and lower Ottawa River valleys in the third quarter of the 19th century. During the same period, a ready market developed in the same region for small birchbark canoes. Sportsmen used these craft extensively for hunting and fishing trips, guided by local native people. Such trips became popular on the tributary rivers of the lower and central Ottawa Valley, with outfitters at Montreal and Mattawa providing the necessary canoes, equipment and native guides for the sportsmen. These trips became especially popular after the railway was completed between Montreal and Mattawa in 1880.[128]

The styles of birchbark canoes which were used for such trips were primarily the Abenaki type and the Algonkin old model. In time, the Abenaki form became predominant; its popularity even caused many Algonkin and eastern Ojibwa builders to switch to this style, since there was a ready market for canoes of this model. The style was called *Wabenaki chiman*, "Abenaki canoe" in the Algonquian languages, by the various native groups that adopted the craft.

The Abenakis at St. François du Lac provided a great many of these canoes for the Montreal market; the manufacture there continued until about 1915. Nicolas Panadis was one of the Abenaki builders at St. François; he reported that he and a partner built thirty such canoes in one year.[129] This production probably involved the assistance of family members, following the traditional division of labor of native canoe manufacture.

LOWER ST. LAWRENCE

The foregoing discussion of voyaging canoes which were built in the St. Lawrence Valley has focused primarily on the craft that travelled westward into the interior of North America. The canoes which were built for the eastern trade of the lower St. Lawrence region still remain to be considered.

The area to the north of the lower St. Lawrence River was designated in the 17th century as the *Domaine du Roi*, the Domain of the King. Its territory extended from Ile aux Coudres, an island in the St. Lawrence near the community of Baie St. Paul, downriver to Sept Iles, near the mouth of the Moisie River. The revenues derived from the fur trade, hunting, fishing and agriculture in this region served to help defray the expenses of the colony of New France.[130]

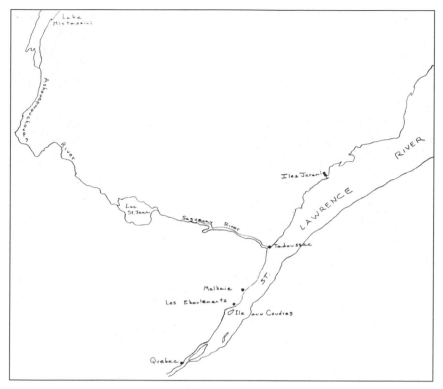

Region of the Domaine du Roi, *the Domain of the King.*

Trading posts were established in the Domain along the northern shore of the St. Lawrence from Malbaie to Sept Iles, up the Saguenay River, and northwest of the Saguenay on Lac St. Jean, the Ashouapmouchouan River and Lake Mistassini.[131] The post at Tadoussac served as the headquarters for these King's Posts, due to its central location. The post at Iles Jeremie, about 75 miles down the St. Lawrence from Tadoussac, was the most productive one for furs.[132] During the French regime and afterward, the King's Posts were leased to major traders or trading companies to operate; the NWC and later the HBC each in their turn leased the fur trade rights of the region.[133]

The native people of the region were the Montagnais. Their economy revolved around hunting, trapping, fishing and a little gathering, plus the fur trade after the arrival of Europeans.[134] A few turned to farming near the mission stations on the St. Lawrence.[135] Their traditional seasonal cycle included a summer gathering during the short summer season at large inland lakes or at the mouths of rivers that emptied into the St. Lawrence River or Gulf. Birchbark canoes were one of the primary modes of transportation of the Montagnais.

During the latter part of the French regime, fur trade canoes appear to have built in the King's Domain at the Tadoussac and Iles Jeremie posts, as well as at a canoe yard operated by three Tremblay brothers from Les Éboulements. The latter community lay within the King's Domain, on the north shore of the St. Lawrence just downriver from Ile aux Coudres. It was about fifteen miles upriver from the Malbaie Post and some 55 miles upriver from Tadoussac, the headquarters of the King's Posts. Peter Kalm, who visited Les Éboulements in 1749, indicated that it was the furthest settlement down the St. Lawrence at which agriculture was practised.[136]

The documentation which reveals the locations of the canoe yards within the *Domaine du Roi* during the French regime is found in a letter that was sent to Canada from France in 1766.[137] This letter has an interesting background.

Canadian-born Joseph Cadet held the office of *munitionnaire* (supply officer) of New France during the 1740s and 1750s, supplying the provisions for the French troops in New France. Ultimately he was convicted of embezzling public funds. For this offense, he was sent to Paris to serve a sentence in the Bastille prison. When he was released in 1766, he purchased land in France, where he planned to build a Canadian style farm. On May 5, 1766, he wrote to a Mssr. Houdin of Quebec, whom he knew was returning to France. (Britain had now taken over New France, after the French and Indian War.) Cadet requested that Houdin bring back to France various Canadian articles, such as a small carriage (*calèche*), horse collars, bearskins to decorate these collars and a plow ("as they are made in Canada"). He even asked Houdin to hire for nine years a good plowman to work on the farm in France.

The most significant items that he requested, in relation to the present study, were the following:

. . . two canoes or at least pre-cut bark to make a 4-place canoe and another of 5 places, and ready-to-assemble frames and ribs of cedar; 200 pounds of canoe gum, the resin to make the canoes and repair them whenever they

should split; and 10 fathoms (brasses) of bark to patch them. In other words, what I am asking you to acquire is pre-cut canoe parts and rolled bark for 2 canoes, ready to be assembled in France. You will contact the Tadoussac post or that of Îles Jeremie for this material; take care to request good quality bark with small grain. Should you be unable to get these articles at those places, you will call on Sieurs Etienne, Louis, or Jean Tremblay, three brothers at Éboulements near Baie St Paul. Write to them in my name; one or the other will supply these items. Make sure to also ask them to supply 40 well-made and polished paddles of maple [translation].

Cadet obviously knew canoe-building, including qualities of bark, as he was confident that he could assemble the pre-cut canoe parts in France. He may have felt that unassembled canoe elements would survive the ship journey to France better than two assembled canoes. The four-place canoe which he ordered was probably about thirteen to sixteen feet long if built in traditional native sizes, or up to 19 to 20 feet long if built in fur trade sizes.[138] It was divided into four spaces for paddlers, passengers and cargo by five thwarts. A letter from New France in 1709/1710 indicated that the four-place canoe was the size normally used when an entire Indian family travelled.[139] The five-place canoe, which Cadet also ordered, was roughly a yard longer. The measurement of the *brasse* (fathom) used by Cadet in reference to the repair bark was equivalent to 5.278 feet in France.[140] Thus, he ordered some fifty feet of bark for making future repairs. When Cadet requested "frames and ribs of cedar," he presumably meant all of the wooden elements that would be required for the two canoes. Therefore, the only items which he did not include in his order were peeled and split roots for the lashings. He must have felt he could acquire these roots, or appropriate substitutes, in France.

Cadet was apparently very familiar with the canoe and paddle production of the three Tremblay brothers of Les Éboulements. He even listed them in descending order of age: Étienne (1690-1766), Louis (1695-1772), and Jean (1701-1783). The builder Étienne Tremblay is a direct ancestor of the present author, separated by a span of seven generations.[141] The three brothers were born at the small village of La Petite Rivière St. François Xavier, on the northern shore of the St. Lawrence, about forty miles downriver from Quebec. They were the oldest three sons in a family of fifteen children. Each of the three eventually married and settled at the village of Les Éboulement, some eighteen miles down the St. Lawrence from La Petite Rivière; they all resided there for the rest of their lives.

The father of the three craftsmen, Pierre Tremblay, purchased the seigneury of Les Éboulement in 1710, when Étienne was age 20. After the father's death in 1736, the seigneury ultimately became the property of Étienne, the eldest son.

It is not known whether the canoe production yard of Étienne Tremblay and his two younger brothers was located near the village of Les Éboulements or at some distance from the community. It is highly likely that they employed Montagnais craftworkers in their yard, for at least some phases of production. This was certainly a well-established practice at numerous canoe yards in the fur trade era, as has been amply discussed. The Tremblays may have hired individuals who lived a settled life at one of the mission stations, or those who lived in the traditional Montagnais lifestyle of hunting, trapping and fishing in the interior, emerging on the St. Lawrence during the summer months.

Church records of the period indicate that the three brothers, Étienne, Louis and Jean Tremblay, and their wives were friends and associates of the native population of the region. From 1737 on, they appeared as god-parents at a number of baptisms of Indian children and as witnesses at several weddings of native couples. The records of these events are found in the record books of the missionary priest who served the parish of Les Éboulements and the posts of the *Domaine du Roi*.[142]

The three French couples witnessed at least twelve baptisms and three weddings of native people at scattered intervals over a span of some thirty years. The records indicate that some of the Indian participants in these ceremonies were from the region, while others resided as far away as Tadoussac, Iles Jeremie and Sept Iles, at the far eastern edge of the Domain. On January 7, 1760, all three of the brothers appeared as the witnesses at Les Éboulements for the marriage of a Montagnais man who resided at Tadoussac and a Mik'maq woman.[143]

By 1747, two churches had been erected in the western area of the King's Domain, at Les Éboulements and at La Malbaie, in addition to the one in the centre of the Domain at Tadoussac. It appears that the above-mentioned baptisms and weddings involving the Tremblays took place in the two former communities, near the western edge of the Domain. These associations at important liturgical occasions between the three canoe craftsmen and the Indian population may be circumstantial evidence that the brothers employed native craftworkers in their canoe and paddle production. This may have involved the gathering of bark, wood and roots, as well as some or all phases of production. It also may reflect business associations which were established by the delivery of their canoes and paddles to widely dispersed posts within the King's Domain.

No notary contracts in the name of Étienne Tremblay have been located (after a thorough computerized search) with either employees of the yard or fur trade individuals who may have purchased Tremblay canoes. Any business arrangements appear to have been made without a legally binding notary contract, as was a common practice during the French regime.

At the time the order from Joseph Cadet for canoes and paddles arrived in Canada, during the summer of 1766, all three of the canoe-builder Tremblay brothers were living with their families at Les Éboulements, presumably in semi-retirement: Étienne was age 75, Louis was 71 and Jean was 65. One can speculate that when Étienne went to his grave the following year, on September 20, 1767, he had the satisfaction of knowing that two Tremblay canoes had brought many happy reminiscences of the Canadian homeland to Cadet, an exiled Canadian in France.[144]

The Representation of Aboriginal Culture within the Canadian Canoe Museum

Shanna Balazs

For many Canadians the canoe is a symbol of national heritage, linking us not only to the environment, but also to the history and cultures of our country. It can draw to mind images of the fur trade, symbolize our northern heritage and connect us to the land. The canoe, an Indigenous creation, is also a meaningful concept within the Aboriginal worldview, the function and significance of these watercraft varying from nation to nation. The beauty and diversity of Aboriginal watercraft is realized in the Canadian Canoe Museum's collection, one third of its total consisting of Indigenous vessels. These craft, from various Aboriginal cultures, are beginning to be presented to the public eye as the development of the Canadian Canoe Museum (CCM) gains momentum. Within the next few years, the dreams of the CCM's original founders finally will come to fruition; the institution will be fully open and operating, having permanent exhibits to present to the Canadian public. This being said, it is evident that now is the time for real planning and organization. In order to "do it right," careful consideration must be given to the presentation and use of the CCM's collection. In particular, the Aboriginal component of the collection must be presented accurately and in an affirmative manner.

The question of representation is a central issue in any museum situation. In contemporary Canadian society, Aboriginal groups are increasingly taking a stand, claiming back not only their land but also their history, material artifacts and identity. Indigenous peoples are demanding control over the production and presentation of their own cultural image, in an effort to counteract the extensive misrepresentation they have experienced throughout history.

The intention here is to describe the very real power held by museums as forums for representing and expressing image and identity, specifically considering Canadian museums and Aboriginal peoples. The issue of representation in museums will be outlined and current research on this topic will be presented in an effort to demonstrate the need for a model concerning Aboriginal involvement within the Canadian Canoe Museum. Before initiating this discussion, however, it is first necessary to examine in more detail the meaning and significance of the canoe within Aboriginal cultures.

As noted in Canadian Canoe Museum promotional literature, the canoe has been developed by Indigenous peoples over several thousand years. Except for the Plains nations, the canoe is a central element in Aboriginal cultures – both in history and in contemporary societies. The canoe certainly continues to be of significance for contemporary Aboriginal nations, often serving as a strong symbol of spirituality and cultural resurgence:

Today, in its renaissance, the canoe carries the knowledge of a millennia-old culture as well as the dreams and aspirations of a younger generation. It is a vessel of knowledge, symbolizing the cultural regeneration of many nations as they struggle to retain and rebuild following a period of systematic oppression and of rapid social and technological change. The great canoe has come back from the abyss a vital symbol for First Nations.[1]

As such, the canoe has also come to symbolize the healing process of Aboriginal nations:

Once a mode of transport, allowing our people to fish, gather food, trade and travel, it has evolved today into a healing vessel, deeply affecting all those who come into contact with it.[2]

It also has been suggested that the contemporary canoe has evolved into an important political tool, functioning to strengthen the existence, adapt-

Dugout canoe exhibit, Canadian Canoe Museum, featuring a late nineteenth century Tlingit canoe and various Aboriginal paddles from the west coast of Canada.

ability, vitality and continuation of Aboriginal peoples and cultures in a socio-political climate which has oppressed them and often rendered them powerless. As an example of the political symbolism of the canoe, David Neel, an Aboriginal author, photographer and canoe builder, refers to the *Luu Tas*, a fifty-foot vessel constructed by Bill Reid and utilized by the Haida Nation to protest unregulated sport fishing within their traditional waters.[3]

The canoe also serves as a metaphor for community to many Aboriginal peoples; in a canoe, as in any community, all individuals must work together and respect one another in order to thrive and succeed. The cooperation achieved through the canoe experience is believed to aid in making contemporary Aboriginal communities strong and vital in tradition.[4] Spirituality is also an integral component of the canoe experience for many Aboriginal peoples, linking them with their traditions, cultures, languages and identities. Furthermore, in contrast to the Euro-Canadian perception of the canoe as a historical symbol and recreational craft, the canoe is perceived as a sacred entity within many Aboriginal cultures:

The canoe is a living entity that provides you with not just transportation but the experience of moving over water and through time. . . . The canoe is just not a boat, it's part of the family.[5]

Considering these disparate perceptions of the function and significance of the canoe, it is evident that interpretation of the canoe must involve multiple perspectives. To illustrate this point, one merely needs to consider that the concept of the conservation, preservation and presentation of canoes within the context of a museum, is in direct opposition to ideas concerning respect for the canoe in Aboriginal cultures – namely, returning the vessel to the earth after it has finished serving the community. In addition, the function of watercraft within Aboriginal cultures does not necessarily reflect the categories of classification utilized by Western society. As an example, the Makah peoples perceive the canoe as a container rather than a means for transportation. Thus, in order to present the Aboriginal component of its collection in an accurate, affirmative and culturally appropriate manner, the Canadian Canoe Museum must directly address concerns of Aboriginal involvement within the institution.

If the CCM is to maintain a legitimate voice in its exhibits, it must address the sensitive issue of Aboriginal representation. To confront this complex issue now, to work in partnership with Aboriginal peoples as the CCM progresses, seems to be the reasoned direction. The Canadian public and the museum community have already been exposed to the events which may transpire in the sensitive realm of cultural representation. The Glenbow Museum's 1988 "The Spirit Sings" exhibition demonstrated how cultural interpretation and political interest can become entangled, while the Royal Ontario Museum's 1989 "Into the Heart of Africa" exhibit illustrated that a museum's message can often be misinterpreted.[6] It is in the best interest of the CCM to create a working partnership with the peoples it intends to represent: to confront the issue of representation in order to present to the public a valid picture of the function, meaning and significance of the canoe in both historical and contemporary Aboriginal cultures.

CANADIAN MUSEUMS AND THE ISSUE OF ABORIGINAL REPRESENTATION

As noted, museums have played a dominant role in both generating and reinforcing stereotypes of Aboriginal peoples. These often represent the obvious extensions of the cultural differences which exist between the two groups. The clash of worldviews is most evident in the interpretation of history, concepts of spirituality and the value of culturally significant sites or spaces. These divergent ideologies have, in turn, strongly influenced the ways in which Aboriginal cultures have been represented through the media of the museum.

More than a simple question of the ownership of cultural property, the issue at hand involves the consideration of who is entitled to control the representation and interpretation of the meaning of objects within the context of museums. The emergence of a new national consciousness in the post-colonial era has strongly impacted the museum, challenging the traditional relationship of "objects and others" within this environment.[7] No museum can escape the inherent problems of the representation of cultural others; both the physical ownership of objects and the right of interpreting their meaning have become points of contention.

The "politics of representation" – who can represent whom, how, where and with what, as well as questions of authenticity, authority, appropriation and ascribed meaning – have therefore become central questions in the museum field.[8] There exists a widespread inclination to question the implicit authority of Western museums to represent adequately the concerns and realities of Indigenous populations.[9] The contemporary museum also has had to account for the potential bias which affects any interpretation. The mode of installation, arrangement and assemblage of artifacts, and the subtle messages created through design and text, actively contribute to the development of meaning ascribed to the cultural data being represented. As such, museums and exhibits always make principled statements and must be recognized as political arenas in which definitions of identity and culture are asserted and contested.[10] Thus, the museum becomes a powerful tool for the communication of ideas and ideals – namely those of the dominant culture. As communities often look to museums as places in which identity is artic-

William Commanda (centre) on the occasion of his investiture in 1995 into the Canadian Canoe Museum's Hall of Honour as its second Canoe Builder Emeritus. Kirk Wipper, the Museum's founder, is on the far right.

ulated, these institutions hold the responsibility of ensuring that exhibitions present other peoples on their own terms – not in comparison with the standards of Western society – and also incorporate dynamic depictions of history and culture, presenting contemporary issues and current realities.[11]

In contemporary society, Aboriginal peoples are becoming more aware of the isolated views of their culture being portrayed to the public within the museum setting. Canada's First Nations are increasingly becoming involved in the struggle to win control and free themselves from their "ethnological fate as museum specimens."[12] Consequently, the relationship between Aboriginal peoples and museums must undergo change. The communication of Aboriginal cultural values has long remained the prerogative of specialists who often are not part of the culture under consideration. It is, however, no longer acceptable for cultural institutions to portray Native culture without, at the very least, the assistance and input of those to whom it belongs. Ideally, control of the Aboriginal image should be returned to its rightful owners. No longer

Birchbark canoe exhibit in the Canadian Canoe Museum.

"guardians," museums must strive to become areas of mutual interest and accurate representation. Partnerships between museums and Aboriginal peoples must be cultivated to meet the demands of contemporary situations. Every effort must be made to create an environment in which Aboriginal culture, historic and contemporary, can be accurately represented and rightfully appreciated.

Many scholars view Glenbow's "The Spirit Sings: Artistic Traditions of Canada's First Peoples" exhibition held in 1988, as a true awakening towards the desperate need to strengthen the interaction between museums and Aboriginal communities. This exhibition, featuring over 650 Canadian Native objects borrowed primarily from foreign collections, was part of the Arts Festival of the 1988 Winter Olympics. The exhibition was designed with the intention of educating the Canadian public about Native heritage and of showcasing the wealth of Canadian Native materials held in foreign institutions.[13]

"The Spirit Sings" was sponsored by Shell Canada and subsequently boycotted by the Lubicon Lake Cree. The Lubicon opposed sponsorship by Shell, as well as by both levels of Canadian government, claiming that it was an attempt to make the sponsors appear supportive of Native people when, in fact, they were contributing to the destruction of Native existence through drilling activities and by contesting Lubicon land claim negotiations. The boycott gained widespread public attention; never before had the issue of Native heritage within museums been the focus of such international concern. As a result of the Lubicon's request for support, academic and cultural institutions worldwide suddenly were faced upfront with a problem not commonly dealt with on a public level.[14]

What "The Spirit Sings" presented to the Canadian museum community was the overwhelming realization that the relationship between Aboriginal peoples and museums was changing. The Lubicon Lake First Nation's boycott ,in turn, was the impetus for the implementation of a series of national discussions between Aboriginal and museum communities. The Canadian Museums Association and the Assembly of First Nations subsequently co-sponsored a national conference in November of 1988, entitled "Preserving our Heritage: A Working Conference Between Museums and First Peoples." It was during this symposium that a strong need for the establishment of a Task Force on the issue of Aboriginal representation in Canadian Museums was identified.

A Task Force of twenty-five Aboriginal and non-Aboriginal individuals was formed in 1989, jointly sponsored by the Assembly of First Nations and the Canadian Museums Association. The identified mission of the Task Force was to "develop an ethical framework and strategies by which Aboriginal peoples and cultural institutions can work together to represent Aboriginal history and culture."[15] During meetings in 1990 at the Woodland Cultural Centre in Brantford and the Royal Ontario Museum in Toronto, three major issues to be addressed were identified: increased involvement of Aboriginal peoples in the interpretation of their culture and history by cultural institutions; improved access to museum collections by Aboriginal peoples; and, the repatriation of artifacts and human remains.[16]

The Task Force on Museums and First Peoples presented the results of their research in a 1992 published document entitled, "Turning the Page: Forging New Partnerships Between Museums and First Peoples." The document reported on the two year process of consultation between museums and Aboriginal communities within Canada, and presented recommendations to be implemented by Canadian heritage institutions.

The regional consultations and responses to the Task Report provided a national perspective on the needs of First Nations with regard to museums. The wide range of needs identified reflects the immense cultural diversity of Aboriginal peoples in Canada. It was also recognized that a common solution was not a possibility. Nonetheless, the need for fundamental change was acknowledged by the Task Force, and recommendations were made in an effort to improve the relationship between the two communities.[17]

Recommendations made in the report involve all aspects of museum work including: interpretation, access, consultation, involvement/training programs, and the repatriation of artifacts.[18] Overall, the active participation and involvement of Native peoples directly within museums was a theme stressed throughout the document.

The ultimate purpose of the Task Force and its report was to suggest ways in which Canadian museums could change their foci and policies of operation to enable First Nations groups to determine the presentation of their own culture. Growing support for cultural self-expression within the museum field maintains that First Nations peoples must present their own image of Aboriginal culture within the context of Canadian museums. Doing this is a first step towards a mutual co-operation and understanding.

In 1995, three years after the publication of "Turning the Page," the CMA circulated a survey throughout the Canadian Museum community in an effort to assess the impact of the principles and recommendations contained in the report. Institutions and individuals, both Aboriginal and non-Aboriginal, were invited to comment on any cooperative projects initiated as a result of the Task Force recommendations. Submissions received by the CMA were compiled as both a record of accomplishment and as a progress report which evaluated the effectiveness of the 1992 recommendations. The survey responses were also utilized by the CMA to identify new recommendations or mechanisms to develop further successful partnerships between museum and Aboriginal communities.[19]

In general, the responses to the 1995 follow-up survey indicated that the framework for collaboration established in the 1992 report was broadly implemented, subsequently influencing the representation of Aboriginal cultures in Canadian museums. The responses were positive in tone, relating the implementation of many proactive policies and projects. These include: cooperative exhibitions and public education programs; involvement of Aboriginal peoples in planning and decision making processes; and financial support for First Nations' museums and institutions. In addition, it was noted by Dr. Trudy Nicks, the CMA council member responsible for the evaluation of the post-Task Force Survey responses, that further proactive policies may have been implemented by some of the institutions since their submissions in 1995.[20]

Several responses noted the mutual benefits achieved through collaborative projects. Through such cooperation, museums receive benefits including a greatly enhanced knowledge of the significance of collections and the objects within them, as well as opportunities for museum staff to develop a greater understanding of Aboriginal culture and values.[21]

The post-Task Force survey has been recognized by Canadian museums as an essential element in implementing the recommendations of the 1992 report. The responses received reflect both the challenges being faced in Canada's museums regarding Aboriginal involvement, as well as the successes and benefits of implemented collaborative initiatives.

In summary, the current issue of Aboriginal representation is linked inextricably to the Canadian museum community. As demonstrated with the 1992 Task Force Report and the 1995 follow up survey, many Canadian

Eastern Arctic kayak exhibit in the Canadian Canoe Museum.

museums are facing this issue head-on; working in partnership with Aboriginal organizations to ensure authentic cultural representations are presented to the public. As an emerging institution, the Canadian Canoe Museum must demonstrate the same commitment to involve Aboriginal groups and individuals. Much more than simple consideration, it is the CCM's obligation to consult with the peoples whose cultural objects it will present.

ABORIGINAL CULTURE WITHIN THE CANADIAN CANOE MUSEUM: CURRENT RESEARCH

The issue of Aboriginal representation in the Canadian Canoe Museum is addressed within current research completed for the Canadian Heritage and Development Studies program at Trent University. The first purpose of this research was an examination of the scope of Aboriginal involvement within selected Canadian museums. Through an evaluation of the CMA Post-Task Force survey responses, three museums currently working in close partnership with Aboriginal communities were identified for research: the Glenbow Museum, Calgary, Alberta; the Manitoba Museum, Winnipeg, Manitoba and the Peterborough Centennial Museum and Archives, Peterborough, Ontario. An additional museum, the Woodland Cultural Centre in Brantford, Ontario also was selected for research based on its reputation as a successful Aboriginal institution.

Research in the identified Canadian museums was conducted in an effort to determine the nature and amount of Aboriginal involvement in each institution, specifically in the areas of: training and employment; advisory committees on marketing, storage, cataloguing, acquisitions and exhibitions; Board members; specific programs designed to reach out to Aboriginal communities; Artists in-residence; the handling of sacred objects; and, repatriation policies. Interviews were conducted at each site with museum staff and members of the local Aboriginal communiy. Open-ended questions included discussion in areas concerning: governance, training and employment, education, collections, access and interpretation. Public representations of Aboriginal culture by the selected museums also were considered, though the study focused on processes and activities which precede exhibit development. The opinions, perceptions and recommendations of Aboriginal peoples are, of course, of great significance for this project and representatives from this group were consulted at each site visited.

Through this research, which included interviews, an analysis of current literature and participant observation in museum settings, successful proactive models of Aboriginal involvment were distinguished. Models were deemed successful, for the purposes of this study, if they presented Aboriginal cultures in a form which Native peoples found both affirmative and acceptable, and which also functioned to involve Aboriginal people in the presentation of their own heritage.

The second purpose of this research involved the modification and adaption of the identified proactive methods of Aboriginal involvement into a model suitable for the Canadian Canoe Museum. Judging the transferability of ideas and methods presented a great challenge, especially considering the specific nature of the CCM's collection. As each museum is unique in nature and operation, a potential problem exists – namely that a model which works at one institution may fail in another. Subsequently, the application of initiatives for Aboriginal involvement to the Canadian Canoe Museum required consideration of the CCM's mandate and collection, as well as consultation with Aboriginal representatives, the institution's staff, their governing board and the Academic Committee. Taking such factors into consideration, the following recommendations were made to the Canadian Canoe Museum in May of 1997:

Short-Term Recommendations Regarding Aboriginal Involvement within the Canadian Canoe Museum:

1) Aboriginal Involvement on the Board of Directors
2) Cultural Sensitivity Training for CCM Board Members and Staff
3) Active Establishment of Institutional Partnerships with Aboriginal Organizations
4) Issues of Access, Repatriation and Loans to Aboriginal Peoples be addressed by the CCM

Long-term Recommendations Regarding Aboriginal Involvement wthin the Canadian Canoe Museum:

1) Maintenance of Partnerships with Aboriginal Organizations and Individuals
2) Development of a Formal Institutional Policy Regarding Aboriginal Access, Repatriation and Loans of the CCM Collection
3) Development of Aboriginal Employment and Training Initiatives, including:
   – Aboriginal Internships
   – Aboriginal Contract Positions
   – Aboriginal Interpreters and Docents
   – Aboriginal Artists In-Residence
   – an Aboriginal Liaison

4) Active Aboriginal Involvement in Interpretation and Public Programming within the Canadian Canoe Museum through:
   – Establishment of an Aboriginal Advisory Council
   – Recognition of multiple perspectives (in the interpretation of canoe history)
   – Development of a separate Aboriginal Gallery (in consultation and collaboration with Aboriginal peoples)
   – Creation of meaningful roles for Aboriginal Peoples within the institution.

RESPONSE OF THE CANADIAN CANOE MUSEUM

Since the grand pre-opening of the Canadian Canoe Museum's Collections Centre to the public in May, 1996, [22] the museum has steadily gained momentum in its development as a national heritage institution, expanding both its staff as well as permanent exhibit space. With regard to the specific situation of Aboriginal involvement within the Canadian Canoe Museum, it is evident that the CCM Board and Staff realizes that this issue must be given consideration now – during the development phase of the institution. What follows is a brief discussion of the ways in which the CCM has initiated this process, in effect attending to many of the previously outlined recommendations.

The first step in this process involved the Museum's Board and Staff becoming fully aware of the significance of the canoe in Aboriginal cultures – both historically and currently. Though the Museum will have a historic focus, the use and significance of the canoe in contemporary Aboriginal cultures also will be highlighted. The Indigenous peoples of Canada are living cultures and the CCM realizes their responsibility to portray them in this manner within the institution. As such, the CCM has come to understand that Aboriginal peoples, both individuals and organziations, must be involved as partners in all apsects of the Museum's operation.

The Canadian Canoe Museum has put forth a sincere effort to address the first issue identified as critical by the 1992 Task Force on Museums and First Peoples, this being the increased involvement of Aboriginal people in the interpretation and representation of their cultures. In addition to becoming fully aware of the meaning and significance of the canoe in Aboriginal cultures[23] the inclusion of a First Nations individual as an active memeber of the CCM's Board[24] has been a significant first step on the part of the institution. In addition, the museum has been working arduously to involve Aboriginal representatives within the CCM's Academic Committee.

More recently, the Museum's Board and Staff have been working to establish positive partnerships with local Aboriginal groups and individuals. In particular, the CCM has formed a Committee for Museum Design, which involves four representatives from the Museum Board and four representatives from local Aboriginal groups, including individuals from Curve Lake, Alderville and Hiawatha First Nations and Métis. The institution also has established a Council of Advisors, which include Aboriginal representatives on a national scale.

In the area of interpretation, Museum Staff actively are involved in cooperative partnerships with local Aboriginal communities (including Alderville, Curve Lake and Hiawatha First Nations) in an effort to present Indigenous canoes and cultures in an accurate and appropriate manner, Furthermore, the CCM's Director consistently works to establish and provide training and employment opportunities for Aboriginal individuals within the institution.

Madeline Katt (Theriault) of Bear Island, Temagami, is of the Teme-Augama Anishnabai people. "There were no docks only the canoes drawn up on the shores. Everyone paddled then. I know. I was there." [25]

Finally, with regard to issues of access, repatriation and loans by Aboriginal peoples, the CCM identifies these as important areas to be considered and discussed in cooperation with Aboriginal groups. Although set insitutional policies to deal with such issues are not in place at this time, the CCM recently demonstrated its willingness to cooperate with Aboriginal groups through the informal loan of a canoe to the Hiawatha First Nation. It has been said to me by members of CCM that this working at the grassroots level with local Aboriginal groups is proving to be a positive process.

Overall, at the time of the 1995 acquisition by the Canadian Canoe Museum, the condition of the collection was generally poor, largely as a result of damage through the neglect of preventative conservation measures and improper handling procedures. The first of several essential tasks recognized by the CCM was, therefore, the stabilization and conservation of the collection. In addition to these conservation initiatives, the Canadian Canoe Museum also identifies as its primary purpose the interpretation and presentation of a spectacular collection of watercraft to the Canadian public, highlighting the significance of these craft in the development of the country and promoting the canoe as a symbol of national identity. Furthermore, the Museum's Board and Staff clearly understand the need to address concerns related to the Aboriginal component of the collection and realize the importance of presenting the significance of the canoe in both historical and contemporary Aboriginal cultures within the institution.

CONCLUSIONS

The importance of the Canadian Canoe Museum's collection as a cultural resource is strongly evident. In addition to providing valuable information to the academic, canoeing and boat-building communities, the collection is also of great appeal to the Canadian public. Furthermore, the collection is of great significance on the national level, as John Jennings notes in this volume, acting as an icon of the Canadian spirit. Certainly, for many Canadians, the canoe is indeed a symbol of national heritage. The canoe, an indigenous creation, is also a meaningful concept within Aboriginal worldviews, the function and significance of these watercraft varying from nation to nation. It is important that the Canadian Canoe Museum consistently gives equal attention to the importance of these varying perspectives within the institution; although the canoe is a link between the peoples of Canada, it is often viewed in a different light according to the worldview through which it is being perceived.

As the Canadian Canoe Museum continues to grow and develop, the need to address the issue of Aboriginal representation will become increasingly critical. This brief outline of current research and contemporary developments in the museum field regarding Aboriginal involvement has illustrated the serious nature of the issue: one that is faced at all levels, from small community museums to national cultural institutions. If the CCM is to establish and maintain respect and legitimacy in the museum community, the Aboriginal community and in Canadian society, it must continue to expend every effort to represent material artifacts and the cultures they are connected to in an affirmative manner.

It is imperative that the CCM realizes the degree of commitment that is required in this process of Aboriginal involvement. This is not a one-time act, nor a process that occurs at a single phase of development. Establishing and maintaining a working partnership will take time, effort

Ojibway canoe headboard.

and much compromise – both for the CCM and for the Aboriginal peoples involved. Although the Canadian Canoe Museum, at this time, remains in somewhat of a developmental stage, it is clear that the institution's Board and Staff fully realize the critical importance of, and need for, Aboriginal involvement. To date, many proactive measures have been initiated in this area, and I remain confident that the Canadian Canoe Museum will continue "paddling" towards full development on the harmonious path of mutual co-operation – in a direction which involves Aboriginal peoples at all levels of institutional operation and presents Indigenous canoes and cultures in an accurate and affirmative manner.

CANADIANS AND THE CANADIAN CANOE IN THE OPENING OF THE AMERICAN MIDWEST

Ralph C. Frese

Of all the watercraft ever designed by the ingenuity of man, none have survived and retained their usefulness throughout history like the canoe. It was the key element in the discovery and settlement of the American Midwest. Champlain once wrote back to France:

With the canoes of the savages, one may travel freely and quickly throughout the country as well as up the little rivers as up the large ones. So that by directing one's course with the help of the savages and their canoes, a man might see all that is to be seen, good or bad, within the space of a year or two.[1]

In 1603, Champlain had no conception of how large the North American continent was but within 40 years after those words were penned, the Canadians had penetrated as far west as Green Bay in Lake Michigan.

The French had discovered the gateway through the eastern mountains, the St. Lawrence River, which led them west to the Great Lakes. From this vast network of inland seas, portage trails led in every direction of the compass to other watersheds. As the traders of New France came in contact with the various native people of the Great Lakes region, they heard rumours of a great river called the Michissippi. Could this be the route to the China Sea they had dreamed of finding? It was a native-born Canadian who discovered the answer.

Louis Jolliet was born in Quebec in 1645, the son of a wheelwright. Educated by the Jesuits, he decided against entering the priesthood in order to follow his older brother, Adrien, and enter the fur trade. Experienced in cartography, wilderness travel and negotiating with the natives, it was natural that Talon, the Intendant of New France, would commission Sieur Jolliet to lead an expedition to search for this great river. Unfortunately, there was no funding available. However, Jolliet was given a trading license which, it was hoped, would bring enough profit to cover the costs of the venture. So, the voyage which was to discover the American Midwest as we know it today, began in Quebec City in October of 1672 with two old Algonquin bark canoes roughly twenty feet in length.

Louis Jolliet owned one of the old canoes and borrowed the second from his sister-in-law. After loading them up with trade goods, he headed west with six companions, following the traditional route up the Ottawa to Georgian Bay, eventually arriving at Sault Ste. Marie. After setting up a trading venture at the Sault and leaving his younger brother, Zacharie, in charge, Louis Jolliet and five voyageurs travelled south to the Jesuit mission at St. Ignace on the Straits of Michigan. Here, he notified Fr. Jacques Marquette that Fr. Dablon, his superior, wanted him to accompany the expedition. It was on the morning of May 17, 1673, that the party of seven men headed south, coasting the northern shores of Lake Michigan to the mission site on Green Bay. They ascended the Fox River, portaging innumerable rapids, traversing huge Lake Winnebago, until they reached the headwaters where they were told by the natives they could portage 2,700 paces to a river that would lead them west. They descended the broad Wisconsin River for ninety miles and reached the Mississippi River on the morning of June 17, the first white men to voyage this far west They were to travel 300 miles down this mysterious waterway before seeing the first sign of another human being. They discovered a path that led to a village of Peoria Indians, near the mouth of the Iowa River where they were made welcome. Jolliet was given a gift of a 10 year old slave boy and Fr. Marquette was given a sacred calumet or peace pipe as a sign of friendship for safe passage among the more warlike tribes to the south. They also were warned of monsters farther down the river that sometimes devoured men and canoes. It was not long before they reached the first one.

Near present day Alton, Illinois, they espied two figures painted high on a cliff. Marquette described them as being as large as a calf, with horns on their heads like a deer, scales, a bearded man's face and a tail so long, it

Launching of the three hundredth anniversary voyage of the Jolliet-Marquette expedition down the Mississippi River. The replica canoe was built by Ralph Frese.

wound around the body and between the legs, ending in a fish's tail. Painted in three colors, red, green and black, it posed a mystery as to whom the artist might have been. The boldest savages dared not rest their eyes on these monsters drawn high above them on the bluffs. They came to the mouth of the Missouri, which was in flood and dangerous and wondered if it might be the passage west they were searching for. They next came to a series of rock islands across the mighty river that, in high waters, caused a whirlpool that could easily swamp a crude native dugout, giving rise to the legend of a monster that devoured men and canoes. After passing the mouth of the Ohio River, they spied natives near the mouth of the Arkansas River. These warlike tribes threatened to kill the strangers, but Fr. Marquette, holding aloft the calumet and repeating the few words of Illini he had learned, persuaded them to let them land safely. These natives, who had only dugout canoes, at first did not believe these strangers had come so far in these fragile craft and wanted to know what animal had such a skin from which canoes could be made? Here the expedition learned that, a few days journey to the south, were more blackrobes, and Jolliet, having seen Spanish trade goods among the natives and having mapped the river's course, realized they must be near the Spanish sea. Fearing they might be stopped by the Spaniards, he decided to return to Quebec with the information they had collected and so the voyageurs turned upstream.

The return upstream was tedious labour and uneventful until they reached the mouth of the Illinois River. The local natives had told them that this was an easier route back to the lake of the Illinois, present day Lake Michigan. Marquette left us this description, "We have seen nothing like this river that we enter, as regards its fertility of soil, its prairies and woods; its cattle, elk. deer, wildcats, bustards, swans, ducks, parroquets, and even beaver."[2] The lands along the Illinois River supported large villages of Indians and it was apparent to Jolliet and his men that this land offered promise. The natives guided them to the Chicago Portage, that crucial link between the Mississippi and the Great Lakes watersheds. Milo Quaife, the famous historian, called it ". . . one of the five keys to the North American continent."[3] Following Lake Michigan's shoreline north to Green Bay, Jolliet left Fr. Marquette, seriously ill with dysentery, at the mission there and proceeded back to the Sault and his trading post. Marquette reported his adventures to his superior, Fr. Dablon. Jolliet left one copy of his maps and journals at the Sault and, with two voyageurs and the Indian boy, headed east to report to Talon in Quebec. At the Lachine rapids, their canoe struck a rock, the two men and the Indian boy were drowned, the tin strongbox with his maps and journals was lost and Jolliet was plucked from a rock by two fishermen who chanced by. Unfortunately, his trading post was later destroyed by fire and the second set of notes and maps also were lost. Only the portion of the Marquette journal Dablon saw fit to include in the *Jesuit Relations* has left us a clue to this important voyage of discovery.

Jolliet now made a verbal report to Talon. It is recorded that he said:

. . . we could go with facility to Florida in a bark, and by very easy navigation. It would only be necessary to make a canal by cutting through but half a league of prairie, to pass from the foot of the Lake of the Illinois [Lake Michigan] *to the St. Louis River, which empties into the Mississippi. We were told of these treeless lands, we envisioned burnt over forest lands, but we have certainly observed to the contrary. No better soil can be found for corn, for vines, or for any other fruit whatever. A settler would not there have to spend ten years in cutting down and burning the trees* (as in Quebec), *on the very*

day of his arrival, he could put his plow into the ground. The river which we named for Saint Louis (the DesPlaines), *which rises near the lower end of the lake of the Illinois, seemed to me the most beautiful and most suitable for settlement [the Chicagoland region].*[4]

Jolliet petitioned the authorities for permission to take twenty men to colonize his discovery, the Illinois Country. He was turned down. France was not ready to expand her presence in North America.

Louis Jolliet's older brother, Adrien, was returning from a voyage to Lake Superior in the fall of 1669 with an Iroquois captive who had been held prisoner by the Ottawa there. The grateful Indian had shown Adrien a new route back unknown to the French, by way of Lake Huron, Lake St. Clair, Lake Erie and Lake Ontario. He showed Adrien the traditional Iroquois portage trail around Niagara Falls. These two brothers of Quebec had discovered a canoe route across North America, from the mouth of the St. Lawrence to the mouth of the Mississippi, that led to the richest lands in North America known as the Corn Belt or the American Midwest, yet had only two barriers to navigation by canoe, Niagara Falls and the Chicago Portage.

The commemorative La Salle expedition of 1676 to the mouth of the Mississippi during a lunch stop at Chicago.

It remained for another who had the proper political connections and the ability to raise the credit necessary for such a great venture, the colonization of the Illinois Country. This was Robert Cavalier de la Salle who subsequently built the first sailing ship on the upper lakes, the *Griffin*. Also he built Fort St. Louis atop of Starved Rock on the Illinois River, built Fort Crevecoeur at Peoria, and voyaged to the mouth of the Mississippi in 1682, claiming the entire watershed for the glory of France. He realized that to secure his colony against British incursions from the east, France needed to establish control of the mouth of the river as well, so he set sail for the gulf coast from France. Overshooting the delta of the Mississippi, and landing somewhere in Texas, he and a party of men attempted to reach the Illinois Country on foot. Enroute, he was assassinated by one of his own men. However, the Illinois colony had been left in charge of an able assistant, Henri de Tonty, an Italian by birth, who inherited La Salle's trading concessions. Inspite of being hampered by the loss of one hand in a European war, Tonty was the primary figure in the Illinois Country for 20 years, during which time it is estimated he travelled over 85,000 miles by canoe and on foot organizing the trade between Canada and the Illinois Country.

Tonty's nephew, Pierre Deliette, joined him in 1687 and left a detailed description of travelling from Chicago to Peoria. He begins his memoir with the statement, "The Illinois country is undeniably the finest to be found between the mouth of the St. Lawrence and that of the Mississippi, which are a thousand leagues apart. You begin to see its fertility at Chicago."[5] His candid observations on the countryside, the game and the habits and mores of the natives have given us a window through which we can peek into the past of 300 years ago. He describes hunting with the Indians for five weeks during which they killed 1,200 buffalo, but did not bother counting the lesser animals they killed, such as the bears, does, stags, bucks, mountain lions, young turkeys and lynxes. Deliette served as the principal French presence in the Illinois Country for over 30 years.

By the 1700s, many Canadians had settled at Peoria and along the Illinois shore of the Mississippi, south of present day St. Louis, on a flood plain known as the American Bottoms. Also at this time, the French were establishing a colony on the gulf coast and supplies were filtering up to the Illinois settlements that heretofore depended on Canada for their needs and, in turn, the fledgling colony depended on the Illinois Country for food supplies. Convoys manned by voyageurs travelled the lower Mississippi between Mobile and the Illinois Country. Until the settlers of Louisiana began to build wooden bateaux, the great bark canoes of Canada were being used up and down the gulf coast as well as on the great river. Diron D'Artaguette, Intendant of the Illinois Country, was ascending the lower Mississippi River to his post in 1720 when he passed a fifteen man birchbark canoe with two nine man piroques of Canadians heading south on a trading mission. The rich and fertile lands of the Illinois Country offered opportunity for many of the voyageurs who declined to go back to Canada when their service was over, and they became farmers and miners as well as traders. Many of them travelled as much as 1,000 miles up the Missouri River and its tributaries, trading with the various native tribes during the early 1700s. An example of colonization is found in official church records in Illinois dating back to the 1690s. There are reportedly more French records in the courthouse of Randolph County in southern Illinois than there are in New Orleans. By 1710, so much wheat was being grown by the settlers, the Jesuits built a post windmill of the type used in France and England in addition to the water-driven grist mill they had first constructed. In 1720, a lead mine was opened on the Meramec River in Missouri and 200 mining technicians and 500 blacks from Santo Domingo were brought in to work the mines. Annually, convoys carried wheat and other products to market in Louisiana and, after a bumper crop in 1747, 800,000 lbs of wheat flour were shipped to New Orleans the following year. A number of villages now existed in the Illinois Country: Cahokia, St. Phillipe, St. Anne, St. Genevieve, Prairie du Rocher, Vincennes, Post Ouiatenon, Fort de Chartres, Peoria and Chicago. A paved road connected several of these villages along the lower Mississippi. The architecture reflected its French-Canadian heritage as the homes had a steeply pitched roof like the homes in Quebec and were built of logs set vertically into the ground. The roofs were supported by heavy oak trusses of the same type used in Normandy in the middle ages and brought to Canada by the early Norman immigrants. The post factor's house at Norway House in Canada is roofed in the same fashion. Because of the hot summers, these homes had a *"gallerie"* around the house as did many of the homes in the French colonies in the West Indies. Many of these buildings are still standing in the Illinois Country, some dating back to 1740, 1770 and 1790.

The Liberty Bell of the West, housed in a small shrine on Kaskaskia Island, Illinois.

Standing on the only part of the state of Illinois that lies west of the Mississippi, is the Church of the Immaculate Conception, founded by Fr. Marquette in 1675 when the Kaskaskias lived near Starved Rock on the upper Illinois River. In La Salle's time, the Kaskaskias were moved down-river by the French to settle them beyond the reach of the Iroquois raiding parties. The town of Kaskaskia, once the largest town in Illinois, now lies some fifty miles below St. Louis and during the exceptional flood of 1889, the great river created a new channel into the nearby Kaskaskia River and severed the town from the rest of the state. In the church is a handcarved walnut altar made by the early voyageurs in 1738. The bronze church bell, cast in 1741, was a gift from Louis XV. It was shipped to Mobile where it ascended the Mississippi River by bateau to grace the Church of the Kaskaskias among the Illinois. It was rung after George Rogers Clark's capture of Kaskaskia during the American Revolution on the 4th of July, 1778, proclaiming freedom from British rule in the Illinois Country, and so is called the "Liberty Bell of the West."

There is not too detailed a record of the amount of canoe traffic on the rivers of the American Midwest, but one occasionally finds a reference to

The Pierre Menard House was built about 1790 by a Montreal trader. It has been referred to as the "Mount Vernon of the West."

the ties to Canada at a time when it was all one vast country. Two brothers started from Montreal in a bark canoe to seek their fortune in the Illinois Country in the year 1787. One, Pierre Menard, settled on the banks of the Kaskaskia and became a successful merchant, farmer and trader, having as many as 60 men employed in his enterprises. He built a lovely home in 1790 on a hillside overlooking the Kaskaskia that is often called "the Mount Vernon of Illinois." Today, Menard's home overlooks the mighty Mississippi because of the channel change in 1889. In 1818, when Illinois became a state, Pierre Menard was elected to be the first Lt. Governor. The state constitution had to be changed to allow this popular son of Canada to be elected to this office as he was not born in the United States.

Peter Pond, fur trader, left an account of trading on the Minnesota River in 1774. Descending the Mississippi after the breakup of the ice, he arrived at Prairie du Chien for the annual rendezvous and wrote:

. . . we saw a large collection from every part of the Mississippi who had arrived before us, even from Orleans eight hundred leagues below us. The Indians camp exceeded a mile and a half in length. Here was sport of all sorts.

The French were very numerous. There was not less than one hundred and thirty canoes which came from Mackinac, carrying from sixty to eighty hundred weight apiece, all made of birchbark and white cedar for the ribs. Those boats from Orleans and Illinois and other parts were numerous . . .[6]

Picture one hundred and thirty canots du maître on the Mississippi in 1774!

One of the most incredible canoe journeys in Illinois history took place in 1827. Chicago fur trader, John Kinzie, was at breakfast in his home across the Chicago River from Fort Dearborn, when he heard voyageurs singing on the river. He rushed out to see a light birchbark canoe rapidly approaching the Fort, manned by thirteen men. It proved to be Governor Lewis Cass and his secretary, Robert Forsyth. Governor Cass had been at Green Bay for a council meeting with the Winnebago and Menominee tribes who, instead, were committing hostile acts on the upper Mississippi. He immediately procured a fast canoe, chose thirteen hand-picked French-Canadian voyageurs to man it, and started up the Fox River, portaging into the Wisconsin River and, upon reaching the Mississippi, followed it down to Jefferson Barracks below St. Louis. Here he ordered troops upriver by steamboat to reinforce the garrison at Fort Snelling in Minnesota and, upon reaching the mouth of the Illinois, he embarked in his canoe to ascend that stream to the Chicago Portage. They reached Fort Dearborn from Green Bay in only thirteen days, the governor's party sleeping only five to seven hours each night and averaging sixty to seventy miles travel each day.

The early settlers of Prairie du Rocher, near Fort de Chartres, brought with them from Canada the tradition of La Guiannee. Since 1722, a motley group of people in grotesque masks and beggar-like costumes gather on New Year's Eve and begin the traditional visit to the homes of townspeople, where they stop quietly in front of the door. They sing the song "La Guianne" in a French patois, wishing the householder and his family good wishes for the coming year. He responds by offering the group drinks and cookies, often made from recipes two hundred years old. Then they move on to the next habitation. This community has been observing this custom for over two hundred and fifty years and this tradition now is being observed by other towns in this French colonial district of southern Illinois.

Illinois has many place names that reflect its French-Canadian beginnings. Its nickname, the Prairie State, is the French word for a meadow or savannah. Communities with French names are numerous, such as: Wilmette, Joliet, Bourbonnais, Au Sable, Papineau, L'erable, Creve Coeur, Renault, Prairie du Rocher and Belleville. Others with French origins have been anglicized. The name Illinois was derived from the French attempt to say the Illini Indians' name for themselves, the Illiniwek, meaning "the men."

Gurdon Saltonstall Hubbard came to Chicago from Montreal via Michilimackinac as a clerk in the American Fur Company's brigade to trade on the Illinois River in 1818. At the tender age of sixteen, he was made clerk for he was the only one able to read and write in the accounting books. He has left the best description of the Chicago Portage, citing the plagues of mosquitoes, the endless mud and the bloodsuckers that left men suffering for days afterwards. As the fur trade declined, Hubbard turned to meat packing, warehousing and other endeavors in the growing village of Chicago and, as a member of the new state's legislature, pushed for the building of a canal across the portage. To drive home the message, Hubbard and his supporters created a canal barge out of one of his fur trade canoes, loaded it onto an ox-drawn wagon and drove it downstate to Vandalia where the legislature was in session.

In the year 1835, a Mr. Edwin Gale and his family arrived in Chicago aboard the little brig *Illinois,* which could not enter the river's mouth because of sandbars thrown up by storms on the great lake. He mentions in his memoirs how they were conveyed ashore by "Frenchmen in their birchbark Mackinaw boats" and brought to Hubbard's warehouse a little way up the Chicago River. The Canadian voyageurs and their huge birchbark canoes were still in use in Chicago as late as 1835.

Interest in the early history of the Illinois Country was renewed when replicas of the bark canoes of the explorers and the fur trade became available and special events at some of the historic sites were begun. One of the oldest of these is the annual rendezvous at Fort de Chartres in southern Illinois, started over twenty-five years ago. This stone edifice, built as a garrison for 400 men and costing a million livres to build in 1756, was the centre of government in the Illinois Country. It also was the last place in North America that the flag of Louis XV flew, for when Montreal

Built in 1756, Fort de Chartres was the centre for the government of New France in the Illinois Country and the last place in North America to fly the French flag.

fell to the British redcoats in 1763, Pontiac would not allow them west across the Illinois Country to take command of Chartres. For two long years until 1765, the lilies of France still flew over Illinois until Pontiac let a detachment of the Black Watch cross the prairies of the Illinois Country to where St. Ange, the commandant of Fort de Chartres, awaited patiently to turn over his command. History comes alive each June during the annual rendezvous as military units from all periods gather. Blanket traders and craftsmen ply their trades, Indians and habitants wander about in colourful costumes for the benefit of visitors, while on the Mississippi, the great canoes of the fur trade gather again for a race down-river to Saint Genevieve on the far shore.

Several other historic sites offer annual gatherings, such as the ren-dezvous at Fort Crevecoeur near Peoria where La Salle built the first European structure in the Illinois Country in 1680. Fort Massac on the Ohio River hosts an annual event on the site of a French post that dates back to 1702. Near the community of Bourbonnais, along the Kankakee River, is the Gathering on the Theatiki, the early cartographer's name for the Kankakee River. Farther upstream is the annual rendezvous at the Grand Kankakee Marsh County Park to commemorate the voyageurs and the importance of the river as a highway for their canoes. Closer to Chicago Portage National Historic Site is the Isle a la Cache Rendezvous, held on an island in the DesPlaines River where, tradition has it, a trader hid his trade goods when warned that the Indians downstream planned to rob him. And another, farther upstream at Columbia Woods on the DesPlaines, attracts thousands each year. While there are many black powder meets and other events of a historical nature held each year in the American Midwest, these are of a particular importance because they focus on a colourful part of our heritage, the voyageur and his canoe, reaching back over three hundred and twenty-five years in our history.

The largest such event is the annual Feast of the Hunter's Moon, staged each year around the first of October on the Wabash River. Near the present day city of West LaFayette, Indiana, is the site of Post Ouiatenon, founded in 1700. It is the largest such assembly of history buffs, craft persons, military units, blanket traders, frontiersmen, voyageurs and other assorted characters, all of whom must conform in clothing and gear to the period of the French and Indians in the Wabash

Valley during the 1700s. Each year they attract over 4,500 costumed participants and close to 70,000 visitors in this two-day festival. The high-
light of each day comes in the late morning when it is announced that the
canoes from Montreal are expected and all retire to the riverbank to await
them. When the brigades are sighted, the cannons and muskets are fired
in a noisy welcome and, as the voyageurs land, a blackrobe leads them in
a prayer of thanks for their safe arrival, and the canoes are brought ashore
to make camp. This beautifully organized festival is the one by which all
others are measured.

I often wonder, as I paddle these historic waterways in our Midwest,
what Louis Jolliet would say if he could return and see what has developed
in the lands he first saw over 325 years ago and how prophetic his words
turned out to be. The beauty of the land mentioned in the writings of
these early explorers is still to be found here and there for those of us who
are willing to search for it. And as we paddle our canoes on our own personal modern day journeys of exploration, we often see the wild iris, commonly called the blue flag, in bloom along our shores and we are
reminded of the *fleur de lis* and of the French-Canadian explorers who
first probed these unknown lands in their canoes.

But let us not forget that they could not have accomplished those great
discoveries without the birchbark canoe of the natives and without the
aid of those dauntless French Canadian canoemen, the voyageurs, who
left an indelible mark in the historic development of the American
Midwest.

Paddling Voices: There's the Poet, Voyager, Adventurer and Explorer in All of Us

Alister Thomas

Paddling is as much an inner journey as it is an adventure of discovery.[1] Over the years there have been opportunities to listen to and collect some extraordinary paddling voices, voices which describe a true sense of personal journey.[2] All speak to their passion for paddling.

There is a sense of connection combined with the sense of canoeing as part of Canadian culture, imagination and identity. James Raffan, the author of a number of books on canoeing, writes:

Canoeing more or less defines who I am. Patched boats in the backyard affirm soul truths. My home, Canada, is not an abstraction; it is kindred canoe spirits and a constellation of sun-alive, star-washed campsites, linked by rivers, lakes, and ornery portages; scapes of the heart, rekindled by sensations that linger long after the pain is gone. When I meet someone, I wonder what they would be like on a trip.

Michael Peake, Governor of the Hide-Away Canoe Club, makes a similar reference to the canoe and one's sense of being a Canadian. Since 1980, members of this club have paddled and walked more than 10,000 kilometres along the routes of our forefathers. "We are Canadians," says Peake, "who have taken the time and hard work to feel history in the stroke of our paddles and blisters in our boots." The HACC's credo, attributed to James Monroe Thorington, an early member of the Alpine Club of Canada, states: "We were not pioneers ourselves. But we travelled over old trails that were new to us and with hearts open. Who shall distinguish?"

Since Canada, the second largest country on earth, is 25% water, canoeing is the most efficient, practical and fun way to get around. And while there are regional variations in our paddling environments – expedition length trips across the North, ocean adventures along all three coastlines, Canadian Shield tripping in the heartland, and fast, icy cold mountain rivers in the West – canoeing is canoeing. Or is it?

Obviously, canoeing as self-propelled travel is self-powering and empowering. But the *experience* is the key. In "Confessions of A Know-It-All Or Why Take A Clinic," Sheena Masson describes a revelation she had on the waterways in Nova Scotia:

Over the weekend I realized what a skilled solo paddler can do – move the canoe sideways, pirouette around the paddle, and turn gracefully with a little forward momentum. Meditation in motion. If whitewater paddling is slam dancing, solo flatwater paddling is ballet. I had discovered another way to have fun instead of just crossing the lake.[3]

More often than not, canoeing is the conduit to heightened perception as well as a sense of renewal. There can be a feeling of flow to the wild in the wilderness and to a deep sense of *being* – a spiritual connection, an immersion. Bruce and Carol Hodgins and their extended paddling family have felt and enjoyed this experience, as this excerpt from Bruce demonstrates:

In haunting memory, the landscape of the Lady Evelyn keeps drawing me back for canoe voyages of both the dreaming and the physical. Often more appropriately called the Trout Streams, its waters are as close to mountain flows as the Canadian Shield can deliver. The Lady Evelyn has so many small, often unnavigatable rapids, so many captivating, high yet small falls, and such rugged Precambrian shorelines and heights. It has such rocks, such white and red pine stands, such cedar, such lily pads, such shallows, such depths, such sunsets, and such portages. I simply must recanoe and reimagine its mysteries.

In order to see what similarities and differences, themes and concerns were running through a selected sample of 37 canoe stories, an independent content analysis was undertaken by Anne Dahlberg, a Calgary researcher (happily, this task renewed her interest in paddling). This analysis revealed four distinct streams of experience – Poet, Voyager, Adventurer and Explorer. There are, of course, other common currents running throughout all four. There is the contrast between pristine, isolated nature and civilization. There is an awareness of the history of the route and with it a sense of timelessness. There is a sense of passing through the wilderness and a shared belief that the land belongs to the flora and fauna.

From Quetico Park and the French River in Ontario to the South Nahanni in the Northwest Territories, Poets describe the canoeing experience as vital to existence. And in this way, the experience is renewing, refreshing and rewarding. Sheila Archer has a series of vivid remembrances on Saskatchewan's Churchill River:

. . . I am walking out of the boreal darkness, late on a September night, the roar of the distant rapids blowing over the lake. The island I'm on is surrounded by brilliant northern lights, a sky so beautiful I cannot stand up. . . . Now it is the morning and there are eagles circling over the channels downstream. The early sun begins to heat the black slope of rock slanting down into the bay. I walk down from the tent and plunge into the river . . .

Soaking up the stillness of an Alberta river.

Each of the Poets describes a close relationship with the land. Descriptions are filled with memories as well as new delights. There are also sensory and historical relationships, and a revelation of truth about life and sometimes self. These are reflective and self-defining trips, yet since these trips are shared with others, the experience is shared by a community. In describing the out-of-the-way places in Algonquin Park, David F. Pelly writes:

[It is] the smaller, less-travelled lakes that draw me back. That's where I find peace. That's where I see old-growth white pine so large that it takes four of us to link hands around its girth. That's where I feel the bond to wild places that stirs deep within us all. For those who know it, the Park provides that primeval connection. It is a steady, reliable friend – a place that is always there waiting for your next visit, a place that never disappoints. While in his ninties, Ralph Bice, the last of the Park's old-time guides and trappers, summed it up nicely: 'Anyone who knows Algonquin Park will be disappointed when they get to heaven.'

For those identified as Voyagers, however, there is a different perspective. From the William River and Bowron Lakes in the West to Harp Lake in Labrador and the Yukon in the North, these paddlers emphasize the land and nature while de-emphasizing the canoe or paddling. After a visit by a silver-tipped barrenland grizzly on the Thelon, Max Finkelstein notes:

It was an apt finale for a magical trip – and a reminder that we were merely visitors here. It was our presence that had interrupted the bear on his regular river patrol. The bear didn't invade our camp; rather, it was we who had intruded on his domain.

For Voyagers the landscape is dynamic and ever-changing. They learn to read the land, taking in and experiencing what it has to offer. They are filled with exploration and discovery. There is a sense of achievement and/or accomplishment where each can look back and see growth over the course of the trip. They realize that the nature of any trip is never the same way twice. On the drive home after a 24-hour solo trip in the tame wilds north of Peterborough, Gwyneth Hoyle remarks, ". . . I had been alive in every fibre of my body, all senses alert, even while I slept. . . . It had

Discovering new landscape.

been an exhilarating and totally satisfying trip."

For those identified as Adventurers, such as Stephan Kesting, who made a solo trip from the Seal River to the town of Churchill on Hudson Bay, personal challenge is the focus. Some Adventurers relate triumph, others defeat, but all impart important lessons learned – the waters warrant respect and require technical skill and expertise. In a surrealistic account of a trip from Shefferville to Ungava Bay, Gino Gergeron shares his experience:

Running down from the land of the Montagnais and the Naskapis to the seas of the Inuit, the George River represents, for me, the road to the Far North. A trip that flows over 600 kilometres allows me to visit the meanders and undertows of my fears.[4]

For Adventurers there is often a transformation from defensive to offensive whereby various paddling skills and the art of reading and listening to the river become second nature. In relating his experience during a nighttime trip down the Ottawa River, Paul Mason explains how he and his paddling partner are able to see the rapids: ". . . as I expected we would be able to see them okay by the light of our white knuckles." A little later he says, "It was now 10:30 p.m. and we were becoming quite adept at sensing the different waves and currents, and reading the rapids by moonlight."

The haunting beauty of the Barren Lands on the George River in northern Quebec.

Explorers include a range of paddlers from Ric Driediger's account of Saskatchewan's Drinking River to Kevin Redmond's description of Newfoundland's Main River. These Explorers have various reasons for paddling. They combine an awe for the pristine land with an appreciation for the challenges, rewards, and surprises of the water. On a trip into the Land of the Midnight Sun in the Yukon, Paula Zybach, writes:

At 2:00 a.m. the pilot has just off-loaded us on Bonnet Plume Lake where we proceeded to set up camp. . . . The first thing unpacked was a good flashlight, complete with new batteries. It would be weeks before night would return to this region. That weight in the barrel should have been chocolate.

Explorers have a deep appreciation for the untouched or barely touched land where one can view extreme and varied landscapes. These expeditions allow unobtrusive interaction with nature and wildlife. "For those who love to travel by canoe it is rare that any trip is not memorable," comments Shawn Hodgins in his writing about a trip on the Snare and Coppermine rivers in the Northwest Territories.

Naturally it is often the most recent trip that you recall most vividly and fondly. . . . Some trips, however, stay etched in your memory for a much longer

The challenge of whitewater.

period of time. A whole combination of factors lead to this -- companionship and group dynamics to physical challenge, scenic beauty, and natural resources such as the weather. Ironically hardships, while not necessarily enjoyed at the time, may be remembered fondly afterwards. A lengthy trip may also be much more vivid. Time gives you much opportunity for reflection.

These are four types of paddling voices I have heard. No doubt you have heard them too. Each voice is individual and unique, yet all are unanimous in their descriptions of the joys and pleasures of paddling. Perhaps a timeless voice that will always be with us best describes this rapture. In *Path of the Paddle* Bill Mason wrote:

The first thing you must learn about canoeing is that the canoe is not a lifeless, inanimate object; it feels very much alive, alive with the life of the river. Life is transmitted to the canoe by currents of air and the water upon which it rides. The behaviour and temperament of the canoe is dependent upon the elements: from the slightest breeze to a raging storm, from the smallest ripple to a towering wave, or from a meandering stream to a thundering rapid.[5]

In *Song of the Paddle*, he adds, "I was elated with my new-found freedom. I was no longer just listening to the song. I was singing it!"[6]

A canoe party on the Kootenay River in British Columbia.

A kayaker on the glacial Arctic waters of the Alsek River.

THE CANOE AS A WAY TO ANOTHER STORY

Bob Henderson

I speculated with a kind of wonder on the strength of the individuality of journeys and stopped on the postulate that people don't take trips – trips take people . . . who has not known a journey to be over and dead before the traveller returns? The reverse is also true: many a trip continues long after movement in time and space have closed.

— John Steinbeck, *Travels with Charley*, 1962

The canoe trip is not often connected to cultural studies. Yet with over 20 years of guiding canoe trips in the Canadian Shield, such an association is all important in designing guiding principles and educational objectives. The association did not just come to me. It evolved over years of watching and responding to students' actions and reflections before, during and after canoe trips. In fact, an analysis of the canoe trip reveals (or sometimes perhaps just introduces) what I call 'another story' to be in; a story that allows for changes in people's self-understanding.[1] This involves, fundamentally, an enhanced awareness of one's situation in the world, where nature is met more openly, more as a place as a Self rather than a space as an Other. Through this process, relationships replace detachments and there is a surfacing of an enlarged/ extended Self. Certainly, poet and essayist Gary Snyder is right, from my evolving understanding of canoe guiding, that, "Wild nature is inextricably in the weave of self and culture."[2]

In this paper I hope to articulate a way of guiding the canoe trip that lies largely outside conventional concepts of the practice of outdoor education, but is central to the shared critical stance of certain academic realms of thought: deep ecology and critical social theory. Deep ecology encourages us to ask more comprehensive questions about our place on the earth. Critical social theory encourages us to consciously change ourselves by changing our situation in the world. Both realms of thought are rooted in a personal and cultural desire to change. By exploring some of these ideas, it is my intention to enlarge an understanding of the outdoor travel guiding process and the potential of the participant's experience beyond the usual justifications.[3] My goal is no less than to suggest that we must change the way we think of ourselves in the world and on the earth. To do this, we must seek a more viable consciousness, one that is ecological not egological. This can only be found, however, in an apprehension of the primacy of the earth and our organic reality with the community of life.[4]

When challenged on these seemingly outlandish sentiments, often in the guise of 'you foolish back to nature freak,' I respond, thanks to cultural anthropologist, Paul Shepherd, with the reminder that should not be necessary; "How can you get back to something you never left?"[5] The rhetorical question is a good one. As a canoe guide, I ask the question, how can the canoe trip help to bring us "home" within the earth? How can we get beyond the illusory dualistic splits (mind/body, culture/nature) that psychologist and canoe guide Robert Greenway calls, "a massive cultural con game"[6] for a rethinking of assumptions that allow us to reshape our practices of living?[7]

One needs look no further than the current social upheaval and the environmental crisis to see why this is a pressing question. Doing what one can in every field of study and vocation does more than make sense, it can be judged as a moral obligation. Certainly teaching and guiding is not an apolitical affair. My "critically pragmatic" view, in fact, assumes an active re-shaping of our inherited traditions. It is a view which assumes an "active social reconstruction . . . as judgements are made about good/bad, beautiful/ugly, true/false in the context of our communities and our attempts to build them anew."[8] Indeed, such dualities can be displaced by a richer, more complex reality. A critical pragmatic view is one that seeks to *produce* culture not reproduce it. We, participant and guide, engage in the possibility of building community anew as we evoke an increased understanding of our situation in the world and the need to rethink our assumptions and practices.

For my students, the task of writing a canoe trip journal is often the first step towards rethinking the assumptions and practices of their life-ways, the first step towards raising their consciousness about the relationship of the travel experience to "everyday life," or, as some students have suggested, "reality."[9] Their journal entries provide a source for what might be used to re-form new possibilities of life. In shaping new stories, one builds upon a practice of questioning cultural assumptions and implementing new life patterns. As E. F. Schumacher writes:

All through school and university, I had been given maps of life and knowledge on which there was hardly a trace of many things that I most cared about and that seemed to me to be of the greatest possible importance to the conduct of my life. I remember that for many years my perplexity had been complete; and no interpreter came along to help me. It remained complete until I ceased to suspect the sanity of my perceptions and began, instead to suspect the soundness of the maps.[10]

For me and for others as evident below, the canoe trip can serve as a critical incidence in questioning the "common sense" soundness of our cultural maps and can help us to find a glowing resonance, vitality and viability in the soundness of canoe tripping perceptions.

In *Pedagogy of the Oppressed*, Paulo Freire writes that "circles of certainty" promote a "culture of silence."[11] As a travel guide and educational researcher, I find that certainty and silence promote a culture that bars me and others from a Self-realization of connectedness to the land and other people. These circles can be transformed if the individuals seek to 1) explore felt greivances, 2) explain the conditions of these frustrations (provide a historical and social context) and 3) seek to express some new program of action to alleviate these greivances.[12] But for these we need transformative education experiences; we need to enter the canoe trip with its circles of ecological engagement. Gramsci spoke of a "praxis in the present" whereby people become increasingly conscious of their situation in the world.[13] Again, enter the canoe tripping group with its circles of human primary community building. These ideas were immediately relevant to me as a canoe travel guide working with groups to seek greater self understanding within the natural world, within the human community, within oneself. "Call it recreation," as novelist Fred Bodsworth once wrote of the canoe trip, "but it involves far more than having fun."[14]

Early on I was taken aback by the students' sentiments of liberation. Now I see them as akin to my own acknowledgement of the need to challenge those aspects of everyday life that deprive us of richer meaning. The travel experience serves as a reprieve from an over-developed, objectified, indoor, detached view of phenomena. We know there is a better story out there; more authentic, more complex, more alive. Many students, it appears, crave to respond to the reprieve, indeed, liberation from these forces. Some, in fact, elect to act on their new insights in order to change their lifeways. In the short passages to follow, from journal entries recorded while on an eight-day canoe trip, this desire for change is a common flow downstream within the watershed of thought connecting the intersubjective dialogue of the guide (who is I) and the students.[15]

STUDENT

Each day we reacted less like tourists and more like tenants.

I will never forget the double-seated outhouse for as long as I shall live.

Again, I thought what have I got myself into? I never, ever, envisioned myself as an outdoor type of person.

I've never been on a hike which didn't involve following an already paved path. The freedom of walking through the woods with a destination, although not a set path, felt like you were really out exploring and discovering something new.

GUIDE

The Norwegian word *Filuftsliv*, means more than outdoor recreation. It means a way home to the open air.[16] Such a participation in our culture demands a stripping off of oppressive forces such as objectivity, consumption, competition: a disorientation leading to a decontextualization. This peeling away of the layers of cultural determinacy leads to a discovery of a

A guitar player, part of the experience.

self that is more connected to self, place, and others. This Self experiences new possibilities, mainly a being at home "with" nature. There is a Self-realization of a "wild" centre to the self as one discovers relationships rather than detachments. There is much to be unlearned along with what will be learned. As we discover a homeness within nature, we are recovering the latent biological being within and we become more wild.

STUDENT

The best part of the day was paddling down the river on a perfectly calm lake with no one around but our three canoes and Bob playing his guitar. My whole body tingled.

GUIDE

Once people get into the swing of travel, travel itself can too easily dominate, limiting perspective. I had a friend who once portaged an island in the middle of the lake to see if the group would notice.

In his case, the group was missing the view in a social excitement. In my case, groups often limit their experience to a task-oriented, "how many miles a day canoe" enthusiasm.

Travelling itself and the social camaraderie associated with travel can be balanced with attention to setting and the joys of stillness. Without a balance of stillness brought to the travel experience, travel can easily so dominate that the setting of travel is lost. The guide must work with this tension between travel and stillness given the particulars of each new group. On day one of the trip, once travel mode is flowing smoothly, I often pull out the guitar and play. For dramatic effect, I have tried this on the last lake of the day, while all are bent on "arriving." Sometimes we drift, sometimes we lillydip. People might be annoyed at first. Nothing is said but the subtle push to relax and look around and enjoy the stillness can do more than simply stall our campsite arrival. It can change the perspective concerning travel itself. People might realize they have already arrived. Pulling out the guitar at that critical, "let's get there moment" is an effort to disorient people. It is an opportunity to let go of business.

STUDENT

We set up camp in the dark. It was a little frustrating but we managed. I like the little snacks around the campfire. Unfortunately we couldn't really stay up around the fire too long. It was raining and everyone was wet and tired including myself. I am enjoying both the physical and emotional or intimate sides of this trip. It is not just what you see and hear out here but it is the aura you feel through your whole body. It's a feeling of freedom. Freedom from the everyday hustle and bustle . . .

I want to write but can't. Don't know where to start. Am afraid to start. How could words explain what has been in the beauty, clarity and depth with which they occurred?

GUIDE

There is a 'deep knowing' experienced on trip to which we are not accustomed. It is a knowing that we experienced with our whole body; mind, body and spirit in a unitary moving meditation. We call it mystical or speak of an aura because we do not have an adequate language and

Recording events in the daily journal.

meaning comprehension to attend to these personal intimacies of self in relationship to surroundings.

STUDENT

. . . It is a caress, welcoming you to become a part. I am sure there are many steps to achieve this sort of relationship, of which the primary ones most of us have only begun to take.

In the end you come to the realization that you revolve around the world rather than the world revolving around.

GUIDE

The suggestion was made within the group to climb the hill across the lake. I cast the odd hint and hoped it would take hold. This hill has great power.

We need to see our canoe route whole, this landscape whole, and perhaps, just perhaps, with that, ourselves whole. Someone could say YES THIS IS IT! and we would all understand what was meant. We ran about, not wanting to contain our contentment, but not knowing fully how to believe such enthusiasm. We played with cameras, looking from many angles. Then we lay on the bald, inviting rock. We relaxed. Resting, sharing a reading from an earlier traveller, absorbing rock, wind, our partners in travel, the setting, ourselves, everything. The cliché would have us say "one with nature," but ecophilosopher Arne Naess puts it in clear terms when he speaks of Self-realization.[17]

STUDENT

During the course of the trip, I was continuously reflecting back to this excerpt, "canoeing is a passage way into man's past." (Sigurd Olson) I could not agree more.

I began thinking about some of the reading we had done, particularly the one about the portage. I was living what that man had described.

GUIDE

A "backpocket" sharing of short vignettes from travel history adds a descriptive historical flavour to our present travels that help dissolve notions of time barriers "to snap the thread of linear time"[18] as Tim Cahill writes.

STUDENT

I learned alot about myself on this trip. My original intention was to learn camping skills and meet new people. I planned to leave (escape) my stresses behind. Instead I brought them along and was able to begin working through them and putting them into perspective. This trip among other things, was not an escape, but a discovery. I did not leave anything, but found something new around me and in myself.

It was an "out-of-this reality" experience for which I am different now.

GUIDE

On a trip we work within a physical reality. Can we hone in on the territory of who we really are? Can we get closer to the genuine territory of where we are? If we can, even for fleeting moments, we learn a great deal. We discover our wild self, our wild centre.

STUDENT

We trundled to the dock and laid out our bags. She-ga, the Husky, had also been beckoned to the place where land met water met sky.

As peacefully as slumber came, it ended with a violent crack. She-ga stirred, as did the bodies around me, but none awoke. This thunderclap was my calling alone. I crawled part way from my down-filled cave to meet the chill of a hurried wind. It was not the night that I remember from one blink earlier.

I looked out across the black abyss of Temagami to witness the rain front racing forward. My sleeping bag dropped to my ankles and I stepped free. I was unshielded from the onslaught. The first patterns of rain slapped against the wooden dock, and spilled on my upturned face. Thunder pounded and lightning exploded, waves crashed and I was alone and unprotected.

I almost bolted. I could be under the tarp in seconds. But I stayed, and I danced. I spun, arms swinging, and head thrown back until the edge warned me not to get too dizzy. It was my rain, lightning and thunder. Like a final explosion of fireworks. The north was saying farewell and I was saying thank you.

GUIDE

The storm woke me up before daybreak. I went out to pee. It wouldn't be much of a daybreak. I noticed a heap of sleeping bags and bodies on the dock. The rain was light, but the mist was heavy. They'll be wet, but they must have worked something out. I investigated, still from a distance. Looks like three bodies tight in their bags with one of the big tarps over all. The wind and mist howled past them. Wonderful!

STUDENT

We paddled past those who would simply have us regurgitate thoughts and feelings that they believe we should think and feel during these moments, past those who would have us believe we were going the wrong way, past the well-lighted areas bustling with self-deception – and into the dark, previously unexplored regions of our being.

It is here where we set up camp, lighting our own fires to show us the way. It may have been uncharted and overgrown, but if we decided to blaze our own trail – to become our own teachers – a sense of our true selves naturally emerged. It was this emergence which allowed us to feel a part of everything because during these moments we took a step closer to understanding what was real.

GUIDE

The guide's role is that of an ambience designer. What is designed is a learning environment that provides both a place and a space for unlearning. The bush and one's life can then be seen anew. This seeing anew is a springboard to new learning or, rather, to an enabling to learn "within" the setting of an enlarged community (social and natural).

When the guide asks the participant, "how was the trip,?" the common response is "it was great." The guide knows, however, that "great" has a lot to do with exploring cultural possibilities, a lot to do with new common sense, a lot to do with exploring authenticity, a lot to do with the question "how are we in relationship?"

STUDENT

Stories. Tangible bits of evidence, validating our experiences – events formulated into words – manipulated into existing grammar and expressions.

In telling my stories, I sometimes feel like I'm "selling out," or "No this isn't what it was all about for me!" But what else do I have? Wait. There is something else. There's the excitement in my tone, my wide quick moving eyes, the fresh glow radiating off my face (or maybe that was sunburn) and the fact that I can't stop talking about it. Was it what I described in my stories that altered my being? Perhaps in a small way, but the profound effect came from another source.

GUIDE

With story, there is the opportunity to build bridges between the personal, the cultural and the natural (the genuine territory of travel). First, we develop meaning by exploring our stories and those of others as part of a living matrix. Secondly, we work to understand meaning in the larger context of culture and/or cosmos, developing our voice as we explain our story. Finally, we initiate action by expressing ourselves with an expanding narrative in a livelier context than before. The guide, attentive to these three E's of storytelling (explore, explain, express) sees and plays the various movements of these three in all experiences of travel. At trip's end, the guide, when asked, "how do I describe all this to those I love?" can best respond simply, "tell your stories." Douglas Coupland, in the novel, *Generation X*, is right when he states, "I'm just upset that the world has gotten too big – way beyond our capacity to tell stories about it."[19] The outdoor travel experience can bring the world into a "smallness," or perhaps proximity, that allows for a congruency with world and self through story such that relationships become more fully attainable within our personal realm of comprehension. All participants revel in the expansion, vitality and challenges of this "closeness" and comprehension.

STUDENT

I felt so good about being me after the trip was over. It was like I took a confidence pill.
    . . . Far behind, you can still see the outpost – a tiny speck on the shore. In your heart there is calm, and that is your link to this place. The doorway you can step into every time you close your eyes. . . . I'll see you there!

The students' field notes and the comments of the guide as co-investigator can never fully speak to the "whole" of the experience and certainly do not speak for all. At best, they serve as a representation of experience from which both general and specific propositional themes can be exposed. In short, I hope they speak to another story to be in. The field notes and guide's comments are like pottery shards to the archaeologist.[20] We do not ask the archaeologist to *give* us the whole pot from the fragments. Rather we accept that the fragments are exemplary and can be used to "construct" a whole or tell a story. The story told here is a critical interpretation offered from a commitment by the researcher, be it archaeologist or canoe travel guide, to tell an actual story, not a freely imagined one. The best story, like the best map, is one that most closely depicts the actual terrain of the experience. The story builds from empirical observation, field notes, and a literature review like a watershed funneling from rivulets to streams to rivers to a single water course. Its direction gathers towards an analysis that provides key distinguishing themes. Themes then provide the guide with clear direction. As the fragments build into themes, compelling revelations emerge from guide and student alike which command our attention.

REVELATION

Revelation is the first emergent and embracing theme throughout this story. Of revelation, Alfred North Whitehead has allegedly said:

Revelation is the primary characterization of the process of knowing. The traditional theory of education is to secure youth and its teachers from revelation. It is dangerous for youth and confusing to teachers. It upsets the accepted coordination of doctrine.

Much of the writing from students and guide recorded here is in the form of revelation as an acknowledgement of grand significance. Indeed, it was revelation that inspired much of the field note writing in the first place and helps to explain the wealth of field notes and completed journals – an assignment that is not graded, and, therefore, by the standard assessment, of little value. Revelation is an emerging, embracing theme of the travel experience because it creates a sharp contrast to the dominant epistemological paradigm that pervades schooling. Revelation makes an epistemological shift from learning that is commonly procedural or prescribed, towards a way of knowing, an individual perception and experience. It is learning that readily celebrates personal meaning and relationship and acknowledges and anticipates revelation. Revelation helps both to explain and expand on the story of teaching and learning in outdoor travel. Camping and travel being para-educational yet holistic of mind, body, and spirit, expose learners to another way of knowing (or of storying) that allows for revelation and is a revelation in itself. The figure below, adapted largely from Noel Gough,[21] highlights the contrast of a transmission-behaviourist classroom learning environment and transformation-ecological camping learning.

COMPARISON OF A TRANSMISSION-BEHAVIOURIST CLASSROOM LEARNING ENVIRONMENT TO A TRANSFORMATION-ECOLOGICAL PARADIGM OF CAMPING LEARNING

Transmission-Behaviourist

Socially structured knowledge (largely theoretical and technical)

Education as distribution of structured knowledge. Emphasis on how to answer questions. Short term view.

Teaching as guided access to the storehouses of propositional knowledge.

Control of learning as
Assymetrical dependence   assessment
Teacher-pupil, external   Competiton among learners

Learning Materials as
Textbooks   Standardized procedures

Learning Activities as
Paying attention   Rote activities
Memorizing   Conservative

Personal Development as
Conformity   Divorce of means and ends
self-centredness

Transformational-Ecological

Individual structured knowledge (practical, personal)

Education as searching environments. Emphasis on how to ask questions. Long term view.

Teaching as creative tools, techniques and settings which sustain learner's perceptual work.

Control of Learning as
Symmetrical dependence   Co-learners, self-assessment
Co-operation among learners

Learning Materials as
Reality-centred projects

Learning Activities as
Discrimination   Searching
Creating   Transcending

Personal Development as
Tolerance of individuality   Depth and integration
Equal consideration of self   and others

If there was a balance of these fundamentally different paradigms for learning in an individual's upbringing, then I would not expect the holistic revelatory response that I have come to acknowledge as an overarching theme. Of course, the classroom can be transformational-ecological and the camping experience can be transmissive-behaviourist. For the school environment, however, transformational learning constitutes an exception. As for the camping environment, the transformational-story paradigm must be understood by the guide who then develops a set of guiding principles. Without such acknowledgement, the transformational curriculum story is largely trial and error rather than structured pedagogy.

Individual seeking perception and experience.

The shift toward a transformational-ecological episteme situates the learner/traveller directly within his or her learning experience. This direct engagement in one's experience offers a re-enchantment with the self. Experience as the concrete apprehension of self as an agent in and of life is a liberating revelation, one that comes from pursuing revelation itself.

There is tension within all of us between *disappearing* and *surfacing*. Disappearing occurs consciously, as in one's willing abdication of responsibility, or unconsciously, as in being unaware of oppressive forces (Freire's culture of silence) when one allows Self to be determined rather than determining oneself.[22] Brian Fawcett defines disappearing as "[undermining] one's psychic and physical autonomy to the point where it is unable to recognize itself or be recognized by its community."[23] A person with the experience of autonomy and personalized learning experiences a re-enchantment with the self in context with the social and physical environment.

This re-enchantment is a *surfacing* and is the key quality behind comments such as "it is not just what you see and hear out here but it is the aura you feel through your whole body," and "it was like taking a confidence pill." These fragments of thought bespeak a surfacing of the self,

Many stories to tell.

but, as mentioned, a self that embodies the primacy of relational knowing/living. They bespeak the revelation of enhanced self-understanding. The detached-from-self individual, the largely culturally determined "disappearing" self is suppressed in celebration of the surfacing Self. This Self, with a capital S, is attentive primarily to community, to an ecology of people, place and the delightful mysteries of feelings of connectedness. Put simply, "being" is a reward in itself. Space and silence become newly sought qualities. Time in the present is gainfully experienced. Storytelling is a dominant means of expression. These themes that emerge with the holistic revelation of the surfacing Self serve as principles to guide the travel guide. Space/ silence/stillness, time, within-ness, authenticity: these are specific sites of thought for revelation and surfacing of self. In terms of guiding, they constitute a pedagogy central to a deep ecological and critical story of changing one's self-understanding. One can only do this for oneself. In this story, the guide and student are co-learners and the canoe trip is a medium, a first stroke, a look at a new map, a smelling of a morning sunrise, a step into unknown terrain, another story to be in.

Historic Canoe Routes of the French River

Toni Harting

S ituated between Ontario's Lake Nipissing and Georgian Bay, a most unusual river system carries the lake's waters west down an intricate collection of channels and lakes, bays and marshes, rapids and falls. This is the French River, which – in spite of its short 100-kilometre length and its modest 19 metre drop – is a major waterway, owing to its strategic location between the Ottawa River watershed to the east and the Great Lakes to the west. The French River shows so much physical diversity and has such a rich history that it is among the most exceptional and fascinating rivers in the province, if not Canada.

It is quite a young river. Only about 2,800 years ago, crevices and faults in the Canadian Shield bedrock, still rebounding after their release from the crushing weight of the ice-age glaciers, filled with west-flowing water and formed the infant French River. Eventually these early channels developed into an intricate river system. Obviously, this is not a typical river carrying its waters from source to mouth in a single stream, but instead a highly complex network of pool-and-drop waterways (see Map 1). The present river's water level is controlled to a large extent by the operation of four dams erected in 1916 and 1950 in the upstream section of the river to manage the water level of Lake Nipissing.[1]

Before the arrival of Europeans in this part of the country, the Native inhabitants had used the river for centuries as part of a major trade route

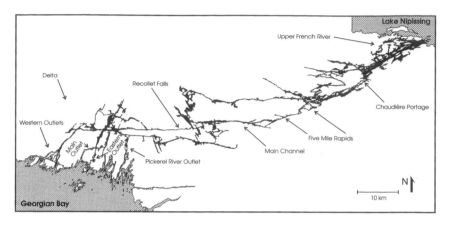

Map 1: The French River System.

which carried them across much of northern North America. This situation started to change dramatically in about 1610 when the first white man came from the east, followed by another some time later, then another and still more, until their light-skinned faces became a familiar sight in the region. These European visitors were explorers, missionaries and fur traders who penetrated deeper and deeper into the unknown, eager to discover other worlds and meet new people. Like the Aboriginal peoples before them, the newcomers travelled in birchbark canoes. They were passionately dedicated to a single-minded search for knowledge, souls and profit, willingly risking their lives in a fierce struggle to fulfill their dreams.

During the more than 250 years of the fur trade, the French River formed a small but vital link in the lifeline between east and west. Its waters were an integral part of the famous and uniquely Canadian fur-trade central mainline, a thin thread of rivers, lakes, and portages stretching like a 4,000-kilometre spine from Montreal all the way to Fort Chipewyan on Lake Athabasca.[2]

Surprisingly, very little physical evidence remains to show that thousands of canoes and tens of thousands of people indeed travelled the French River system in past centuries. Several pre-contact Native archaeological sites have been discovered and these should yield interesting information once they are explored fully. But as far as the presence of non-Natives is concerned during the seventeenth to nineteenth centuries, no campsites, no notes, no graffiti, no marks, no footsteps, no garbage, no

Replica of a North canoe of the voyageurs navigating rapids in the French River.

graves; practically no visible signs of any kind have been found along the shores of the river to attest to the passage of so many people. The only tangible proof that fur-trading canoeists travelled the French River are a number of artifacts (such as kettles, axes, musket balls, glass beads, guns, awls, ice chisels) found under water by divers below several rapids and falls since the early 1960s.[3]

In several old trip journals, including Alexander Mackenzie's *Voyages from Montreal* and Angus Mackintosh's *Journal from the Enterance* (sic) *of the French River*,[4] brief descriptions can be found of the routes selected by past travellers, mostly dating from the British period after 1760. When studying these narratives, it becomes evident that they do not provide a clear and trustworthy answer to the question of which routes were followed. Place names and locations, in particular, can be confusing because there were no detailed maps of the French River included in these old documents. Thus, while the journals are of limited use in the search for historic canoe routes, they nonetheless provide a rare insight into wilderness canoe tripping during the fur trade years.

Eric Morse, in his famous publications on the Canadian fur-trade routes, was the first researcher to provide a broad outline as well as some fascinating details of the routes the voyageurs might have used on the French River.[5] There is, however, much to be discovered about the routes of the voyageurs and my work is a contribution toward presenting a detailed description of possible routes. One way to determine how canoeists in previous centuries probably travelled the river, is to imaginatively accompany them in their canoes and apply one's knowledge of canoeing, camping and portaging techniques, as well as an understanding of the French River system from a canoeing point of view.

In a typical year the fur-trade brigades left Lachine just west of Montreal after ice break-up in early May. They paddled and portaged up the Ottawa and Mattawa rivers and arrived at Lake Nipissing about three to four weeks after leaving Lachine. For the voyageurs coming off the large expanse of Lake Nipissing, the Upper French River was a simple, 19-kilometre flatwater paddle to the start of the river proper.

The first obstacles the voyageurs encountered on their trip down the French River were the unrunnable Chaudière Rapids, located at the top of the Main Channel of the river on the southeast side of Okikendawt Island. Here the travellers were forced to make a 420-metre portage, the longest one on the river (see Map 2).

Various Aboriginal peoples,[6] however, during their history on the river, had discovered a simple, relatively short and reasonably flat trail leading from the southwest shore of Portage Bay to Bruce Bay. Once this portage had been pointed out to the Europeans, travel between Lake Nipissing and Georgian Bay became much more straightforward. As Robert Seaborne Miles, a secretary working for the Hudson's Bay Company, matter-of-factly noted in his journal on 7 June 1818: "Twenty minutes to eleven reached Portage Chaudiere de Francois, carried the baggage (sic) and gummed the canoe and left at twenty-five minutes to twelve."[7] From May until October, it remained the most effective way to move trade goods, fur and people down and up the French River.

Tragically, the Chaudière Portage was all but destroyed in 1949 and 1950 by the construction of the dam-controlled Portage Channel. The trail is now to a large extent covered by rock debris, trees and bush, while part of it has even been cut away by the channel itself. Only two sections at the beginning and end of the portage are in reasonable shape, looking approximately as they did so many years ago. It is a disgrace that this mag-

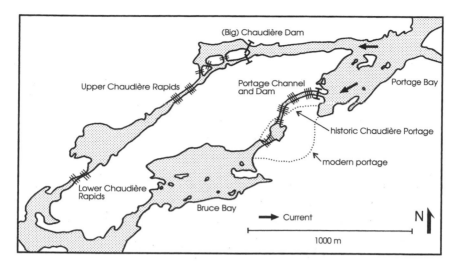

Map 2: Chaudière area of the French River system.

nificent, ancient and historically meaningful trail has been all but ruined in the name of progress. Instead, the Chaudière Portage ought to be part of a national monument dedicated to the unique activities of past travellers who helped to lay the foundations of Canada.

About 15 kilometres below the Chaudière Portage are the Little Pine Rapids, the first of the Five Mile Rapids in the Main Channel running south of Eighteen Mile Island (Map 3). The runnability of all the rapids in this section, and the rest of the river, for that matter, depends to a large extent upon the water level of the river which is determined by the amount of precipitation and the setting of the dam controls and, thus, can vary tremendously in a short period of time.

At the high water levels in May when the first brigades came down from Montreal, the large, heavily loaded canots du maître, also called Montreal canoes, often would have been able to run these rapids fully loaded, provided they stayed clear of the big standing waves. In low water, several of the rapids in this section would have to be portaged, lined, poled or waded. Going upriver would also have meant some hard work to get the canoes with their precious cargo safely portaged or lined up the rapids.

Roughly 29 flatwater kilometres below the Five Mile Rapids, the voyageurs encountered the scenic, and notorious, Recollet Falls (see Map 1), which could not be run by canoes at any water level. The voyageurs, there-

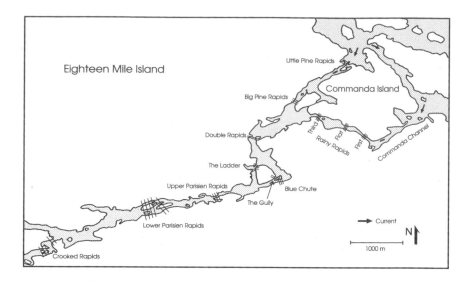

Map 3: The Five Mile Rapids section of the French River system.

fore, would have had to takeout on the left side of the river, just a few metres above the 2.1-metre falls. At high water with a strong river current, this could be very dangerous indeed. If they were not extremely careful, the current could easily sweep their heavily loaded boats down the nearby falls, leading to almost certain death for the unlucky travellers. There are various indications that Recollet Falls claimed quite a few casualties over the years.

The original portage trail was about 50 metres long and followed the same route as the wooden boardwalk today. The water coming off the falls flows against the vertical rockface on the south side of the river causing tricky crosscurrents and eddies that require great care when paddling across. Frances Simpson, the wife of the Governor of the Hudson's Bay Company, George Simpson, on an excursion down the river, gives some indication of the anxious moments the voyageurs in their heavy, deep-lying canoes would have experienced in her diary entry of 11 May 1830:

At the Recollet Portage breakfasted, and the weather clearing up, changed our wet for dry clothes, but on going from the root of the Récollet fall, were very nearly drawn under it, by a strong Eddy; indeed so near, that the Spray from the fall showered over, & gave us another drenching; but by the exertions of the men at the paddle, regained the Stream, and got into Lake Huron at 2 O'clock.[8]

About 14 kilometres below the Recollet Falls the voyageurs came to the Ox Bay / Wanapitei Bay area. Here a crucial decision had to be made regarding the route they ought to take, depending upon the level of the water. If the brigade guide thought that the water was high enough to carry the boats safely down the Old Voyageur Channel, they would continue west from Wanapitei Bay to the point where the Western Channel divides into the Western Outlets. But, if the water level was considered to be too low, the voyageurs would turn south at Wanapitei Bay into the Main Channel and follow it to the Main Outlet, where the Dalles Rapids form the last obstacle before the river waters flow into Georgian Bay.

At the Dalles Rapids the canoes could be run or possibly lined down the relatively deep major channel on the south side without much of a problem (see Map 4). If necessary, the voyageurs could follow the 180-metre portage trail that would take them safely around the rapids. This was likely to happen more often when going from the Bay back up to the river later in the year. Lining the canoes up the rapids was another possibility, especially attractive when the water was not too high. When going downriver, the standing waves that can exist in Little Dalles Rapids when the river water level is high would not have posed any real problems for the big canoes.

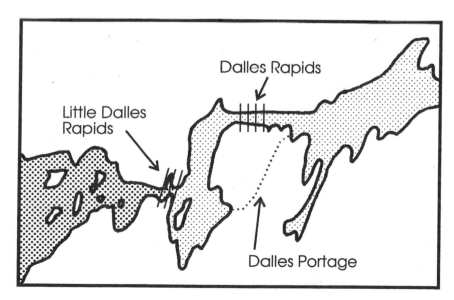

Map 4: Main Outlet section of French River.

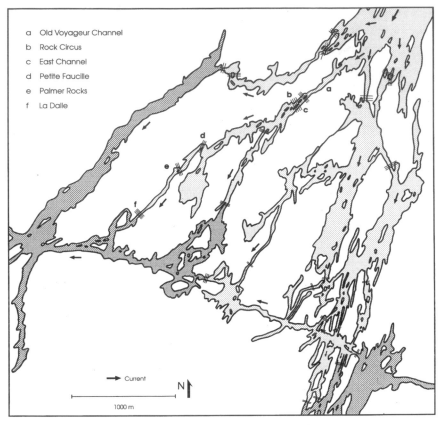

a Old Voyageur Channel
b Rock Circus
c East Channel
d Petite Faucille
e Palmer Rocks
f La Dalle

Current

N

1000 m

Map 5: Western Outlets, French River system.

If the voyageurs decided at Wanapitei Bay that the river water level was high enough to run a channel of the Western Outlets, they would have continued west via the Western Channel. The only outlet channel with the right physical properties to be of use to at least some of the voyageurs is the Old Voyageur Channel (see Map 5). In several of the historic narratives this channel is indeed mentioned as the one followed by various fur traders. However, closer study of this route from a canoeing point of view reveals some serious difficulties that would have been encountered by travellers in big canoes, limiting the use of this route to periods of sufficiently high water levels. This would especially have been the case with large brigades going upriver.

Depending upon the water level, there are four places in the Old

Voyageur Channel which are potential trouble spots for big canoes. The first is the East Channel of the Rock Circus, a narrow, almost straight passage between sloping rock walls and connected to the western part of the Rock Circus by three openings through which water can flow. In some studies this channel is called La Dalle, but the true location of that section appears to be further down the Old Voyageur Channel.

The East Channel is an interesting passage with obvious possibilities for canoe travel, but unfortunately several rocks sticking up from the channel floor obstruct canoe traffic at medium to low water. Even at relatively high water the big voyageur canoes, lying deep because of their heavy loads, would not have been able to negotiate this channel without running serious risks. The East Channel, therefore would have been used by the fur traders only at quite high water levels. Upriver travel would then have been difficult because of the strong current as well as the steep walls of the narrow channel, which would have made lining up troublesome but by no means impossible.

The second obstacle in the Old Voyageur Channel is the Petite Faucille, or Little Sickle, a tightly curved and unrunnable drop with an average height of less than a metre, where the canoes had to be unloaded and carried over the rocky peninsula to the south for about 20 metres. The existence of the Petite Faucille is reported a few times in the journals of several of the travellers. Muskets and other artifacts found in the late 1960s below the drop on the river bottom are another indication that this route was used by the fur traders.

The third serious obstacle voyageurs would face in the Old Voyageur Channel, the Palmer Rocks, can cause severe problems for passing travellers if the water level is not high enough. They consist of a rock ridge made up of several parts crossing the channel at an angle, and make it practically impossible for big boats to pass in low to medium water levels. Portaging this section is extremely difficult because of the inhospitable terrain.

Finally, a few hundred metres below the Palmer Rocks, the voyageurs encountered a scenic and comfortably straight channel about 100 metres long that could be run at any water level by canoes of all sizes. Going upriver at high water levels, the big boats could be lined up against the strong current by walking on top of the elevated west bank. This may be the famous La Dalle, the Trough or Gutter, mentioned in several of the old trip journals, although it is possible that in the fur trade days the whole Old Voyageur Channel was sometimes called La Dalle and not just any small section of it.

A rare insight into the use of the Old Voyageur Channel is given in the journal written by the North West Company agent, Angus Mackintosh, who on 14 July 1813 travelled upriver from Georgian Bay:

This morning left our encamping ground and proceeded up the river, came to the Dalle a rapid of 50 feet of very strong water where the canoe was dragged up by the line (5 codelines twisted together). Soon after getting up this rapids we came to Le Petit Faucille a rapid and carrying place of 60 feet . . .[9]

Below La Dalle, the waters flow into the West Cross Channel and the travellers would have to decide whether to go west on this channel or to take the Fort Channel directly to Georgian Bay.

When returning from the western fur country at the end of September or early October, the voyageurs encountered a serious complication. They immediately had to decide on the correct channel to take the canoes back upriver without knowing the actual water level in the river. The choice depended upon their intimate knowledge and understanding of the weather and the topography of the country.

Using the Old Voyageur Channel had several advantages over the Main Outlet via the Dalles Rapids. For one thing, they did not have to travel as far along the treacherous section of the Georgian Bay north shore. They also had easy access to the western end of the West Cross Channel where the Prairie des Français offered shelter in case of inclement weather.

Little or no information exists about other locations along the French River where the fur traders might have camped. There must have been several campsites because of the time it would have taken the brigades to travel the river. The campsites would also have been quite large to accommodate the often considerable number of canoes involved. Fur fleets with sixty canoes or more occasionally have been reported going upriver.

Under the right circumstances, the voyageurs paddling express canoes apparently made it downriver in one day, as mentioned in several of the old journals. But going upriver, especially at high water, would have taken several days. The regular big freight canoes surely would have needed a few days to travel the river because of the cargo that had to be portaged.

What conclusions can be drawn from these observations? Obviously, when speaking about the French River voyageur routes, one is talking in general terms. The Delta and mouth of the river are complicated and offer too many options to restrict the travellers to one specific route. The paths the voyageurs chose would depend upon a number of factors such as: time of year, weather conditions, canoe type and loading, canoeing experience, brigade size, freight type, down or upriver travel and destination. But above all, water level was the overriding factor in deciding where to go and what to do on the river. The voyageurs wanted to travel as quickly and efficiently as possible. They were in the business of transportation, of making money and did not intend to waste precious time sightseeing, loafing around or waiting for each other in traffic pile-ups.

Taking all these factors into account and assuming that the water levels in those days followed roughly the same cycle they do now, a few broad conclusions can be made regarding the routes the fur trade voyageurs might have used. The route from Lake Nipissing down to Wanapitei Bay in the Delta would have been a straightforward following of the Main Channel after first crossing the Chaudière Portage into the river proper. At Wanapitei Bay the large fur-trade freight brigades would go south to the Main Outlet and descend or portage the Dalles Rapids. The Old Voyageur Channel in the Western Outlets probably was used primarily by the voyageurs at quite high water levels and not by the large brigades of fur-trade canoes. Smaller fur-trade canoes and specialized big canoes carrying only passengers, mail and other important cargo would also have used this channel. These express or light canoes had less weight to carry and therefore enjoyed more freeboard to run rapids and shallow parts. They were also easier to handle in the narrow channels and to portage. The same procedures would be followed by canoes travelling upriver. However, if the water levels in the past were consistently higher than they are now, especially during spring high-water, greater numbers of the large freight canoes could have used the Old Voyageur Channel.

The French River at the end of the day.

These main conclusions are of course tentative. However, they offer at least a general idea of the situation and may serve to open the door to future research into how the voyageurs really operated during the years of the fur trade, as well as into the behaviour of the French River before modern society began to interfere with its natural flow. This is an important river, and we should clearly recognize the essential role its trade routes have played in Canadian cultures.

THE DARK SIDE OF THE CANOE

Gwyneth Hoyle

Much has been written about the healing powers of the wilderness experience.[1] The spiritual power of nature and the strength gained from overcoming a challenge are often implicit in even the most straightforward account, from the classic epic journeys to the short articles appearing in canoeing magazines. When people commit their lives and comfort to the basic baggage that can be carried in a canoe or a pack, and embark on a journey, they have expectations of coming back spiritually restored and revitalized after the experience of living close to nature.

In a recent television interview Canadian artist, Mary Pratt, spoke of being drawn to painting by the need to depict light. When she begins a painting the light is all important to her. But shadows are an essential part of light and she has found that in the shadows are fascinating depths and hidden messages, where the paintings take on new and unexpected meanings.

There are shadows in the journals of wilderness travellers as well and these dark patches occur most often in the area of interpersonal relationships. There is great satisfaction to be found in surviving a battle with the elements or in negotiating a stretch of treacherous white-water, but when partnerships turn sour, a cloud descends over the journey that is not easily dispelled. Examples of dissension can be found in a number of books. For example, Eric Sevareid in *Canoeing with the Cree* writes:

Gradually our dispositions gave way under the strain. We became surly and irritable. The slightest mishap set our nerves jumping. At first all this went on only in our minds, but each knew the other's thoughts and it was only a matter of time before it came to words. Like children, we bickered. And then we came to blows. One cold morning as we prepared to load the canoe, a trifling incident occurred . . . we leaped at each other. Hitting and twisting violently as though we were fighting for our lives, we rolled over and over until we struck a tree trunk. The same thought must have come to each of us at the same moment and we were sane enough to recognize it . . . : separation here in the wilderness would mean but one thing – death to both. Without speaking a word, we released our hold, staring at each other as if we had been having a bad dream.[2]

Christopher Norment from *In the North of Our Lives* is less violent and more subtle, but disruptive nonetheless:

Our rest day was a welcome break for most of us, yet it had unexpected consequences that were completely out of proportion to their seeming importance and dogged us for the rest of the journey. . . . Over the next few weeks we battled out the issue – sometimes arguing, more frequently resorting to quiet gestures of defiance. Eventually, we effected a compromise. . . . And as is true of many compromises, no one was completely satisfied.[3]

George Grinnell in *A Death on the Barrens* shows conflict building:

We all loved Art in those early days as if he were not the leader of an expedition, but of a religious cult and we his five anointed disciples. Skip commented on how well we were all getting on. 'Enjoy it while it lasts,' Art replied.[4]

Then a few weeks later:

Art smiled at Skip, and Skip smiled at Art; but beneath the surface their attitudes . . . were all very different. As the days passed into weeks, these differences began to surface with ever-increasing frequency.[5]

The following quotations are from two books written by Victoria Jason and Don Starkell about a trip the authors undertook together. In *Kabloona in the Yellow Kayak*, Jason writes: "Again he [Don Starkell]

Victoria Jason and Don Starkell, an amicable start to a stormy voyage.

started cursing and yelling. I hated the way he exploded when things weren't just right."[6] And here is Don Starkell's comment in his account called *Paddle to the Arctic:*

Victoria bit her tongue many times and put up with my remarks – most of which were not called for. My intentions were not bad, I was just too tense. Victoria has ... performed ... better than most of my previous paddling companions. She deserves a medal for putting up with me. She never complained, so I didn't realize how much extra pressure I was putting on her.[7]

Finally from a trip on which things were going awry before the trip had really started, Robert Cundy in *Beacon Six:*

It was the stowage problem which caused the first real friction. The rations were in neat parcels just as they left the factory. Robin worked out our daily rations and declared that no one was going to open the parcels until they reach the Barrens. . . . It is impossible to argue with Robby once he has made up his mind – he hunches his enormous shoulders and shuffles away to sulk, becoming as unapproachable as a wounded animal.[8]

None of the above quotations refer to an average recreational canoe trip. The participants were either attempting something unique, not following an established route with a written history to guide them, or attempting an unusual combination of routes. All the trips were lengthy, extending through at least a whole season, and some stretching beyond a year. All except one person survived, but a few suffered physical or psychological damage. While interpersonal relationships can degenerate even on average trips, the reactions quoted above are magnified and heightened by the more extreme nature of the adventures.

There are two major sources of tension that can be identified as creating the kind of friction we have just seen. These are present to some degree in all of the stories, and indeed, are sources of tension in everyday life. Since a journey is a metaphor for life itself in which the elements of life are compressed, the experience heightens the perceptions of those participating.

The first cause of tension is fear. Admitted or not, fear of death lurks somewhere in the deep recesses of all our psyches. Fear can bedevil everyday life or it can be a healthy emotion, acting, when necessary, as a cautionary brake. On a river, fear in the midst of a set of rapids, for example, releases adrenalin, which for a time sharpens the reactions and enhances the experience. But fear from which there is no escape loses its edge of pleasure and grinds down the spirit. When the situation is out of control and danger is real, fear rises to the surface and reactions to it become unpredictable. On a wilderness trip, it often begins as anxiety about the schedule, which is just another form of the fear of starvation or fear of being caught by the approach of winter. Fears of being lost, of accidents or of animal attack may exist, but none are so powerful as the concern about the amount of food left in the packs, or by the sighting of snowflakes in the air when the journey's end is nowhere in sight.

Like fear, the second cause of friction, the inherent differences in people, happens everyday. Personality differences give life flavour and texture. Ironically, in a vast expanse of empty wilderness, two persons confined to the small space of a canoe can find their personality differences become magnified to the point of hostility. At the onset of an Arctic winter, living with a trader, Gontran de Poncins in his book *Kabloona* describes this feeling:

. . . our world narrowed until it was reduced to the dimensions of a trap, I went from impatience to restlessness, and from restlessness finally to monomania. I began to rage inwardly, and the very traits in my friend which had struck me in the beginning as admirable, ultimately seemed to me detestable. The time came when I could no longer bear the sight of this man who was unfailingly kind to me . . .[9]

With differences in physical strength and experience added to variation in personality, the possibilities for tension are increased. Elliott Merrick has a story in his book *True North* that illustrates the eruption of blind rage when physical endurance was pushed to the limit. Even though his experience is of sledding with a Labrador trapper, the intense feeling can be translated to a tough portage or a hard paddle:

For hours we never spoke, afraid of the words of weakness we might say if we opened our lips. . . . I was ahead for a long stretch and I commenced to leave him behind. When two men are travelling under such terrific stress . . . it unfortunately becomes a contest. . . . I cannot explain it, nevertheless the feeling is tremendously powerful. As I commenced to draw away I looked back and saw that Henry was pale and had his teeth in his lip. A gust of blinding passion shook the sanity right out of me and I thought as my teeth ground savagely, 'Now I can leave you if I want. You have left me behind so many times on these sled hauling trips, now it is my turn for once. Ah God, I don't care if his sled is running harder than mine and he's sick. I wouldn't care if he had a broken leg. . . . I can leave him, I can leave him. I don't care why!'. . . . I had no intention of leaving him or even showing him that I could. It was simply that I knew for the first time in my life that I had the power. I could have held up my fists to the sky and screamed with evil joy. . . . For a moment there was not one spark of goodness in me. I found myself trembling and afraid. Henry hauled up alongside and we stopped and ate bread and sugar to keep us going. After that he was as good for it as I was.[10]

In their light-hearted instructional book, *The Complete Wilderness Paddler,* Davidson and Rugge have anticipated the problems that can be sparked by personality differences on a remote wilderness trip:

. . . throw a group of people together without benefit of organization, uniforms, or the flag, deprive them of outside contact, and then put them at hard labor hauling around edibles that they have to ration among themselves. You have just rolled gunpowder. Now forbid these people the use of hot emotion – no anger, no resentment, no irritation, no conflict of any kind. You have just spiked that keg of powder. We will put the problem as directly as we know how: the rigors of a wilderness trip will draw out differences among fellow human beings, and the wilderness paddler is well advised to prepare for them.[11]

One of their suggestions to break the tension, is to change the routine with a day off, giving people a chance to escape into their own worlds from the rub of being yoked together by the journey.

While fear and human variation are the prime sources of trouble, another problem occurs when members of the group have different goals. This is especially true when the goal has no connection with wilderness and is strictly self-serving or even mercenary. As Margaret Atwood

Eric Sevareid and Walter Port prepare to leave on their epic journey.

pointed out in her book *Strange Things,* "... real goal of the Franklin expedition was financial – to get to India and China faster."[12] The wilderness,
particularly in the far north, is a law unto itself and cannot be influenced
by the whims of mere mortals. The native people who depend on trapping
and hunting know the risks they take and observe the laws of the wilderness. Those who expect to pay for their trip with the story, film or glory
they bring back must pay attention to nature's timetable.

By examining the stories behind the first five quotations, it is possible
to recognize that in varying degrees fear and personality difference were
root causes of friction. Conflicting goals or self-interest are present in
some cases but not in others.

When Eric Sevareid and Walter Port set off from Minneapolis to go to
Hudson Bay, they were seventeen and nineteen respectively. Strong and
husky, and with a contract with the *Minneapolis Star* for the story, they
had no idea of the immensity of their undertaking. Port was the stronger
of the two, Sevareid was the dreamer. Sevareid said that before leaving "...
just for an instant he went cold to the pit of his stomach,"[13] but Port
seemed less concerned. When they finally reached the confusing waterways between God's Lake and York Factory, it was late in the season, the
weather had broken, they were short of food and, with only crude maps,

they were lost. The fight occurred when they were at their lowest ebb. In Sevareid's words written years later, the fight simply had relieved the terrible pressure of built-up tensions. "When you are lost, when you are hungry, when the rivers and woods become your enemy, waiting for you to die, none of the senses discovers pleasure. For years afterwards a visit to the woods produced a moment of nausea."[14] Sevareid and Port returned to the area fifty years later on a flight provided by the Audubon Society, which allowed Sevareid to put to rest his obsession with God's River.[15]

While the two young men had a contract with the *Minneapolis Star* to write the story of their trip, this played no part in the tension that arose. As the wilderness closed in on them like a trap, their personality differences were rubbed raw. At the same time, fear of death was their constant companion and they were in despair of getting out alive. What had begun as a school-boy dream had turned into a nightmare.

In his book, *In the North of Our Lives,* Christopher Norment tells of the fourteen months spent canoeing from the Yukon to Hudson Bay, wintering at Warden's Grove in the Thelon Game Preserve with five companions. It was planned as a retreat from the rush of urban life, with an opportunity to experience the wilderness in all its seasons. It was also a commemoration of the fiftieth anniversary of John Hornby's fateful last trip into the Barrens. Some of the group had met through Outward Bound, others were friends. All had outdoor skills and strong egos, but different physical capabilities and different ideas about the nature of the trip.

They began with an upstream slog and portage across the watershed onto the Nahanni River. This was punishing work at the beginning of a trip when the food packs were heaviest, but the group worked hard and pulled together. But there was a fly in the ointment. One of the strongest and hardest working members of the group had his own agenda. He was committed to reaching the Thelon early enough in the season to build a memorial cabin to John Hornby and his two unfortunate companions. The other five had signed off from their professional lives for the chance to immerse themselves in wilderness. The conflict came after the first, much needed rest day on the Nahanni when the group was slow to move. The irritation continued to build as one member continually urged the group to move faster, while the others felt they were missing the hoped-for experience in the rush. The harmonious Utopian dream was tarnished and never recovered its original lustre. Differences in personality and purpose were magnified as winter confined them to close quarters for longer periods.

Fear did not play a large part in the disturbance that boiled beneath the surface of this story, although it may have been present at times. The group had prepared very carefully for every eventuality. The friction between personalities, the clash of egos, came from the frustration of not achieving the different purposes on which they had built their hopes. This cast a shadow near the beginning of this otherwise successful expedition, and the shadow remained throughout.

The Arthur Moffatt trip across the Barrens in 1955 stood out as a cautionary tale to every canoeist planning subsequent trips in the area. The Albany River was Art Moffatt's spiritual home since his first solo trip on it when he was seventeen. He loved the wilderness and the Cree families that he met along the way. He had attempted to earn a living by guiding trips of young American college students on the Albany and had made a movie of it. With a wife and two young daughters to support, he needed a larger project. He hoped that leading a similar group of college students on a more spectacular trip across the Barrens and additionally making a movie of the wildlife would be the answer to his problems. No such trip had been made since the days of the Tyrrell brothers.

Art Moffatt's style of leading was extremely passive in a way that confused his five companions. He wanted to blend into the wilderness and issue no orders. Breaking camp in the mornings, he moved with deliberate slowness, soaking up the last peaceful moments with his cup of tea. On the early portages, climbing the watershed, he was burdened by the extra weight of water-proof camera equipment and film. In fact, the making of that film to support his family became like a millstone around his neck throughout the trip.

As the food ran out and the season advanced, the lack of leadership and the slow pace drove the members of the group to open rebellion. Fear of death stalked the campsites. After a feed of caribou, when the weather turned benign, Art Moffatt's charisma beguiled some of them into forgetting their dissension, but it was never far below the surface. When the accident happened and Art died of hypothermia, the survivors found the solidarity and strength to complete the trip to Baker Lake under terrible conditions, but some continue to bear psychological scars.

That fear of death was Art Moffatt's companion from the outset can be seen in the first foreboding entries made in his diary before the trip was under way.[16] Anxiety caused by the slow schedule surfaced early in the trip and, as the food packs shrank and the weather turned colder, the fear spread to all members of the party. Art's concern about making the film slowed progress further and, finally, personality differences were like sand in the gear box.

Horrendous conditions marked the completion of Don Starkell's crossing of the Arctic by kayak. Starkell admits that he is driven by obsessive stubbornness; without it he would not have survived the frigid end of his trip. At the same time, it is a trait which makes him a difficult kayaking companion as Victoria Jason quickly learned.

Fear played a large part in Don Starkell's reactions. His first solo attempt at kayaking on Hudson Bay had ended in a near-death experience. Fear never left him and underlay many of his explosive reactions when he travelled with this companion. Being in the *Guinness Book of Records* for his paddle to the Amazon, gave Starkell the motivation to push the limits of physical endurance to make another record-breaking trip. This extraneous purpose, combined with his fears and the differences in their physical strength and personality made friction between him and Victoria Jason inevitable.

Finally we come to the story of *Beacon Six*. It was organized by Robert Cundy, a young, restless London lawyer, seeking adventure on the rebound from a rejected marriage proposal, who put an ad in the personal column of *The Times*, "Adventurous, photogenic young people needed to join owner of a 16 mm Bolex to make TV travel films. Keen, rough travellers, share expenses."[17] This would seem to be a recipe for trouble from the start.

The group which made the trip down the Back River in 1962 consisted of two Royal Marines and two officers from the Army's Special Air Service. The stated purpose was to investigate the cairn on Cape Britannia at the end of Chantrey Inlet, in the hope of finding a message from Sir John Franklin. (The Canadian Geological Survey had already explored this cairn and found nothing.) This was to be the first trip down the Back River in over 100 years and they expected to pay for it with the film they would make, as well as with magazine stories and still photography. Unfortunately an American group was on the river with the same idea at the same time.

Robert Cundy, David Gordon-Dean and Robin Challis, disconsolate and cold as they leave the Lentz camp on the Back River.

One of the Marines tried to withdraw just before the start of the trip, but pressure from his Colonel prevented him – it was to be a joint service venture. Friction within the group was building even before they left Montreal. To soothe his hurt feelings over the unpackaging of the supplies, Rob had got himself an underwater camera and diving outfit plus oxygen tank, promising that it would add to the value of the film. They were to be travelling in two-man collapsible kayaks, but in view of the extra weight of equipment Rob felt they should bring along a third kayak. They were also carrying a heavy radio in its waterproof case and a generator, which required pedalling like a bicycle.

With all the filming, the packing problems and the radio schedule to be maintained, it was three days before they put their kayaks into the waters of Beechey Lake. For the first hour paddling was idyllic, but boredom and exhaustion soon set in. In the problems of packing the kayaks, there had been another fight with Rob, who, in spite of his underwater equipment, wanted to leave behind some of the cooking pots and a sack of flour. By the second day out, the tents were being pitched far apart and, by the third day, the Marines and the SAS were cooking separately as well.

The four Americans in two open canoes, who had started farther upriver, soon caught up with them, averaging twenty-nine miles a day, while the British group had achieved eleven miles in four days. The British rate of progress improved and they sometimes camped with the Americans, envied their camaraderie, their food and their efficiency. The British were travelling as two separate expeditions. The trip was organized and led by one of the Army officers, while the Marines disputed everything from the navigation to the camp sites. Paddling separate kayaks, the Marines were slower and had to work harder. They also were sleeping in leaky tents without flies, because in Montreal they had painted their tents bright yellow for visibility and destroyed the waterproofing. Filming produced its own frustrations and slowed progress, so it was the end of August, late in the season, before they reached the end of the river.

Personality conflict and film-making played havoc with this trip. Fear lurked underneath. The Marine who wished to withdraw, for example, fully expected to die on the trip. They had narrow escapes in the rapids, completely destroying one of the kayaks. There was no special interest in the Canadian North, it was just a venue for an adventure and a pseudo-military exercise.

Mismatched as some of the people on these trips were, they were boon companions compared to the combination of characters in M.T. Kelly's latest novel, *Into the Whirlwind*,[18] in which two biologists, who experiment on live animals and an animal-rights activist, hire a young Métis from Fort Smith to take them on a canoe trip on the Thelon. The results are predictably unpleasant, but become totally bizarre when one of the party secretly throws the food pack into the river. For once fiction is stranger than truth, but fear, personality conflict and hidden agendas are all part of the fiction.

In all of this conflict nature itself is neutral. The wild winds, the unexpected storms, the tides have been there since time immemorial. They do not provide the dark side to the canoe. That comes from the shadows cast by large egos, by people intent on self-centred designs, trying to impose their wills on the vast immutable presence that is the essence of the north. Those who choose their companions carefully, who travel in harmony with their surroundings, will travel lightly through our great wilderness landscape, leaving no foot-prints and casting no shadows.

THOUGHTS ON THE ORIGINS OF THE CANOE

Kirk Wipper

R eference to the probable experience of humankind with the canoe is relevant as a beginning to this story on propelled watercraft. Admittedly, it is speculation shrouded by the mists of time, but it is useful to imagine the circumstances shaping the lives of the dawn of man. There is what may be referred to as the everlasting quest to see what is around the bend or on the other side of the waterway. The temptation to satiate curiosity would, perhaps, prompt those early people to venture onto a floating log and experience the delight of being carried along by wind or current. Some means of propulsion of that log or logs soon followed and we have then the first water transportation, primitive as it was. The real story will never be known but there is the possibility that something of that first flirtation with floating on water may have occurred as proposed.

The canoe, from a variety of points of view, is the true symbol of Canada. For thousands of years, perhaps even 15,000 years, in what is now Canada, the canoe and the kayak were essential to the survival of the people who built and used them intensively. Hunting, trapping, fishing and moving families to winter or summer grounds required a means of transport for which the canoe was ideally suited. Although one must hypothesize because there are no written records except for pictographs and petroglyphs, there is growing evidence, as well as sheer logic, that the canoe and the kayak in some form have been intimately intertwined with the daily lives of those early humans.

This very distinctive Kutenai pine bark canoe from the interior of British Columbia is unlike all other bark canoes in North America. It closely resembles the canoes of the Amur Valley in Siberia, a feature which leads to some interesting speculations.

In the very long journey, there were a number of factors which contributed to the scope and nature of hand-propelled watercraft. High on the agenda of possibilities is that of purpose. In addition to the needs mentioned above, we might add the desire to find new tribal locations and exploration as requirements for the use of watercraft. A second consideration was the availability of materials. For the Canadian Aboriginal, there was at hand a rich variety of very desirable gifts of nature for the task of canoe building. Among the several types of bark used, that of the birch tree became the most preferred material. With the grain of the bark going around the tree instead of vertically, it was durable and resistant to splitting and decay. The nature of waterways at hand had much to do with the size and shape of canoes. The Canadian landscape offered a broad spectrum of navigable waters. Tribal traditions also had a profound influence on design and construction modes. The Kutenai canoe is a fine example of a canoe that originated in the Amur River Valley and at least two other locations nearby in Mongolia. The idea of the canoe was, no doubt, brought with migrants over the Bering Strait and eventually transplanted in the Kootenay Valley of British Columbia. Respect for those who had gone before and the urge to create an ancestral tribute had much

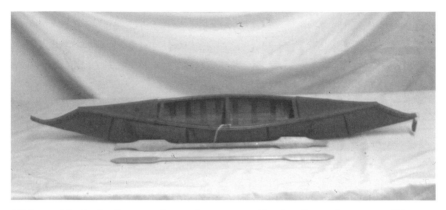

This model of a bark canoe from the Amur Valley in Siberia bears a striking resemblance to the Kutenai canoe of British Columbia. Also, its closed decks are very similar to those of the bark canoes of the Canadian northwest.

to do with the art work and overall shapes of many canoes from the Aboriginal culture. Striving for excellence and ingenuity of the builder can be identified in a detailed examination of their handiwork.

Not to be overlooked is the possibility that outside influences have had an impact on the canoe. Did the carpathian arch of a Viking ship have any relationship to the Beothuk canoe of Newfoundland? Did the Irish coracle trigger in some way the shape of the Mandan bull boat of Alberta and Montana? Did the Irish curragh have any linkage to the umiak of the Arctic? Did the Polynesian, Melanesian or Micronesian dugouts have some bearing on the great dugouts of the West Coast? In these and other uses, the possibility is there and careful examination points to more than coincidental invention. In all of the study of watercraft and the contributing factors, it is clear that generally form follows function. This is especially true in the more recent history of watercraft.

It is no small wonder that the basic canoe shape has endured for so long. There are definite advantages to the materials used, the mode of construction as well as the propulsion of the canoe. Such attributes as weight-carrying capacity, maneuverability, portaging convenience and the ability to paddle a canoe forwards, backwards, or even sideways, are all good examples.

Although the long Aboriginal experience with canoes deserves much more exploration and analysis, it is appropriate to turn to the relatively

A Welsh Coracle. Very similar craft also are found in Iceland and England and represent an universal type of watercraft.

A Mandan Bull Boat. This coracle-type craft of buffalo hide and willow was developed by the Mandan people of the Upper Missouri River.

short period of recorded history. In this reference, it is significant to note that the canoe is a symbol that joins the founding peoples of this country namely: Aboriginal nations and immigrants of French and English origin. In the time of the first explorers, the watercraft and the ways of the wilderness were adopted by the early visitors with good result. In the arms of the Aboriginal canoes, there were waves of Europeans venturing into the vast Canadian wilderness. Their hope was to seek a short route to India and the Orient to glean riches from that part of the world. In addition to explorers, there were missionaries, the military, (including the North West Mounted Police and the RCMP who in 1998 celebrated 125 years of service), railroad builders, surveyors, settlers and, of course, those hardy, persevering paddlers in the fur trade. The voyageurs endured severe, adverse conditions to accommodate those who, in the zeal for wealth, did not understand the human cost inherent in their demands.

Two examples of quite different venturers in the canoeing world may help to appreciate the distinguished contributions that were made over a long period of time. The first is David Thompson who, in 28 years surveyed, plotted and mapped almost two million square miles of territory. To accomplish this, he travelled more than 50,000 miles by canoe, and sometimes on foot or horseback. Often he has been described as the greatest land geographer who ever lived. Earlier, however, little was known about his remarkable achievements especially in the mapless void of the great Canadian West. In 1786, with a few belongings, the 16-year-old set off for the west on the turbulent Hayes River toward Lake Winnipeg with 800 lbs of cargo. It was a tortuous journey of lining and tracking upstream. Through all the ensuing years, Thompson struggled, utilizing his newly acquired mapping skills from his generous mentor, Philip Turnor. His mapping and recording of a seemingly endless territory was done accurately much to the amazement and appreciation of those who benefitted from his work. Thompson's exploits included the location of the Columbia River source, a river which he followed to the Pacific Ocean. His work was so remarkable that it evoked the admiration of other great explorers including Alexander Mackenzie and Simon Fraser. Thompson and his canoes made an extraordinary impact on what is now Canada! About the time of Thompson's death in 1857, a relatively unknown canoe-

The Peterborough Canoe Company factory.

maker was building a reputation for fine canoe construction along the shores of Rice Lake at Gore's Landing.[1] William McBride is described by Reginald Drayton as follows; "I used to go to the village (Gore's Landing) every day and visit the canoe (and skiff) shop and the boat builder who came out from Ireland." In a further reference in 1852 it states that the William McBride boat and coffin shop was a gathering place for both gentry and working classes…According to McBride's grandson, Charlton McBride, the shop had a verandah on the south side where the canoe forms were stored…In 1852, an Irish Catholic, Daniel Herald joined McBride as an apprentice. After eight years, Herald left to build his own shop next door below his house. This move was made by the time of his marriage in 1861. During the time he was with McBride, Herald built the first known canoe signed "Herald Canoe" and dated 1854. This early record ushers in the beginning of a whole group of individual builders, and then companies, to produce the finest canoes and skiffs in the world. It also contributed to Peterborough's reputation as a canoeing mecca. More than 100 years later, it was entirely appropriate to have the Canadian Canoe Museum (formerly Kanawa International Museum of Canoes, Kayaks and Rowing Craft) established in Peterborough, to house the finest collection of hand propelled watercraft in existence. In part it serves as a tribute to the outstanding craftsmen who lived and worked in the Peterborough region.

Canoe built by the Peterborough Canoe Company in 1948 as the City of Peterborough's wedding present to the future Queen Elizabeth.

For the most part, the works of those builders are well known; Herald, Gordon, Stephenson, English, O'Dette, Pengelley, Gates and Dean, to name a few. The companies that followed have long and distinguished records of building watercraft: Rice Lake, Lakefield, Peterborough, Canadian, Brown and Chestnut (Chestnut Canoe Co. of Fredericton, New Brunswick amalgamated with the Peterborough Canoe Company in the 1920s); all were respected for their fine products. Examples of their remarkable craftsmanship may be seen in the Canadian Canoe Museum. They always will serve as an inspiration for contemporary builders and paddlers who seek to continue a great tradition in canoe construction. There is still a demand for canoes built by those who have persisted in fine construction.

There has been a subtle transition in Canada from a utilitarian approach for canoeing to an ever-increasing emphasis on leisure applications. As society became more complex, the desire to experience beauty, peace, freedom and adventure grew in significance. A continuum of values associated with canoeing can be devised to describe the range of activity under the leisure umbrella. From the quest for serenity and intimacy with the small quiet voices of nature to the tumult and excitement of adventurous pursuit can all be identified. I am reminded of an experience at Sigurd Olson's "Listening Point" in the boundary waters where he lived and wrote his famous series of books born out of his canoeing experiences. His works came to life for me once more in 1997 when I spent a most memorable time contemplating the source of Olson's inspiration.

In the transition identified above, it is appropriate to note that the canoe has not diminished in its importance to Canadians and to their wilderness-bound guests. It is that way for the most numerous watercraft in the country today. All indications are that it will continue to be so.

Part of the leisure expression has ushered into being an extraordinary diversity to accommodate the broad spectrum of activity in canoes or canoe-like craft. Examples are many; racing, slalom, white water, freight canoes, duck boats, sectional canoes and sectional freight canoes. In addition to modification in design, there has been an introduction of interesting materials including aluminum, fibreglass, kevlar, graphite, A.B.S, and combinations of these. Motivation for some of the material used was based on durability, ease of portaging and accommodation for mass production. Again it can be seen that form continues to follow function.

There are, in addition, to the observations made above, some resurgences of long-standing traditions. For example, the North Canoe of the fur trade has sprung into popularity across the nation and dugout canoes are being made again on the North West Coast. I had the privilege of being a guest at Bella Bella (Waglisa) for Quatuwas (the gathering, in 1996). All of the dugouts were constructed and paddled for that inspirational, historical event.

Not to be overlooked is the prominence of the canoe in art, music, drama, carving, film and advertising. A few examples are appropriate here. In the art of former and contemporary artists, we see a variety of ways of depicting the canoe or rather the spirit of the canoe, all fascinating and informative, but widely different. Witness the works of Krieghoff, Heming, Colville, Carr, Jeffreys, Hopkins, Gagnon, Verner, Kane or contemporaries like Mason, Wilson, Robinson or Broadfoot to discover the variety of canoe depictions. In the sphere of art, the long lasting Aboriginal pictographs come to mind as part of the Canadian scene. The essential point is that these and other artists saw the canoe as a significant part of the Canadian landscape and culture.

Similar observations can be made for poetry, music and drama. The works of E. Pauline Johnson or Longfellow are relevant here. Carvers also have responded ably to the canoe theme. Consider here the works of Bill Reid, Adams, Self or Bourgault and his fellow sculpteur-de-bois at St. Jean Port-Joli in Quebec. Coins and stamps have done much to reveal the importance of the canoe in Canada. In 1998 a postage stamp was introduced to mark the distinguished contributions of Bill Mason.

Recently the advertising sector has chosen to refer to the canoe as a typically Canadian object. Although some portrayals of the canoe are a deviation from reality, the prevailing impression is that the canoe is truly Canadian. So it is with film. Inclusion of the canoe in that medium presents far too many examples to attempt an exhaustive list here. Some remarkable episodes, however are: *Black Robe, Last of the Mohicans, Impossible Dream, Rose Marie, The Voyageurs, Paddle to the Sea* and in 1999 the awaited *Grey Owl*.

What is the abiding impression of all of the foregoing discussion? I hope and trust that the canoe will be regarded as a product of the wilderness. It is after all a thin veneer of material that allows us to be close to the wilderness, to feel the pulse of the earth and water. In the arms of a canoe we learn what it is to be Canadian. The maple leaf is important to much but not all of Canada. Similarly, the beaver signature became popular especially during the fur trade. However it was the canoe that made it so. The true symbol of this nation is, indeed, the canoe which has been an essential part of life for so long from sea to sea to sea!

Because of the creative, ingenious achievements
of those who have gone before
We go
Not in their footsteps
It is their stars, we follow!

CANOESCAPES AND THE CREATIVE SPIRIT

Becky Mason

Many knew my father, Bill Mason as a filmmaker and author but not as a painter. While filming he was compulsive about getting the "perfect shot," spending hours even days waiting for the right light or reshooting until he got the perfect sequence. I believe that he was trying to capture on film the endless images in his imagination and it often seemed to me that he used his camera as a brush and the film as his canvas.

Dad actually was drawing and painting long before he picked up his first camera. He trained and then worked as a commercial artist in Winnipeg, but as his career diversified into animation and then into film, he found it harder to do what he loved most, to paint. Of the few earlier works he did for pleasure in the fifties and sixties, the one entitled *Quetico* is among my favourite. Unlike his later style, in this painting he applied very heavy thick layers of paint onto the large canvas, giving it an almost three-dimensional quality. I find the results striking because the canoe in the painting constantly beckons me. I feel I could just walk into the picture, pluck the canoe off the shore and paddle off into the distant reflections.

Dad always had a dream to write a book about his paintings in order to share his thoughts of the land, water and the canoe in paint, just as he had done in film years before. He had put together numerous mock-ups as far back as I can remember, but when he was diagnosed with cancer we felt an urgency to help him finish. Before his death, he managed to complete the paintings, the book design and most of the text. In the spring of

Bill Mason painting by the Pukaskwa River.

1995, my family contacted a publisher and to our surprise and pleasure *Canoescapes* was in bookstores by Christmas.

Dad was quite shy about divulging his technique when asked how he painted. However, one day he took me aside in his studio and guided me step by step through his palette knife on paper technique. First, he lined up various colours of oil paint on his glass palette and taking his small palette knife, mixed about five shades of colours. Then he took each mixed colour and piled them carefully, one on top of the other. Lifting the large blob of layered paint from the glass he scraped it once across the surface of his smooth paper. For the following palette knife stroke he would start his mixing process all over again in preparation for the next application. I remember being amazed at how haphazardly the paint appeared to be applied and still create a detailed painting.

Dad had a bit of a dilemma in his painting style. What drove him to distraction was that he couldn't seem to paint larger than six inches in the loose, free style he liked. I think some of his best paintings range in size from one square inch to three inches square and he would agree, except he thought they were too small! We would argue into the night, talking about large versus small and which is considered to be "art." I kept telling him, "Dad, it's not the size of the painting, it's what people feel about it."

Dad's thoughts about the painting *Precambrian Reflections* indicate the direction he wanted to go in his painting.

When confronted with a scene, I can look at it from a distance or I can walk into it and examine the minute details that make the scene what it is. Years ago I discovered quite by accident that it was possible to do the same with many of my paintings. Using a magnifying glass or a camera close-up lens, one can explore my paintings and find colours and compositions within each painting. With most painting techniques, close examination usually reveals brush or palette knife strokes. But with my paintings, close examination does not reveal how the paint was applied, there are no brush strokes.[1]

There was nothing Dad loved better than to pack up his sketch books and painting box and set off on some wilderness canoe trip. I joined him on some of these painting trips and one excursion in particular on the Petawawa River sticks in my mind. After a morning of painting, we brewed up a cup of soup and, over lunch, discussed our mornings work. Both of us realized that although we had been deliriously happy painting out in the bush, our finished products were not satisfactory, so we pitched our paintings into the fire and headed out to try again that afternoon. Producing work was not the important thing – it was the stopping, looking and listening that we loved. We were always storing up our memories and experiences and most of the time we would let them out on paper *after* we got back to our studios. We both created a few memorable pieces on canoe trips but rarely more than two or three.

Dad loved canoes in all shapes and sizes and was passionate about collecting, paddling and going on trips in them. In *Canoescapes* he wrote:

I have always believed that the Canadian canoe is one of the greatest achievements of mankind. There is nothing so aesthetically pleasing and yet so functional and versatile. It is as much a part of our land as the rocks, trees, lakes and rivers. Most of my enjoyment and creative endeavours in the Canadian widerness have been from a canoe.[2]

Dad named each of his canoes, names which usually gave a hint as to how he acquired them. I remember the day he found a beautiful Peterborough cedar-rib canoe. He was driving on a road north of our house in Quebec looking for a stretch of rapids someone had told him about, when he spotted a lady planting flowers in a canoe on her lawn. He slammed to a halt, jumped out of his car, marched up to the lady and told her, "You can't plant flowers in a canoe!" She replied, "Oh, yes I can!" After an animated argument, Dad struck up a deal. If he supplied two flower barrels she would give him her flower-pot canoe in exchange. I'm sure Mom's flowers were flying that day! When he returned, Dad shovelled earth from the canoe into the barrels so she could plant her flowers. I still remember the look of pleasure on his face when he returned with that trophy which he christened the "flower pot canoe."

I always admired my Mom and Dad's relationship and I learned a lot from them. Sometimes they would take the afternoon off from their hectic schedule and go for a paddle or take one of their favourite sailing canoes out on the lake where there were no phone calls or demands, just the quiet, peaceful sounds of water lapping on the canoe hull; Dad with his cup of tea and Mom with her book. They would chat and relax and unwind. It seemed like any worries just washed away and they would always come back refreshed. I also have learned to return to the canoe to refuel and rejuvenate my creative spirit, sort out my troubles and just take time to enjoy life. Every spring I'm out on the water, breaking up the ice to get my first Classic Solo canoe course under way at Meech Lake. When autumn arrives I close up shop for a couple of weeks and take a trip down a wilderness river with my husband, Reid. As soon as Meech Lake freezes over I hang up my paddle for the winter and paint my experiences and memories of the canoeing that I've stored up from the summer months.

One of my family's favourite places to paddle is the rugged north shore of Lake Superior, in particular Cascade Falls. Dad liked to grade each of his campsites giving them an A, a B-, or maybe a C+. Cascade Falls, however, went right off the scale. It was an A+++. It was given this rating mainly because Cascade Falls plunges directly into Lake Superior and Dad could stand in it and have his head pounded by the water. Cascade Falls also has a beautiful sandy beach on which to camp and enjoy the dazzling sunrises and sunsets. It took some nerve to get to because you could be wind-bound for days on the shores of the lake. We thought that was the best part, having to overstay your scheduled visit at a campsite where few would go.

When I look at my dad's paintings I am reminded of the many rivers, lakes and campsites that we travelled together. They remind me of how important it is to slow down and wonder at the natural beauty of the land. As a child I remember the portage with the bugs, the heat and all the things to carry as something to be dreaded. I was puzzled why my dad liked portaging so much. As I followed him on the trails through the years, however, I began to see and understand what he was doing. For him, portaging a canoe was a change of pace and scenery and a way to retreat deeper into the wilderness. In *Canoescapes* he says:

The price you must pay for a spectacular waterfall is a long and arduous portage but I wouldn't want it any other way. . . . The part I like best about portaging is the walk back for the second load. You see things you would never see while staggering under a ninety-pound pack or eighty-pound canoe. . . . On a river journey by canoe, doing a portage properly and enjoying the scenery along the way is just as important as paddling the canoe. Not that you would catch me portaging a rapid that was runnable, unless it was to carry the canoe back up to run it again. If it weren't for rapids, falls and their accompanying portages, there would be no wilderness, no place to hear the cry of the loon. Let's keep our portages wild, the wilder the better.[3]

Of course, if there is portaging on a river there is also the temptation of being lured into running rapids. It was natural that Dad loved whitewater paddling. He really craved the adrenaline rush he would get when "hot-dogging" (as he called it) with friends on a sunny day. He enjoyed the camaraderie and the thrill of pushing his skills and his canoes to the limit in the "big stuff!" But he also recognized that he really needed the quiet solitude of a wilderness journey to nourish his soul. This he passed on to me.

A year after my father's death I was upstairs in his studio and found the special wooden box that held his small unframed paintings that I loved so much. I opened the box and, as I looked through them, I came across a painting called *Old Woman Bay, Morning Mist*. The painting reminded me of the day we said a final good-bye to Dad. Along with a few of my dad's closest friends, my family had set out in canoes one calm misty morning on Lake Superior and paddled to the cliffs of Old Woman Bay, one of my dad's most cherished places to which he would return year after year. My mom conducted a beautiful ceremony bidding Dad farewell and let his ashes slip through her fingers into the clear green water. I remember watching them float down, meeting the white rocks far below. I closed the wooden box with the bitter-sweet memory of saying goodbye to Dad from his canoe.

My dad, Bill Mason, taught me that a canoe trip, be it an afternoon paddle or an expedition north of 60, is not a race. Nor is it another check mark on a rivers-to-do list. It is a journey of looking, listening, and learning a journey of discovery. Like him, I find that paddling can take you on a voyage of creativity where you store experiences in your memory to treasure for a lifetime.

The Canoe as Chapeau

The Role of the Portage in Canoe Culture

Bruce W. Hodgins

The canoe represents Canadian heritage. An almost perfect vessel, the canoe can not only be paddled, but it is designed and built to be carried. It can be flipped and worn, in effect, like a hat or a chapeau. Indeed that duality is almost the definition of canoe.

Hats have hat racks; canoes have canoe racks. Racks traditionally hold hats and canoes for long periods of time between wearings, carryings and travels. The Canadian Canoe Museum now has some canoe racks and will have many more to gather, display and store its hundreds of canoes. It may be said that canoes, in a heritage museum, are symbolically resting, it is to be hoped permanently, on an interrupted long, perhaps never-ending portage. And this is fitting because, to my mind, the portage is a metaphor for Canada and its people. The land with its heritage of great waterways, like the canoe, supports us as we move about upon it. Yet so often we must carry the land, care for it, exhibit it, wear it. For what is the canoe if not a product of the land?

My favourite canoe song is the old haunting and melancholy poem by George Marsh, written about 1890, called "The Old Canoe." It talks of grief, but since we all must die, I define the grief in the song as emotionally reflective heritage:

My seams gape wide as I'm tossed aside to rot on the lonely shore,
And the leaves and mould like a shroud unfold,

Carol and Bruce Hodgins on a portage on the Clearwater River which runs west from Saskatchewan into Alberta.

for the last of my days are o'er,
But I float in my dreams on northern streams that never again I'll see,
As I lie on the marge of the old portage with grief for company.

The song then carries on about the canoe's memorable voyage – on Temagami and the Lady Evelyn to James Bay, on the Montreal River and Temiscaming, concluding:

Tho' the death-fraught way from the Saguenay to the storied Nipigon,
Once knew me well, now a crumbling shell I watch as the years roll on,
And in memory's haze I love the days forever gone from me,
As I lie on the marge of the old portage with grief for company.

Which end of the old portage, before or after the carry, was the open grave for the rotting old canoe? The Museum, for a few old canoes, is the open, preservative heritage portage, the gathering place, the celebratory mausoleum.

For my wife and me, some of our best tripping moments have taken place on great portages: carrying the canoe and gear in 1959 across the divide from the Lady Evelyn River watershed to the Montreal ("Sunnywater Carry") and then from its upper Ottawa watershed to the James Bay-Arctic watershed ("the Grassy Lake Carry"); walking in 1982 much of the Methye Portage, with the canoe already resting on the Clearwater, while we travelled down from the latter's headwaters – the Methye Portage being the link between the Churchill-Hudson Bay watershed of old Rupert's Land and the Athabasca Country of the Mackenzie watershed, roughly the divide between the Cree and the Dene; crossing in 1972 the historic Carry from the Broadback River to Lake Nemiscou on the Rupert; carrying by Bloody Falls in 1979, the last portage on the Coppermine where in 1771, with Samuel Hearne watching, the Chipewyan guides ambushed the hapless Inuit; and the zig-zag, descending carry in 1976 into the canyon by Virginia Falls on the South Nahanni.

For Bill Mason, as Becky Mason points out in this volume, it was the same. In his writings, Mason emphasized the need to take a few portages to enjoy the wilderness, God's country.[1] Note the opening scenes, for instance, in James Raffan's biography of Bill Mason, the scene set in 1988 four months before Mason's death:

A single red canoe pivots playfully next to the Mississippi River in Carleton Place, southwest of Ottawa. Evening light warms its chipped wooden gunwales and shadows its gentle curves from stem to stern. Starbursts of tiny cracks and scratches in the patina of painted canvas give a sheen to the boat as it turns in rhythm with the music. Underneath, balancing the canoe on his shoulders, blasé about poise or whom he might hit in the process, is a diminutive man in grey flannels, white shirt and burgundy tie. It is only when the twirling canoe narrowly misses the bride, clapping in a joyous circle of family and friends, that someone grabs the dangling painter as it sweeps across the polished dance floor, stops the pirouette and leads the man outside and back to the river. A spontaneous cheer rises above the music. People applaud and hoot for the spirit of the man, Canada's own Mr. Canoehead – Bill Mason – dancing as only he would, at his son's wedding.[2]

When I think of that great canoeist, Grey Owl, the old moving pictures I remember most are those of him helping to load up his beloved Anahareo, and then lifting his own huge pack and flipping the canoe. I see him striding off into the bush of the portage, moving further into the great land back of beyond. Then there is in our Wanapitei Wilderness Centre brochure, the photograph of the happy, confident young woman heavily-loaded down with packs and other equipment, ready for the great portage.[3] Furthermore, many paintings of the voyageurs or Aboriginal canoeists have them depicted on a carry or camping at the end of a portage.[4]

As Glenn Fallis of the Voyageur Canoe Company reminded us, when he delivered his 36-foot "canot du maître" to the paddlers at Ste. Marie-Among-the-Hurons for the Champlain-Huron 1615 commemorative trip to Peterborough in 1996, the high pointed ends of this fur-trade canoe existed in part to be able to take the weight when the vessel was upside down on the land. It also made possible the initial grip for those on the down side to commence the carry. Even the heavy Montreal canoe was built thus to be portaged. Indeed, the Museum's 1996 heritage trip on the Severn-Otonabee was unforgettable because it was portrayed and not locked through its twenty odd obstacles.

Let us look at a few more classic portages, in addition to the Methye Portage. Perhaps the most important historically was Lachine, the place where the voyageurs and their brigades repeatedly began their epic canoe journeys to the northwest. To the east of Lachine was Montreal and Europe; on the west, toward Lac-des-Deux Montagnes, were Oka-Kanasatake, the Ottawa and the "pays d'en haut," perhaps China (la chine). Then there is the voyageurs' LaVase portage through present day North Bay, the link between the Mattawa-Ottawa Valley and the French River[5] of the upper Great Lakes – a portage now struggling to be restored. There is also the Grand Portage and, later, Fort William, the two carries across the divide between the Lake Superior watershed and the Hudson Bay watershed, between pork eaters and pemmican eaters, between summer paddlers and wintering partners, the symbolic source of the Métis nation and the real divide or cross over between East and West in Canada.

But let us not forget the Winnipeg street corner of Portage and Main, close to the spot where the Assinaboine empties over rapids into the Red River. In Hull, opposite the Parliament Buildings, there is Place Portage around our Capital's great rapids. In Peterborough, situated at the lower end of two portage routes from its own "pays d'en haut," there is Portage Place, on the upstream route to Chemong Lake. In the Temagami Country, the Wanapitei Wilderness Centre is close to the Red Squirrel Falls Portage, the summer and winter *nastawgan*[6] to the Anima Nipissing and a great route north. Nearby, to the west, is Sharp Rock, the short local Temagami portage from the Georgian Bay watershed to the Ottawa Valley. In the Maritimes there are the Tantramar Marshes, now the border between New Brunswick and Nova Scotia, once the border between the French Empire and the British Empire and once the great Mik'maq portage route from the Gulf of St. Lawrence to the Bay of Fundy. Far to the northwest there is the breathtaking beauty of Summit Lake, experienced by Carol and me and our group in 1983, the lowest continental divide in the Rockies, on the border between the Yukon and NWT, the divide between the Rat and Bell-Portage. Happily, (unlike Eric and Pamela Morse) we were flown in from Fort McPherson and only had the short portage from the Lake into the Little Bell, before the long paddle descent to Old Crow (and a simple paddle through to Fort Yukon in Alaska). And on it goes.

Noted photographer and canoeist, Toni Harting on the French River, demonstrating the art of carrying a canoe.

The canoe carries us on the water. On the portage we must carry the canoe. Canada carries Canadians: Canadians must also carry Canada.

Big and small, great and minor, we have the portage experience, the portaging culture. How many "Carrying Places" (and "Carrying Lakes") in how many languages are there in Canada? Even Toronto was the traditional gathering place at the end of the crossover on Lake Ontario leading from what became Lake Simcoe, when Lieutenant Governor Simcoe was escorted over the Yonge Street route more than two hundred years ago. Then there is Upper Canada's London, in the southwest by the Forks of the Thames, at "the head of navigation," meaning that from here on up east it was portage and paddle by canoe, until Dundas Street could be built. "Streets," canals and early railways were along major portage routes. Most of these portages, or linkage routes in the south came to be institutionalized almost out of memory. This is part of what I meant in my paper for *Canexus I*, entitled "Canoe Irony: Symbol of Wilderness and Harbinger."[7]

As a secondary metaphor, the portage represents the tribulations of life. For many, portages involve four letter epithets, bugs, burdensome weight, moose muck, loon faeces, sweat, rotting logs, disappearing trails and burnt bush. Then there is the struggle to single-carry a canoe longitudinally sideways through the narrow gap between a tree and the heavy branches from a tangled windfall. What indeed is worse than carrying a heavy canoe over a rough, hilly and overgrown portage in a July heat wave, with both mosquitos and black flies chewing your wet face, crawling into your ears and nose and mouth, if you dare to open it to curse or gasp. Yet what an accomplishment when you finally set down the craft, breath heavily and perhaps wade into the shallow water to cool off. Then think of that magnificent hike back up the trail, without extra weight and bareheaded to get a second load. So light that you can see, hear and feel the living landscape! What an accomplishment, and it is not masochistic or macho. It is, instead, important culturally, and any reasonably strong and healthy individual of either gender can accomplish great carries. But I still have small scars from the removal of two lypomas below the back of my neck, created from stupidly carrying heavy, wet, wood-canvas Peterborough canoes "bareback" (without yoke, paddles or tump) before I was fifteen. No more of that! At least I never suffered from lifting too-heavy loads, and acquiring the voyageur's curse of the hernia.

Wanapitei's full summer trips for 17 year olds in the Northwest Terrritories usually involve fantastic up-hill-over-tundra travel to Arctic headwaters before the great descent. The first half of such trips have sometimes been characterized as cross-country hiking treks with canoes. Yet for the young and skilled, these trips are extremely popular. Again we have canoes worn like chapeaus.

When seriously ill in 1988 with pulmonary emboli and thinking my canoe tripping days, indeed my life, might soon be over, I did ride about in a canoe a little, and I even softly paddled a bit. Then, after waiting, I underwent elective surgery. Afterwards, during recovery, my fixation was with the portage. Could I again carry a canoe? Could I perhaps even flip it? That would be full recovery. Recently, several friends have mentioned the same apprehensive longing, following great physical ailments.

Let me conjure the feel, smell and sounds (somewhat muted now when we more often carry plastic rather than traditional wood-canvas canoes) as you walk wearing the canoe as chapeau. There is the gentle creaking of the thwarts, gunwales, ribs and planking stimulated by the lashed paddles. There is the sweat rewetting and reviving the smell of the leather tump on the top of your own wet hair, until the moisture runs lightly down your face. Most canoeists can smell and feel that heritage in their memory nostrils.

Portaging is an integral part of canoe culture, and the portage is a cultural metaphor for Canada and Canadians. Canoes spend most of their existence on racks, on interrupted carries – like automobiles in garages. The Canadian Canoe Museum is better than the marge of the old portage. The rot might be arrested or at least slowed down. But like hat racks, the Museum's canoe racks signify the interrupted carry.

The message of "The Old Canoe" slightly mars our metaphor, because in the poem the old canoeist has finally become the rotting canoe itself, left there on the marge, with only nostalgic grief for company. Yet through the canoe, on marge and in the Museum, Canada and Canadians (both Aboriginal and "Settler") are symbolically joined. Not a perfect country, says anglo William to franco Jacques; there still will be the GST.[8] Yet through the heritage of the canoe, the vessel invented by Aboriginal people and built to be carried, there can be new vistas and ongoing national life.

R.M. PATTERSON'S PADDLING PASSION

David Finch

"A river is still a river, and a canoe can still go where no other craft can follow," wrote R.M. Patterson in 1963.[1] The Athabasca River, the Peace and the Bow, the South Nahanni, Liard and Mackenzie, the Stikine, Kootenay and the Columbia, all share one thing in common: over their waters Patterson paddled his favourite cedar and canvas Chestnut canoes. And he wrote eloquently about these western Canadian waterways, preserving in his books their unspoilt beauty and leaving a record that continues to inspire paddlers to explore these rivers.

Raymond Murray Patterson is best known for his classic tale of the South Nahanni River, *The Dangerous River*. But the British-born immigrant had never touched a canoe paddle before the day he began his quest for gold on the South Nahanni in 1927. Patterson's only boating experience before 1927 consisted of punting at Oxford on the Isis River – Latin for Thames – and a few sailing trips with friends along the English coast. Unlike his adopted home, England had little need or use for the open Canadian canoe. By the early 1900s, roads and railways criss-crossed the United Kingdom, moving trade and people around a populous country. Canals and rivers still boasted watercraft, but canoes were virtually unknown.

Patterson's early years in England, however, prepared him to take advantage of the opportunities the canoe provided an immigrant to the colony after World War I. When Henry Foote Patterson left his wife and their three year old son, Raymond, in order to pursue adventure in South

Africa, his example challenged his only offspring to seek adventure too. Patterson's education at Rossall, an English public school, taught him discipline and accustomed him to poor food and extreme physical exertion. A short career in the artillery during World War I and months as a prisoner of war also hardened the young man. Oxford then expanded his imagination by awarding him a degree in modern war history and two years as a cadet at the Bank of England convinced him that success as a banker was failure at life. Finally, Patterson escaped what his father called the "desert of stone" in London and took advantage of a Soldier's Settlement provision and the Canadian government's willingness to grant him a half section of land as a homestead in northwestern Alberta.

Survival became an important theme in Patterson's life and his Canadian adventures provided new ways to test his skills. He walked long distances to the nearest community and rode a horse to the closest railway station, but when it came time to heed the call of the north, the only highways were rivers. And the canoe was the time-honoured way to travel the Canadian wilds.

Unable to swim, scornful of life jackets – he thought they were for "tourists" – and never before in a canoe, Patterson launched an overladen canoe into the waters of the Athabasca River and headed North. His reading of Jack London's *Call of the Wild* was partly to blame for this rash expedition to the South Nahanni which had enchanted him since childhood. Patterson also found inspiration in Sir William Butler's *The Wild North Land*, Warburton Pike's *The Barren Grounds of Northern Canada*, Stefansson's *Hunters of the Great North* and Pirsson's *Rocks and Rock Minerals*.[2]

In Patterson's *The Dangerous River*, Michael H. Mason's description of the Nahanni people in *The Arctic Forests* (which must have prompted him to see them himself) intrigued him:

They are a hardy, virile people, but have suffered much from white influence. They are hostile to strangers, and many white explorers have been done to death by them. This tribe was for many years under the complete domination of one woman, supposed to be partly of European descent.[3]

Nearing his late twenties, Patterson vowed to explore the Canadian North for himself before settling down to married life in the late 1920s.

With a fiancée and widowed mother awaiting him in England, he set off into the unknown in the early days of July, 1927 with boyhood acquaintance, Denis France. At Waterways, Alberta, near today's Fort McMurray, they unloaded an 18 foot cedar canvas Chestnut Prospector at the end of the train track and packed it with a summer's provisions. Down the Athabasca River they paddled, greenhorns in a land that often swallowed seasoned wilderness travellers without a trace. Luckily, the novice paddlers followed a regularly travelled route down the Athabasca, Slave and Mackenzie rivers to Fort Simpson in the Northwest Territories. There they parted company and Patterson traded in the large Chestnut for a 16 footer before ascending the Liard to the South Nahanni.

Although paddling unmapped rivers, Patterson was not alone on the River of Death. Albert Faille, whose red pants were so loud that even a blind man could see him, was also on the river. He loved reading, had visited England and France and knew much about the world. On into the long summer nights they talked in camp. But try as he might, Patterson could not convince Faille of some basic truths: his diary rings with appreciation for the old trapper, a man who ". . . will argue at any time & prove – that the Earth is not round & that there is an undiscovered hot continent hidden away in the South Pacific."[4]

Faille was also a skilled paddler and he taught Patterson many valuable lessons as they ascended the South Nahanni. After Patterson failed to reach the Falls of the Nahanni alone in early August, Faille encouraged the disheartened novice and accompanied him in his own 18 foot Chestnut to the mysterious cataract on August 25, 1927. Patterson's diary notes the smoke had cleared and all that remained was a tough day of slogging "up through the cañons with much swearing & damning" until they reached Patterson's turnback camp, where they lunched. Cold and wet, they built a blazing fire and recuperated. Back into the water they went after lunch, crossing to river left and continuing upstream, Patterson tracking, Faille steering.

We heard the roar of the falls simultaneously & shouted. I was first round the bend & saw them first – I hauled on the trackline & pulled Faille into view. They were within less than half a mile of my last camp – their thunder had been choked off from me by the deep twisting cañon & the mists that I had seen in the early mornings were their spray floated down the valley. A sight

R.M. Patterson's photo of Virginia Falls on the South Nahanni River.

worth travelling to see – counting the cataract above the drop must be 200 ft. or over & they are split in the middle by a great tower of rock.[5]

Together Patterson and Faille explored the environs of the waterfall that was indeed in excess of 200 feet; it drops 392 feet from the calm lake-like river above the canyon to the roiling valley floor below. They paddled back to Faille's camp on the Flat River and Patterson continued down-stream, making notes in the little diary that later helped him write *The Dangerous River*, an account that also includes stories of his adventures with canoes on northern rivers when he returned with Gordon Matthews to trap and prospect in 1928 and early 1929.

Although Raymond Patterson married Marigold Portman in 1929 and the newlyweds moved to a sheep ranch near Calgary, he did not quit canoeing. For the next two decades he paddled rivers that drained to the Hudson Bay instead of the Arctic Ocean. Near Cochrane, Alberta the Pattersons bought additional pasture for their sheep along the steep banks of the Ghost River and built a small log cabin in a canyon that reminded Patterson of the South Nahanni.

When the stock market crashed and their investments and sheep ranching ventures failed, the Pattersons borrowed money from his mother and bought George Pocaterra's decrepit Buffalo Head Horse Ranch on the Highwood River. They carefully nurtured the ranch to financial success southwest of Calgary by building a herd of cattle and by taking in guests to entertain at one of Canada's best-known dude ranches. Contributing to the reputation of the Highwood Valley as Loony Lane, Patterson sometimes took dudes down the canyons and over the ledges of the Highwood River in a 16 foot Chestnut, thrilling himself and onlookers when he dumped in rapids.

Patterson also paddled the Bow River while living in southern Alberta. Using a Chestnut and a two-person folding boat, he explored the river from Lake Louise to Calgary as well as its headwaters at Bow Lake. Always one to take advantage of unusual opportunities, he also loaded the collapsible boat on a packhorse and took it to isolated lakes high in the Canadian Rockies, and over the continental divide to the Elk Lakes in British Columbia.

In 1946 the Pattersons sold the Buffalo Head Ranch and moved to Vancouver Island. From a waterfront home, the wanderer began writing articles about his adventures in the Canadian west for *Blackwood's Magazine* and the Hudson's Bay Company publication, *The Beaver*. Canoes played an important role in many of these stories and accounts of incidents on the South Nahanni attracted the attention of British publishers, requesting Patterson to write a book about the romantic Canadian north. The result was *The Dangerous River* in 1954.

Patterson's name also graced another book in the early 1950s and it prompted him to place his Chestnut canoes into more rivers while conducting research. With wife, Marigold, or eldest son, Alan, as paddling companion, Patterson canoed the tributaries of the Peace River in order to better understand the exploratory work accomplished by Samuel Black in the early 1800s. As a result, in 1955 the Hudson's Bay Records Society published *A Journal of a Voyage from Rocky Mountain Portage in Peace River to the Sources of Finlays Branch and North West Ward in Summer 1824* by Samuel Black. The title page lists an introduction by R. M. Patterson and, in the "Preface," the General Editor, E. E. Rich, wrote: "Mr. Patterson, bringing to his task the enthusiasm and the knowledge of one who had himself travelled the same route, has without any doubt put the Journal, the journey, and Samuel Black into their correct relations." The carefully written 98 page introduction proved Patterson's passion for research, skill at writing and vigour as a traveller. Dr. Douglas Leechman, president of the Glenbow Foundation read the volume with great interest and wrote Patterson immediately to commend him on the project. Patterson wrote Pocaterra, "I'm glad he was pleased – writing that d – introduction took me, on & off, four years of work & correspondence & was worse than writing 21/2 ordinary books. A history of the fur trade, it is a limited edition, to subscribers only & universities & libraries (Calgary amongst others)."[6]

Patterson's next book, *The Buffalo Head*, includes a few chapters of autobiographical material and stories of life on the ranch. It first went to the publisher in 1956, but did not arrive on bookstore shelves until 1961. *Far Pastures* followed in 1963 and its edited versions of several articles include many stories based on canoe trips on western rivers. *Trail to the Interior* came out in 1966 and includes accounts of his adventures on the Stikine, Dease, Liard and Mackenzie rivers. *Finlay's River* in 1968 arrived in bookstores just as the W.A.C. Bennett Dam flooded the Finlay and other tributaries of the Peace River in British Columbia, all of which Patterson paddled as part of his research.

By the 1960s, paddling had become so important to Patterson that the Canadian Broadcasting Corporation interviewed him paddling a canoe on a Vancouver Island river. In a letter to Pocaterra he recalled the events of February 18, 1963: ". . . a most interesting day . . . fooling around in a light canoe below the outlet from Lake Cowichan." Two riverboats held nine crew, complete with cameras and recording equipment. A cable running under the canoe and up through his clothing connected to a microphone hidden in Patterson's sweater. "Just how the hell any man could be expected to give a sane answer to an impromptu question under those circumstances I do not know."[7] The CBC, however, loved the result.

As he aged, Patterson found he could no longer paddle long distances. Undaunted, he continued plying the waters of the British Columbia interior in a square-sterned, 20 foot, Chestnut Ogilvie Special, powered by an outboard, sometimes taking his grown children along on summer camping expeditions exploring rivers and lakes.

R. M. Patterson died on October 20, 1984. For more than five decades he had explored the wild lands in classic cedar canvas canoes, and a quote from his 1927 South Nahanni diary shows the depth of the passion that grew from exploring the Canadian northwest in a Chestnut canoe.

Raymond Murray Patterson after his retirement in Victoria, British Columbia.

I am the better for the trail I have made – in every way. A little stronger & heavier, more obstinate, quicker to think & act alone & able to do without things & to drive myself on against my own will. I know the way into the gold rivers – & I have seen very great beauties in a wonderful mountain world.[8]

END NOTES

1. THE CANADIAN CANOE MUSEUM AND CANADA'S NATIONAL SYMBOL (JOHN JENNINGS)

1. Pierre Elliott Trudeau, "Exhaustion and Fulfillment: The Ascetic In A Canoe" in *Wilderness Canada*, Borden Spears, ed (Toronto: Clarke Irwin 1970) 4
2. All international and Olympic canoe races, C1, 2 and 4, are named for Canada. The "C" stands for Canada, not canoe, as most people suppose.

2. BEING THERE: BILL MASON AND THE CANADIAN CANOEING TRADITION (JAMES RAFFAN)

1. The *Dictionary of Canadian Biography* (reference) lists three eminent William Masons and not one of them paddled a canoe. There was Mason the merchant; Mason the missionary; and Mason the rioter. As chance would have it, William C. Mason the film maker and canoeist embodied characteristics of all three. He sold dreams of a uniquely Canadian way of life that integrated people and nature and in doing so became one of Canada's most influential conservation writers. He proclaimed that wilderness was clear evidence of The Divine on earth. Bill Mason was not a rioter, like the Lower Canadian exile of the same name killed in insurrections following the Rebellion of 1837, but he was a rabble rouser of sorts with more than a touch of rough-spun charm. Sooner or later, the *Dictionary of Canadian Biography* will list a fourth Mason.
2. Details about Mason's accomplishments are available in many popular articles and in my 1996 biography entitled *Fire in the Bones: Bill Mason and the Canadian Canoeing Tradition* (Harper Collins 1996).
3. "The Perfect Machine," a CBC Radio program in the *Ideas* series first broadcast May 23, 1995.
4. Since Confederation, Canada has commissioned twenty five stamps containing canoe imagery of some kind. The first of these stamps, issued on July 16th, 1903 was valued at 5¢. It was Canada's first bilingual stamp and shows canoes on the shore of the St. Lawrence River beside Champlain's habitation in Quebec. Based on the explorer's original sketch it commemorates the 300th anniversary of the first permanent European settlement in Canada. Other early Canadian canoe stamps affiliate the boats with Aboriginal and European people but, by 1989, the boats themselves are

celebrated in a variety of different issues featuring both traditional and modern designs and construction techniques. And in 1994, a punchy and colourful rendering of a stylized bark canoe flying through the night sky, celebrates the canoe in the Quebecoise folk tale "La Chasse Galerie." A definitive source regarding Canada's philatelic history from pre-Confederation to the present is *Darnell Stamps of Canada Complete Listing to the end of 1994*, edited by Lyse Rousseau-Darnell and Emanuel Darnell (Montreal: Darnell Publishing Inc., 1994) which shows all Canadian stamps in colour with much supporting detail.

5. In an attempt to settle the attribution of this quote once and for all, I wrote to Pierre Berton to ask when and where he made this quip. In a letter dated 7 March 1996, he replied: "Although I have been for the last twenty years, credited with the quote you use 'A Canadian is someone who knows how to make love in a canoe,' it is not actually my own – at least I don't think so, it's been so long. It seems to me I saw it somewhere else and I used it with attribution, but the attribution has long since been lost and I'm tired of telling people I didn't actually think of it. So I'm afraid I can't help you much. I notice I'm even in the Canadian Book of Quotations as having said that; so at this late stage it's difficult for me to say I didn't. Maybe I did, but I don't think so."

6. Philip Chester, "Motives for Mr. Canoehead" in *Canexus: The Canoe in Canadian Culture*, James Raffan and Bert Horwood, eds., (Toronto, Betelgeuse Books, 1988) 93.

7. Latterly, books about rivers and canoeing have nodded deferentially, but in a general way, to the contribution of Canada's First Nations people to the Canadian canoeing tradition. A "special acknowledgement" in Bruce Hodgins' and Gwyneth Hoyle's 1994 book, *Canoeing North into the Unknown* (Toronto: Natural Heritage Inc.) takes this a step further in acknowledging the contribution of individuals "from Akaitcho, the Beaulieus, English Chief to George Elson and Bert Blake of recent times." (iii).

8. Chester, 99.

9. Northrop Frye, *The Educated Imagination*, The Massey Lectures, Second series (Toronto: CBC Enterprises 1963),6. Frye goes on in the first essay in this series, called "The Motive for Metaphor," and uses this tripartite distinction in types of language to differentiate art from science. Says Frye, "Science begins with the world we have to live in . . . trying to explain its laws . . . [and] moves towards the imagination. . . . Art, on the other hand . . . starts with the imagination, and then works towards ordinary experience . . . one starts with the world as it is, the other with the world we want to have."

10. "The Perfect Machine," (CBC)

11. A gem in this regard is a 1951 book *The Romance of the Canadian Canoe* (Toronto: The Ryerson Press) by John Murray Gibbon, which contains the most engaging collection of text and artwork concerning the canoe excerpted from a wide range of Canadian sources.

12. LePan, Douglas, "Canoe Trip."

13. Philip Chester's "Motives for Mr. Canoehead" provides an engaging lament on this point.

14. Hugh MacLennan's *The Watch that Ends the Night* as excerpted in *Marked by the Wild*, edited by B. Littlejohn and J. Pearce (Toronto: McClelland and Stewart 1973) 153.

15. William C. James, "The Canoe Trip as Religious Quest," *Studies in Religion/Sciences religieuses* 10, 2 (Spring 1981), 151-166. This essay was republished in slightly different form as "The Quest Pattern and the Canoe Trip" in Bruce Hodgins and Margaret Hobbes, eds. *Nastawgan: The North by Canoe and Snowshoe* (Toronto: Betelgeuse, 1988), 9-23.

16. Bert Horwood, "Doors to the Primitive" in *Canexus: The Canoe in Canadian Culture*, 133.

17. Northrop Frye, "Haunted by Lack of Ghosts: Some Patterns in the Imagery of Canadian Poetry" in *The Canadian Imagination: Dimensions of a Literary Culture*, David Staines, ed (Cambridge: Harvard University Press, 1977), makes a similar point by asserting that European settlers built palisades and developed a "garrison mentality" to protect against Canadian nature which was seen as fundamentally hostile, as monster or leviathan.

18. Margaret Atwood, *Survival: A Thematic Guide to Canadian Literature* (Toronto: Anansi 1972) 32.

19. Northrop Frye, *The Great Code* (Markham: Penguin Books Canada 1981), xviii.

20. F.S Colwell, *Riverman: A Romantic Iconography of the River and the Source* (Kingston: McGill-Queen's University Press, 1989) 3-4.

21. Simon Schama, *Landscape and Memory* (Toronto: Random House 1995), 247.

22. There is also a river connection through Mason's espoused love of the 18th century British painter William Mallord Turner. Very few people knew about Mason's love of art or about his wish to be a painter (until the release of "Waterwalker") but those who did, and who knew about Turner's misgivings about the industrial future (and his stance, as such, as an early environmentalist) and his love for painting river and seascapes, saw instantly another connection between Mason and the abiding connections between people and place through rivers. His connection to Turner was just another way in which Mason unwittingly authenticated and expanded his scope and range in public consciousness.

23. Simon Schama, 5.

24. There is an excellent treatment of this succession and evolution of wilderness spirituality in Alston Chase's, *In a Dark Wood: The Fight over Forests and the Rising Tyranny of Ecology* (Boston: Houghton Mifflin Co. 1995) 42-44.

3. EXTREMELY CRANKY CRAFT: THE JAMES W. TYRELL KAYAK, BIG ISLAND, HUDSON STRAIT (KENNETH LISTER)

1. Al Purdy, *North of Summer: Poems from Baffin Island* (Toronto/Montreal: McClelland and Stewart 1967) 57.

2. John A. Livingstone, *Roque Primate: An Exploration of Human Domestication* (Toronto: Key Porter Books 1994) 8.

3. Kenneth R. Lister, "Water for the Phalarope: Kayak Design and Cultural Values among the Tununirusirmiut," *Museum Small Craft Association Transactions 1995* 2 (1996), 49-51.

4. Philip Goldring, "Inuit Economic Responses to Euro-American Contacts: Southeast Baffin Island, 1824-1940," in Kenneth S. Coates and William R. Morrison, eds. *Interpreting Canada's North: Selected Readings* (Toronto: Copp Clark Pitman Ltd. 1989), 260-264; Cornelius H.W. Remie, "Ermalik and Kukigak Continuity and Discontinuity in Pelly Bay, Northwest Territories, Canada," in Cunera Buijs, ed. *Continuity and Discontinuity in Arctic Cultures: Essays in Honour of Gerti Nooter, Curater at the National Museum of Ethnology, 1970-1990* (Leiden: Centre of Non-Western Studies 1993) 84-85.

5. Knud Rasmussen, *Across Arctic America: Narrative of the Fifth Thule Expedition* (New York: Greenwood Press Publishers 1969) 68.

6. For a similar situation among the Aivilingmiut see Cunera C.M. Buijs, "Disappearance

of Traditional Meat-Sharing Systems among the Tinitekilaamiut of East Greenland and the Arviligjuarmiut and Iglulingmiut of Canada," in *Continuity and Discontinuity in Arctic Cultures,* 122; Therkel Mathiassen, *Material Culture of the Iglulik Eskimos,* Report of the 5th Thule Expedition 6,1 (1928), 92; W. Gillies Ross, *An Arctic Whaling Diary: The Journal of Captain George Comer in Hudson Bay 1903 - 1905* (Toronto: University of Toronto Press 1984) 19-21.

7. Andrew Oyukuluk, personal communication 1993.

8 Tugaq Tunraluk, personal communication 1993.

9. Gaynor Kavanagh, "Objects as Evidence, or Not?" in Susan M. Pearce, ed., *Museum Studies in Material Culture* (Leicester and London: Leicester University Press 1989), 127.

10. Thomas Fisher Rare Book Library (TFRBL), University of Toronto, Henry Grattan Tyrrell Papers, Box 6, James W. Tyrrell, "Explorations and Adventures in Northern Canada." n.d. (MS 24/a).

11. Debates of the House of Commons, *Official Report of the Debates of the House of Commons.* Second Session - Fifth Parliament, 47 Victoriae, 15 (1884) 204.

12. Charles Tuttle, *Our North Land* (Toronto: C. Blackett Robinson 1885) 25.

13. Debates of the House of Commons (1884) 203.

14. Debates of the House of Commons (1884) 1379.

15. James W. Tyrrell, *Coast and Harbour Surveys in Hudson Bay and Strait* (Toronto: C. Blackett Robinson 1890), 4.

16. A. R. (Lieut.) Gordon, *Report of the Second Hudson's Bay Expedition under the Command of Lieut. A. R. Gordon, R.N.* (Ottawa: Department of Marine and Fisheries 1885).

17. TFRBL, James Williams Tyrrell Papers, Box 3, Notebooks and Diaries, 1878-1941, "Notes by James W. Tyrrell, Weston, Ontario Canada June 3rd, 1883 - April 1887," (MS 310/a).

18. TFRBL, Henry Grattan Tyrrell Papers, Box 6, James W. Tyrrell, "Explorations and Adventures in Northern Canada," n.d., 15 (MS 24/b).

19. TFRBL, Henry Grattan Tyrrell Papers, Box 6, James W. Tyrrell, "Explorations and Adventures in Northern Canada," n.d., 17 (MS 24/c).

20. A.R. (Lieut.) Gordon, *Report of the Hudson's Bay Expedition of 1886.*

21. TFRBL, Henry Grattan Tyrrell Papers, Box 6, James W. Tyrrell, "Explorations and Adventures in Northern Canada," n.d. (MS 24/d).

22. TFRBL, James Williams Tyrrell Papers, Box 9, Articles and Speeches, 1885-1931, File 9:6, "Hudson Bay and Churchill: Our New Canadian Sea Port." n.d., 7; (MS 310/b); Henry Grattan Tyrrell Papers, Box 6, James W. Tyrrell, "Explorations and Adventures in Northern Canada," n.d., 267 (MS 24/e).

23. TFRBL, James Williams Tyrrell Papers, Box 9, Articles and Speeches, 1885-1931, File 9:10, "Hudson Bay and Churchill: Our New Canadian Sea Port." n.d., 3; (MS 310/d).

24. TFRBL, James Williams Tyrrell Papers, Box 9, Articles and Speeches, 1885-1931, File 9:1, "Hudson Bay and Churchill: Our New Canadian Sea Port," n.d., 3 (MS 310/d).

25. Board of Grain Commissioners, *Annual Report of the Board of Grain Commissioners for Canada, 1932* (Ottawa: Department of Trade and Commerce 1933) 10.

26. TFRBL, Joseph Burr Tyrrell Papers, Box 8, "To Joseph from James, June 15, 1891 - November 29, 1891," Letter to J. B. Tyrrell dated October 25, 1891 (MS 26/a).

27. TFRBL, Henry Grattan Tyrrell Papers, Box 6, James W. Tyrrell, "Explorations and Adventures in Northern Canada," n.d., 77 (MS 24/f).

28. TFRBL, James Williams Tyrrell Papers, Box 4, Ashe Inlet Materials, 1885-86, "Station Provision List," (MS 310/e).

29. TFRBL, James Williams Tyrrell Papers, Box 9, Articles and Speeches, 1885-1931, File 9:6, "Hudson Bay and Churchill: Our New Canadian Sea Port," n.d (MS 310/f), 10.

30. TFRBL, Joseph Burr Tyrrell Papers, Box 8, "To Joseph from James. June 15, 1891 - November 29, 1991," Letter to J. B. Tyrrell dated November 29, 1891 (MS 26/b).

31. Jean-Paul Sartre, *Being and Nothingness: A Phenomenological Essay on Ontology* (New York: Washington Square Press 1956) 754.

32. TFRBL, Joseph Burr Tyrrell Papers, Box 8, "To Joseph from James, June 15, 1891 - November 29, 1891," Letter to J.B. Tyrrell dated October 25, 1891 (MS 26/c).

33. TFRBL, Joseph Burr Tyrrell Papers, Box 8, "To Joseph from James, June 20, 1889 - March 25, 1890," Letter addressed to J.B. Tyrrell dated June 20, 1889 (MS 26/d).

34. TFRBL, Henry Grattan Tyrrell Papers, Box 6, James W. Tyrrell, "Explorations and Adventures in Northern Canada," n.d., 52 (MS 24/g).

35. E.Y. Arima, *Inuit Kayaks in Canada: A Review of Historical Records and Construction*, Canadian Ethnology Service Mercury Series Paper 110 (Ottawa: National Museums of Canada 1987), 98-100.

36. Ibid, 100; Kenneth R. Lister, "Water for the Phalarope," 49.

37. William E. Parry, *Journal of a Second Journey for the Discovery of a North-West Passage from the Atlantic to the Pacific; Performed in the Years 1821-22-23 in His Majesty's ships Fury and Hecla under the Orders of Captain William Edward Parry R. N., F. R. S., and Commander of the Expedition* (New York: Greenwood Press, Publishers 1969), 14.

38. TFRBL, Henry Grattan Tyrrell Papers, Box 6, James W. Tyrrell, "Explorations and Adventures in Northern Canada," n.d., 52 (MS 24/h).

39. Appreciation is extended to numerous colleagues who have provided insightful comments over the course of this research. The author pays particular homage to Eugene Arima and Rebecca Duclos. This project would not have been possible without the support of John Summers and the Marine Museum of Upper Canada who have provided unlimited access to the James W. Tyrrell kayak. Their support is very much appreciated. An expression of gratitude is given to the officials of the Thomas Fisher Rare Book Library for permission to study and cite the Tyrrell family papers. Finally, appreciation is extended to Emil Huston who under numerous pressures devoted his time and skill to producing the artwork for this paper.

4. BARKLESS BARQUES (EUGENE ARIMA)

1. James Hornell, *Water Transport: Origins and Early Evolution* (Cambridge: Cambridge University Press 1946), 1-20. In the two-sided equation, man and canoe might be defined provisionally. Canoe may be taken to be a vessel shaped with a hollowing to some degree, an essentially simple boat design propelled by muscle power and/or wind often enough. Man, *Homo sapiens*, is a little difficult to define despite the past half century's great advance in knowledge of his ancestry or because of it, with differing views as to "where to draw the line." Most would now include the Neanderthals but not the Australopithecines, with a split on the Pithecanthropines, a few not even granting him Homo classification. But we probably are safe in saying Homo erectus since his brain by the crude measure of size reaches near our range, and he shaped stone tools and used fire as indicated by half a million years old burnt hearth remains. Indeed, some speak of *Homo sapiens erectus*, along with *Homo sapiens neandertalensis* and *Homo sapiens sapiens*. Erectus, if accepted as human, would take us back 2-3,000,000 years. But watercraft is another matter, at least forms developed enough to

be called canoes and not just devices for the occasion. Only from around 40,000 years ago is the existence of comparatively simple boats granted fair certitude by archaeologists on circumstantial grounds, for lack of direct physical evidence.

2. Hornell, 92-154.

3. Ibid, 140.

4. Mike Morgan, personal communication, 1998)

5. Waldemar Jochelson, "The Koryak," *Jesup North Pacific Expedition 6, American Museum of Natural History Memoir 9* (Leiden and New York, 1905-08), 543, fig.80.

6. Georg H. von Langsdorff, *Remarks and Observations on a Voyage Around the World from 1803-1807* (Kingston: Limestone Press 1993) plate 39.

7. Hornell, 178.

8. Pirjo Varjola, *Alaska: Venäjän Amerikka/Russian America* (Helsinki: National Board of Antiquities), 32, fig. 41.

9. Henry B. Collins, "Archeology of St. Lawrence Island, Alaska," *Smithsonian Institution Miscellaneous Collections* 96, 1 (1937) plate 84, #4.

10. H.C. Petersen, *Skin Boats of Greenland* (Roskilde: National Museum of Denmark, National Museum of Greenland and Viking Ship Museum of Roskilde 1986), 178, fig. 202.

11. William S. Laughlin, John D. Heath and Eugene Arima, "Two Nikolski Kayaks," in *Contributions to Kayak Studies* (Ottawa: Canadian Museum of Civilization Mercury Series 122), 163-209.

12. J. Louis Giddings, *Ancient Men of the Arctic* (New York: Alfred A. Knopf 1967) 223-245.

13. H.C. Petersen, *Skin Boats of Greenland*, 15.

14. Bjarne Grønnow, "Prehistory in Permafrost: Investigations at the Saqqaq Site, Qeqertasussuk, Disco Bay, West Greenland," *Journal of Danish Archaeology* 7 (1988) 37.

15. S.A. Arutyunov, M.G. Levin and D.A. Sergeyev, "Ancient Burials on the Chukchi Peninsula," in *The Archaeology and Geomorphology of Northern Asia*, Henry N. Micheal ed. (Toronto: University of Toronto Press 1964), 342; David W. Zimmerly, *Qajaq: Kayaks of Siberia and Alaska* (Juneau: Division of State Museums 1986) 3.

16. Zimmerly, 13.

17. Petersen, 101, fig. 106.

18. Edward W. Nelson, "The Eskimo about Bering Strait," *Smithsonian Institution, Bureau of American Ethnology Annual Report, 1896-97* 18,1 (1899), 346, fig. 134.

19. Henry B. Collins, "Archeology of St. Lawrence Island, Alaska," *Smithsonian Institution Miscellaneous Collections* 96, 1 (1937).

20. Ibid, plate 59, no.1.

21. Zimmerly, 12.

22. Ibid, no.13.

23. Ibid, plate 83, no.5.

24. Hans-Georg Bandi, *Eskimo Prehistory* (College: University of Alaska Press 1969), 80 and Moreau Maxwell, *Prehistory of the Eastern Arctic* (Orlando:Academic Press 1985), 252-253.

25. The Birnirk model may be seen as ancestral to the historical muti-chines from Kotzebue Sound, Alaska, north of Bering Strait to West Hudson Bay and Foxe Basin. James A. Ford, "Eskimo Prehistory in the Vicinity of Point Barrow, Alaska," *American Museum of Natural History Anthropological Papers* 47, 1 (1959), 157, fig.78.

26. Collins, no.4.

27. Ibid, no.6.

28. Canadian Museum of Civilization NaPi-2-29.15.
29. Zimmerly, 9.
30. Langsdorff, plate 39.
31. Zimmerly, 16.
32. Smithsonian Institution, *Arctic Research of the United States* 8 (Fall 1994), 110.
33. George Dyson, *Baidarka* (Edmonds, Washington: Alaska Northwest Publishing Co. 1986), 24.
34. von Langsdorff, plate 30.
35. Zimmerly, 29.
36. John Brand, *The Little Kayak Book*, (Colchester: John Brand 1984) 31.
37. Heath in Knut Bergsland, "Aleut Kayak Terminology," in *Contributions to Kayak Study* (Ottawa: Canadian Museum of Civilization Mercury Series 122) 136.
38. Graphic illustrations are scarce for this section, but an excellent source for them is Kenneth G. Roberts and Philip Shackleton, *The Canoe: A History of the Craft from Panama to the Arctic* (Toronto: MacMillan 1983).
39. E.Y. Arima, "A Report on a West Coast Whaling Canoe Reconstructed at Port Renfrew, B.C.," *History and Archaeology* 5 (1975) 101.
40. Ibid, 142, fig.50.
41. Bill Holm, "The Head Canoe," *Faces, Voices and Dreams* Peter L. Corey, ed. (Juneau: Alaska State Museums) 143-55.
42. Roberts and Shackleton, 107.
43. Ibid, 122.
44. Holm, 154.
45. Roberts and Shackleton, 99
46. Ibid, 105.
47. Wilson Duff, *Thoughts on the Nootka Canoe* (Victoria: British Columbia Provincial Museum 1965).
48. Roberts and Shackleton, 105.
49. John Dewhirst, personal communication, 1984.

5. THE DAO OF PADDLING (BERT HORWOOD)

1. James Raffan and Bert Horwood, eds. *Canexus: The Canoe in Canadian Culture* (Toronto: Betelgeuse 1988)
2. I am conscious that Aboriginal value systems within Canada, while unique, are highly compatible with aspects of Daoist philosophy.
3. T. Bender quoted in Dolores La Chapelle, *Earth Wisdom* (Silverton, CO.: Fine Hill Arts 1984) 158.
4. Dao is the official Chinese transliteration of the word that was formerly written "Tao" and is approximately pronounced "dow."
5. Alan Watts, *Tao, the Watercourse Way* (New York: Pantheon Books 1975), xiv.
6. Tai ji (formerly t'ai chi) is approximately sounded as "tie jee."
7. Bob Henderson, "Confessions of a Bannock Baker," in *Canexus: The Canoe in Canadian Culture.*
8. James Raffan, *Summer North of 60* (Toronto: Key Porter Books 1990) 167.
9. Daniel Vokey, personal communication, 1996.
10. Raffan, *Summer North of 60*, 69.
11. M. Csikszentmihalyi, *Beyond Boredom and Anxiety* (Washington, D.C.: Jossey-Bass

Publishers 1977).

12. Grey Owl, 1938.

13. Raffan, *Summer North of 60*, 117.

14. W.C. James, "The Quest Pattern and the Canoe Trip," in Bruce Hodgins and Maragaret Hobbes, eds., *Nastawgan; The Canadian North by Canoe and Snowshoe* (Toronto: Betelgeuse 1985) 9-24.

15. C.E.S. Franks, "Bonnet Plume: Home of the Loucheux," in James Raffan, ed. *Wild Waters: Canoeing Canada's Wilderness Rivers* (Toronto: Key Porter Books 1986) 113.

16. Martha Craig, "My Summer Outings in Labrador," in Judith Niemi, ed., *Rivers Running Free: Stories of Adventurous Women* (Minneapolis, Minn.: Bergamot Books 1987) 232.

17. D. LePan in Bruce Littlejohn and Jon Pearce, eds., *Marked by the Wild* (Toronto: McClelland and Stewart 1973) 52.

18. Thomas Merton, *The Way of Chuang Tzu* (New York: New Directions Press 1969).

19. Deng Ming-Dao, *365 Tao: Daily Meditations* (San Francisco: Harper San Francisco 1992) 113.

20. Thomas Merton, *The Way of Chuang Tzu*.

6. TRADITIONAL LONGBOATS OF ASIA PACIFIC (ADRIAN LEE)

1. Kenneth Roberts and Philip Shackleton, *Canoe: A History of the Craft from Panama to the Arctic* (Toronto: Macmillan 1983; George Dyson, *Baidarka* (Edmonds, Washington: Alaska North West Publishing Co. 1986).

2. "Vancouver Presented with Chinese Dragon," *Vancouver Sun* (October 10, 1945) 6.

3. Ibid.

4. John Dowd, *Sea Kayaking: A Manual for Long Distance Touring* (Vancouver: Douglas and McIntyre 1997).

5. Robert Bringhurst and Ulli Steltzer, *The Black Canoe: Bill Reid and the Spirit of Haida Gwaii* (Vancouver: Douglas and McIntyre 1991) and David Neel, *The Great Canoes: Reviving a Northwest Coast Tradition* (Seattle: University of Washington Press 1995).

6. Hiromitu Hakari and Erika Kaneko, eds. *Dong Son Drums in Viet Nam* (Tokyo: The Vietnamese Institute of Technology 1990).

7. See Yin Zhihui and Wang Yingheng, eds. *Sports in Ancient China* (Hong Kong: Tai Dao Publishing 1986).

8. Joseph Needham, *Science and Civilization in China*, Vol.4. *Physics and Physical Technology Part III: Civil Engineering and Nautics* (Cambridge: Cambridge University Press 1971), Table 71, 384.

9. See Arthur Waley, *The Nine Songs: A Study of Shamanism in Ancient China* (London: Allen and Unwin 1955).

10. Yang Xin, Li Yihua and Xu Naixiang, *The Art of the Dragon* (Hong Kong: The Commercial Press 1988).

11. Tun Li-ch'en, *Annual Customs and Festivals in Peking* (pub.1936) trans. Derk Bodde (Hong Kong: Hong Kong University Press 1987)

12. "Kerala: Jewel of India's Malabar Coast," *National Geographic* (May 1988), 593.

13. *Vancouver Sun* (August 8, 1998), C5.

14. Elsdon Best, *The Maori Canoe*, Dominion Museum Bulletin No.7, (Auckland: A.R.Shearer Government Printer 1925, reprinted 1976); Ann Nelson, *Nga Waka Maori: Maori Canoes* (Auckland: Macmillan 1991).

15. Tommy Holmes, *The Hawaiin Canoe* (Hawaii: Editions Limited 1981).

7. THE CANOT DU MAîTRE: MASTER OF THE INLAND SEAS (PETER LABOR)

1. Grand Portage was the inland headquarters of the North West Company until 1801. Due to border problems with the United States, a new post, Fort William, was built on the shores of the Kaminsitiquia River near modern day Thunder Bay, Ontario.
2. Approximately 9 kilometres per hour.
3. K.G. Roberts and P. Shackleton, *The Canoe: A History of the Craft from Panama to the Arctic* (Toronto: Macmillan of Canada 1983) 197.
4. Peter Bakker, "The Mysterious Link Between Basque and Micmac Art," *European Review of Native American Studies* 5, 1 (1991) 23.
5. Commonly 26' long, the north canoe was primarily used for trade and exploration west of the Great Lakes.
6. Hugh MacLennan, *Seven Rivers of Canada* (Toronto: Macmillan of Canada 1971), viii.
7. I was a member and leader of the 4 year and 15,000 km Canada Sea to Sea Expeditions, between 1989-93, during which groups of students paddled from Montreal to the Arctic and Pacific Oceans in replica voyageur canoes to commemorate, on its 200th anniversary, Alexander Mackenzie's first recorded crossing of the continent.
8. "La Chasse Galerie" is a popular French Canadian legend of a young voyageur who makes a deal with the devil to travel home to his loved one in a flying canoe.

8. MANUFACTURE OF BIRCH BARK CANOES FOR THE FUR TRADE IN THE ST. LAWRENCE (TIMOTHY KENT)

1. Louise Phelps Kellogg, ed. *Early Narratives of the Northwest, 1634-1699* (New York: Barnes and Noble 1967), 170-72.
2. Louis Callières, National Archives of Canada (NA), "Letter to the Court, 1702," MG1, C11A, F-20, fol.160.
3. Bacqueville de la Potherie, "History of the Savage Peoples who are Allies of New France," in Emma H. Blair, ed. *The Indian Tribes of the Upper Mississippi Valley and Region of the Great Lakes, as described by Nicolas Perrot, French Commandant in the Northwest,* Vol.1&2 (Cleveland: Arthur H.Clark Co., 1911), 228; Yves Zoltvany, ed. *The French Tradition in North America* (Columbia: University of South Carolina Press 1969), 105.
4. Beauharnois and Daigremont, Archives Nationales du Quebec, Quebec, "Letter to the Court, 1 October, 1728," *Manuscrits Relatifs a l'Histoire de la Nouvelle-France,* 3me Serie, vol.2, No. 2269 (1728-1729).
5. Edwin Tappan Adney and Howard I. Chapelle, *The Bark Canoes and Skin Boats of North America* (Washington, D.C.: Smithsonian Institution 1964 and 1983) 13, 135.
6. George Heriot, *Travels through the Canadas* (Rutland, Vt. and Tokyo: Charles E. Tuttle Co. 1971), 115-16; William N. Fenton and Elisabeth Tooker, "Mohawk," *Handbook of North American Indians, Vol.15, The Northeast* (Washington, D.C.: Smithsonian Institution 1978) 473.
7. John Thompson, "The Treaties of 1760," *The Beaver* (April/May 1996), 23-24.
8. Ibid, 26.
9. Conrad Heidenreich, *Huronia, A History and Geography of the Huron Indians, 1600-1650*

(Toronto: McClelland and Stewart 1971) 259.

10. Ibid.

11. John Gilmary Shea, *History and General Description of New France, by Rev. P.F.X. Charlevoix*, Vol.3 (Chicago: Loyola University Press 1870) 282-283.

12. Christian Morissonneau, "Huron of Lorette," *Handbook of North American Indians, Vol.15 The Northeast* (Washington, D.C.: Smithsonian Institution Press 1978), 389-390; Fenton and Tooker, 470.

13. Ivy A. Dickson, trans. *Letters from North America by Father Antoine Silvy, S.J.* (Belleville, Ont.: Mika Publishing Co. 1980) 218.

14. E.B. O'Callaghan, ed. "Enumeration of the Indian Tribes Connected with the Government of Canada; the Warriors and Armorial Bearings of Each Nation, 1736," *Documents Relative to the Colonial History of the State of New York*, Vol.IX (Albany: Weeds, Parsons and Co. 1855), 1052.

15. Heriot, 80.

16. Dickson, 218.

17. Claude LeBeau, *Avantures du Sr. C. LeBeau, avocat en parlement, ou Voyage curieux et nouveau parmi les sauvages de l'Amerique Septentrionale*, Vol.1 (Amsterdam: Herman Uytwerf 1738), 94-96.

18. Morissoneau, 390.

19. Capitaine Leduchat, National Archives of Canada, "Relation de Mr. Leduchat, Capitaine au Regimt. de Languedoc Infanterie, a Mr. Lamy de Chatel, 15 Juillet 1756," MG 4B, SerieA1, Vol. 3417, microfilm F-666, p. 182 on.

20. Fenton and Tooker, 469-71.

21. Dickson, 218-219.

22. Fenton and Tooker, 469-71.

23. Heriot, 116.

24. Bruce G. Trigger, ed. "Key to Tribal Territories" Map, *Handbook of North American Indians*, Vol.15 The Northeast (Washington, D.C.: Smithsonian Insitution 1978), ix.

25. William N. Fenton, "Northern Iroquoian Culture Patterns," *Handbook of North American Indians*, Vol.15 The Northeast, 303.

26. André Vachon, *Dreams of Empire, Canada Before 1700* (Ottawa: National Archives of Canada, Ministry of Supply and Services 1982) 134.

27. Walter Kenyon and J.R. Turnbull, *The Battle for James Bay 1686* (Toronto: Macmillan 1971) 40-41.

28. Fenton and Tooker, 470.

29. André Vachon, *Taking Root, Canada from 1700 to 1760* (Ottawa: National Archives of Canada, Ministry of Supply and Services 1985) 297.

30. Pierre Larousse, *Petit Larousse Illustré* (Paris: Librairie Larousee 1980) 1024.

31. Fenton amd Tooker, 472-473; Dickson, 218-219.

32. Fenton and Tooker, 472.

33. Ibid, 472-473; Heriot, 237.

34. Heriot, 237.

35. Fenton and Tooker, 473.

36. Vachon 1985, 281.

37. Jean Baptiste Perrault, "Narratives of the Travels and Adventures of a Merchant Voyageur in the Savage Territories of Northern America Leaving Montreal the 28th of May 1783," *Michigan Pioneer and Historical Collections*, Vol.37 (1909-1910) 515.

38. Charles M. Gates, ed. *Five Fur Traders of the Northwest* (St. Paul: Minnesota Historical Society 1965) 68-71.

39. Alexander Henry, *Travels and Adventures in Canada and the Indian Territories Between the Years 1760 and 1776* (New York: I. Riley 1809, reprinted by Reader Microprint Corp. 1966) 17.

40. Adney and Chapelle, 136.

41. Jean Lunn, "The Illegal Fur Trade out of New France, 1713-60," *Canadian Historical Association Papers* (1939) 61-76.

42. Elaine A. Mitchell, *Fort Temiskaming and the Fur Trade* (Toronto and Buffalo: University of Toronto Press 1977) 34-35.

43. Ibid, 85-89.

44. Ibid, 89.

45. See "The Late Years" this chapter.

46. Philip Burns, Hudson Bay Company Archives, Winnipeg "Letter to Edward M. Hopkins, 19 August 1848," D.5/22/fo.530, Microfilm 3M82.

47. K.C. Tessendorf, "George Simpson, Canoe Executive," *The Beaver* (Summer 1970), 39; The Prince of Wales's North American Canoe.

48. Gordon M. Day and Bruce G. Trigger, "Algonquin," *Handbook of North American Indians, Vol.15 The Northeast* (Washington, D.C.: Smithsonian Insitution 1978),792-795; O'Callaghan, 1052; Louis Antoine de Bougainville, "Special Return of the Indians,"in "Letter of M. de Bougainville to the Minister . . . 19th August, 1757," *Documents Relative to the Colonial Historiy of the State of New York*, Vol. X (Albany, N.: Weeds, Parsons and Co. 1858), 607.

49. Col. Louis Franquet, "Voyages et Mémoires sur le Canada, par Franquet," *Annuaire*, (Quebec: Institut Canadien de Quebec 1889), 29-129.

50. Detailed biographical information on the LeMaître, Auger, Lottinville, Leclerc, DuGuay, and Jutras canoe builders of Trois Rivières and the Lac St. Pierre area can be found in Timothy Kent's *Birchbark Canoes of the Fur Trade* (Ossineke, Michigan: Silver Fox Enterprises 1997) with explanations of the linkages between the families.

51. Isaac Weld, *Travels through the States of North America, and the Provinces of Upper and Lower Canada, during the Years 1795,1796, and 1797* (London, Picadilly: John Stockdale 1799), 17-18.

52. Marie Gerin-Lajoie, "Canoes," Report, ms., Montreal Merchants Records Project, Research File, c.1968-1977, 25 L 13.9, Box 1, Minnesota Historical Society, 1975, pp.80, 82.

53. Gordon M. Day, "Western Abenaki," *Handbook of North American Indians*, 149-51.

54. M. de Denoville, "Memoir Respecting Canada Prepared for the Marquis de Seignelay in January, 1690," *Documents Relative to the Colonial History of the State of New York*, Vol. IX, 440-441.

55. O'Callaghan, 1052.

56. Fenton and Tooker, 473.

57. Montreal Merchants Records (MMR), Monière, Vol. 4, 471-472; National Archives of Canada, MG 23/G111 25: microfilm M848.

58. Rene Jette, *Dictionnaire Genealogique des Familles de Quebec* (Montreal: Université de Montreal 1983), 292-293.

59. Jette, 704; Cyprien Tanguay, *Dictionnaire Genealogique des Familles de Quebec* Vol. 5 (Montreal: Eusebe Senecal et Fils 1871-1890), 331; Gerin-Lajoie 1975, 13.

60. Jette, 704.

61. Perrault, 514-515.
62. Trudel Atlas, 182
63. Archives Nationale du Quebec, Montreal, Notary François Leguay, 2 November 1785.
64. Archives Nationale du Quebec, Trois Rivières, Notary Badeaux, 9 April, 1792.
65. Jette, 704; Tanguay, Vol.5, 331 on; Gerin-Lajoie 1975, 13.
66. Jette, 704; Gerin-Lajoie 1975, 82.
67. Archives Nationale du Quebec, Trois Rivières, Notary Pillard, 19 November, 1765.
68. Horace Dourthser, *Dictionnaire Universel des Poids et Mesures Anciens et Modernes*, 1840 (Amsterdam: Meridian Publishing Co. 1965, rpt.); Leo-Guy de Repentigny, "Eqivalences,"Annexe 14, *La Ferme d'en bas du Cap Tourmente* (Environment Cananda, Canadian Wildlife Service 1989) 280.
69. Franquet.
70. MMR, Monière, Vol.8, 224; NAC, MG 23/GIII 25: Microfilm M849.
71. Archives Nationale du Quebec, Montreal, Notary C.J. Porlier, 30 May 1742, Deed No. 871.
72. Archives Nationale du Quebec, Trois Rivieres, Notary Caron, 27 September, 1745.
73. Gerin -Lajoie 1975, 11.
74. Bulletin Recherches Historiques, Vol. XXII, 237-237.
75. MMR, Monière, Vol.4, 594; NAC, MG 23/GIII 25: Microfilm M848.
76. MMR, Monière, Vol.4, 794; NAC, MG 23/GIII 25: Microfilm M848
77. NAC, MG 19 F 22. ms.
78. Gerin-Lajoie 1975, 83.
79. MMR, Monière, Vol.4, 593-600; NAC, MG 23/Gm 25: Microfilm M848
80. MMR, Monière, Vol.4, 692; NAC, MG 23/GIII 25: Microfilm M848
81. John Long, *Voyages and Travels of an Indian Interpreter and Trader* (New York: Johnson Reprint Co. 1968), 4, 38.
82. Philip Shackleton and Kenneth G. Roberts, *The Canoe, A History of the Craft from Panama to the Arctic* (Toronto: MacMillan 1983) 197.
83. Archives Nationale du Quebec, Trois Rivieres, Notary Badeaux, 25 January, 1795.
84. Marius Barbeau, "Country-Made Trade Goods," *The Beaver* (September 1944), 16-19.
85. Anne Morton, Archivist of H.B.C. Archives, Winnipeg, personal communications of March to May 1996.
86. Barbeau, 19.
87. Morton.
88. Archives Nationale du Quebec, Montreal, Notary Andre Jobin, 30 May, 1816.
89. Archives Nationale du Quebec, Montreal, Notary N.B.Doucet, 5 January 1820.
90. H.B.C. Archives, D.4/98 fos. 14-16.
91. Mitchell, 157.
92. Ibid, 224.
93. Ibid, 225.
94. H.B.C. Archives, Search File "Three Rivers", 4-5.
95. H.B.C. Archives, Three Rivers Correspondence Inwards 1837-1860, B.216/c/1.
96. Burns (a), H.B.C. Archives, D.5/9 fos.210-211, Microfilm 3M66.
97. Burns (a), H.B.C. Archives, D.5/11 fo.73, Microfilm 3M66.
98. Burns (a), H.B.C. Archives, D.5/11 fo.94, Microfilm 3M66.
99. Burns (b), H.B.C. Archives, D.5/22 fo.530, Microfilm 3M82.
100. Burns (a), H.B.C. Archives, D.5/40 fo.422, Microfilm 3M108.
101. Burns (a), H.B.C. Archives, D.5/40 fo.476, Microfilm 3M108.

102. Burns (a), H.B.C. Archives, D.5/39 fo.371, Microfilm 3M106.
103. Burns (a), H.B.C. Archives, D.5/40 fo.341, Microfilm 3M108.
104. Burns (a), H.B.C. Archives, D.5/22 fo.618, Microfilm 3M82.
105. Burns (a), H.B.C. Archives, D.5/22 fo.691, Microfilm 3M82.
106. Burns (a), H.B.C. Archives, D.5/23 fo.84, Microfilm 3M83.
107. Burns (a), H.B.C. Archives, D.5/23 fo.189, Microfilm 3M83.
108. Burns (a), H.B.C. Archives, D.5/36 fo.208, Microfilm 3M102.
109. Burns (a), H.B.C. Archives, D.5/39 fo.638, Microfilm 3M107.
110. Burns (a), H.B.C. Archives, D.5/31 fo.211, Microfilm 3M96.
111. Burns (a), H.B.C. Archives, D.5/30 fo.599, Microfilm 3M94.
112. Burns (a), H.B.C. Archives, D.5/31 fo.231, Microfilm 3M96
113. Burns (a), H.B.C. Archives, D.5/31 fo.527, Microfilm 3M96.
114. Burns (a), H.B.C. Archives, D.5/37 fo.741, Microfilm 3M104.
115. Burns (a), H.B.C. Archives, D.5/38 fo.20, Microfilm 3M105.
116. Burns (a), H.B.C. Archives, D.5/38 fo.78, Microfilm 3M105.
117. Morton.
118. Burns (a), H.B.C. Archives, D.5/39 fo.95, Microfilm 3M106.
119. Burns (a), H.B.C. Archives, D.5/39 fo.371, Microfilm 3M106.
120. Burns (a), H.B.C. Archives, D.5/39 fo.407, Microfilm 3M106.
121. Burns (a), H.B.C. Archives, D.5/40 fo.332, Microfilm 3M108.
122. Burns (a), H.B.C. Archives, D.5/40 fo.341, Microfilm 3M108.
123. Burns (a), H.B.C. Archives, D.5/40 fo.367, Microfilm 3M108.
124. Burns (a), H.B.C. Archives, D.5/40 fo.390, Microfilm 3M108.
125. Jette, 773.
126. Burns (a), H.B.C. Archives, D.5/40 fo.476, Microfilm 3M108.
127. Burns (a), H.B.C. Archives, D.5/40 fo.500, Microfilm 3M108.
128. David Gidmark, "The Passion of E. Tappan Adney, the Caretaker of America's Canoe Legacy," *Canoe* (October 1987), 20; Adney and Chapelle, 88.
129. Gidmark, 20; Adney and Chapelle, 93.
130. Vachon 1985, 121.
131. Saguenay Region History Exhibit, Musée du Saguenay-Lac St.Jean, Chicoutimi, Quebec, 1994.
132. James McKenzie, "Some Account of the King's Posts, the Labrador Coast and the Island of Anticosti, by an Indian Trader Residing there Several Years," *Les Bourgeois de la Compagnie du Nord-Ouest*, Vol.2, L.R. Masson, ed (New York: Antiquarian Press Ltd. 1960), 439, 449.
133. Heriot, 52.
134. Edward S. Rogers and Eleanor Leacock, "Montaignais-Naskapi," *Handbook of North American Indians*, Vol.6, Subarctic, (Washington, D.C.: Smithsonian Institution 1981), 169.
135. Ibid, 171.
136. Ibid, 170.
137. Justice Baby, "Une Lettre de Cadet, le Munitionnaire de la Nouvelle – France," *The Canadian Antiquarian and Numismatic Journal*, Third series, 1, 4 (October 1898), 173-187.
138. Adney and Chapelle, 114, 116, 123-25, 127, 139. Nineteen-foot fur trade craft located by Adney on St. Maurice River.

139. Gerin-Lajoie 1975, 15.

140. Larousée, 138.

141. Jette, 1089; Tanguay, Vol.1, 572, Vol.7, 336-37; Drouin Institut, *Dictionnaire National des Canadiens Francais* (Montreal: Institut Genealogique Drouin 1955)

142. Hubert Charbonneau et Jacques Legare, *Le Repertoire des Actes de Bapteme, Mariage, Sepulture, at des Recensements du Quebec Anciens* (Montreal:Les Presses de L'Université de Montreal 1978).

143. Ibid, Vol.32.

144. An additional note must be included in the discussion of builders of voyaging canoes in the St. Lawrence settlements. Adney and Chapelle's volume portrays the Tete de Boule people as major builders of such canoes. The book relates a story in which the Iroquois taught the Tete de Boule to construct fur trade canoes, and it even identifies the Tete de Boule as the builders in the St. Lawrence settlements of the Type B-1 style of expedition canoe.

The Tete de Boule were widely-dispersed native people who inhabited the upper watershed regions of the St. Maurice, Gatineau, Lievre, and Dumoine Rivers and beyond, in an area well north of the St. Lawrence and east of the Ottawa River in Quebec. They hunted, trapped, fished, and moved about in the interior regions and traded on the St. Lawrence at Trois- Rivieres and on the upper Ottawa at Temiscamingue.

During the entire era of fur trade canoe construction in the St. Lawrence communities, the Tete de Boule did not settle in the St. Lawrence valley or frequent the trading centers for any extended periods of time. Even by the middle of the 19th century, they still led a roaming existence. Those living in the upper St. Maurice watershed region in the early to mid1800s traded at the main post of Weymontachingue, while maintaining their traditional nomadic lifestyle ten to eleven months per year. It was reported in 1845 that their economy did not allow them to remain around the post as a group for more than five weeks at a time, or their food supplies would run out. A reserve was established for them at Weymontachingue in 1851.

The Tete de Boule people were definitely not a settled labour force which was available to work at the established canoe yards in the St. Lawrence valley. Various Indian groups produced voyaging canoes in this region – Algonkins, Hurons, Iroquois, Abenakis, Montagnais – but not the Tete de Boule.

A study of the correspondence of Tappan Adney reveals that he carried out the majority of his research on fur trade canoes in the mid-1920s. In the process, he located a single full size fur trade canoe, slightly over nineteen feet long, at Grand Piles, Quebec. This community lies a little up the St. Maurice from Trois-Rivieres.

At the time of Adney's research, the last of the Algonkins of the Trois-Rivieres area had been gone since the 1830s, after having lived there among the French for some two centuries. The Tete de Boule had been living on their reserve on the upper St. Maurice only since its establishment in 1851. Thus, during the era of Adney's research, the Algonkins had been long absent, and the Tete de Boule were present in the region. This apparently led Adney to incorrectly attribute the manufacture of the fur trade canoe which he had located on the lower St. Maurice River to the latter native group. See Adney and Chapelle, 136-37, 151; Gerard E. McNulty and Louis Gilbert, "Attikamek (Tete de Boule)," *Handbook of North American Indians*, Vol. 6, *Subarctic* (Washington, D.C.: Smithsonian Instituition 1981) 208-212.

9. THE REPRESENTATION OF ABORIGINAL CULTURE WITHIN THE CANADIAN CANOE MUSEUM (SHANNA BALAZS)

1. David Neel, *The Great Canoes Reviving a Northwest Coast Tradition* (Vancouver, Toronto and Seattle: Douglas and McIntyre and the University of Washington Press 1995) 1.
2. Neel, 1-2.
3. Neel, 4.
4. Neel, 2.
5. Neel, 18.
6. Michael Ames, *Cannibal Tours and Glass Boxes: The Anthropology of Museums* (Vancouver: University of British Columbia Press 1992), 147, 157.
7. George Stocking, "Museums and Material Culture", 3-14, in *Objects and Others: Essays On Museums and Material Culture*, (Wisconsin: University of Wisconsin Press) 11.
8. Ames, 146.
9. Michael Ames, *Museums, the Public, and Anthropology: A Study in the Anthropology of Anthropology* (Vancouver and New Delhi: University of British Columbia Press and Concept Publishing 1986) 77.
10. Ivan Karp, "Culture and Representation," in *Exhibiting Cultures: The Poetics and Politics of Museum Display* (Washington and London: Smithsonian Institution Press 1992) 13-14.
11. Christine Mullen Kreamer, "Defining Communities Through Exhibiting and Collecting," in *Museums and Communities: The Politics of Public Culture* (Washington and London: Smithsonian Institution Press 1992) 371.
12. Ames, 1992, 79.
13. Julia D. Harrison, "The Spirit Sings and the Future of Anthropology," *Anthropology Today* 4, 6 (1988) 6-9.
14. Ibid.
15. Assembly of First Nations and the Canadian Museums Association, *Turning the Page: Forging New Partnerships Between Museums and First Peoples* (Ottawa: third edition, Canadian Museums Association 1994), 1.
16. Ibid.
17. AFN & CMA, 4.
18. AFN & CMA, 4-6.
19. Canadian Museums Association, "The Next Chapter: Task Force on Museums and First Peoples Update." Unpublished summary of survey responses, 1995.
20. Ibid.
21. Ibid.
22. The theme of this CCM event was "A Museum in the Making."
23. It has been suggested to me by a CCM Board Member that a more informal process of becoming aware of, and sensitive to, alternate interpretations of canoe culture – for example through interaction and cooperation with Aboriginal groups and individuals – has been more appropriate and beneficial to the CCM's Board and Staff than the formal cultural sensitivity training I included within my recommendations.
24. This recommendation was fulfilled by the CCM as of February, 1997.
25. Madeline Katt Theriault, *Moose to Mocassins* (Toronto: Natural Heritage 1992) 11.

10. CANADIANS AND THE CANADIAN CANOE IN THE OPENING OF THE AMERICAN MIDWEST (RALPH FRESE)

1. John Murray Gibbon, *The Romance of the Canadian Canoe* (Toronto: The Ryerson Press

1951) 16. The quote is from the translation by H.H. Langton in the Champlain Society's edition of *Des Dauvages au Voyage de Sieur de Champlain fait en l'an 1603*.

2. Reuben Gold Thwaites (ed.), *Voyages of Marquette*, (Cleveland: The Burrow Brothers Co. MDCCC). Author's copy printed by the Ann Arbor University Microfilms Inc. in 1966.

3. Milo Milton Quaife, *Chicago's Highways Old and New*, 14.

4. John W. Larson, *Those Army Engineers*, (U.S. Government Printing Office 1979)

5. Milo Milton Quaife (ed.), *The Western Country in the 17th Century* (The Lakeside Classics, R.R. Donnelley and Sons Co. 1947)

6. Charles M. Gates (ed.), *Five Fur Traders of the Northwest* (Minnesota Historical Society 1965)

11. PADDLING VOICES: THERE'S THE POET, VOYAGER, ADVENTURER AND EXPLORER IN ALL OF US (ALISTER THOMAS)

1. I came to this realization after editing a book for the Canadian Recreational Canoeing Association. This book, *Paddle Quest*, forthcoming in the fall of 1999, has three major sections: 37 outstanding canoe trips in Canada, 21 distinguished paddler profiles, and a bold blueprint for waterway stewardship.

2. All unattributed quotes are from interviews for the aforementioned *Paddle Quest*.

3. Sheena Masson excerpt from "Confessions of a Know-It-All OR Why Take A Clinic" to appear in *Paddle Quest*.

4. Thanks to Gaye Wadham Gagnon of Douglastown, Quebec for translating Gino Bergeron's George River story from French to English.

5. Bill Mason, *Path of the Paddle – An Illustrated Guide to the Art of Canoeing*. (New York: Van Nostrand Reinhold Ltd. 1980) 5.

6. Bill Mason, *Song of the Paddle – An Illustrated Guide to Wilderness Camping*. (Toronto, Key Porter Books 1988) 1.

12. THE CANOE AS A WAY TO ANOTHER STORY (BOB HENDERSON)

1. The concept of culture as story is derived from Daniel Quinn, *Ishmael* (New York: Bantam Books 1993). Connelly and Clandinin point out that we call the phenomenon of telling, *story* and the inquiry into story, *narrative*. "Thus, we say that people lead storied lives and tell stories of those lives, whereas narrative researchers describe such lives . . . and write narratives of experience." F.M. Connelly and D.J. Clandinin, "Stories of Experience and Narrative Inquiry," *Educational Researcher* 19, 5 (1990) 2.

2. Gary Snyder, *The Practise of the Wild* (New York: North Point Press) 68.

3. For a more complete gathering of evidence see Bob Henderson, "Outdoor Travel: Explorations for Change," Ph.D dissertation, University of Alberta, 1995.

4. What started for me as youthful curiosity with only confused observations has evolved into a commitment to inductive reasoning, to develop and articulate a valid method of systematizing the potential life changing experiences of the canoe trip. Mind you, the understanding I offer is not static, just as a story continues to develop. Unlearning and learning are a part of the same weave of wild nature, self and culture.

5. Paul Shepherd, *The Tender Carnivore and the Sacred Game* (New York: Viking Press).

6. Robert Greenway, "Healing by the Wilderness Experience," in *Wild Ideas*, ed. David Rothenberg (Minneapolis: University of Minnesota Press 1995), 185. Greenway

offers a more complete view of dualism, of transference of new perceptions from the wilderness experience back into everyday life and of the very real possibility of post-camping depression. As he notes, " . . . it is not safe to keep one's sensory processes open in the city." I, myself, have been asked to address long canoe tripping staff at an Ontario summer camp on how to help campers avoid post-camping depression or camper's inability to "re-enter." The camp was having complaints of teens camping in their backyard, dropping out of school, and continuing to wear "tripping" clothes. I would suggest much is right on such trips, but some things are wrong too. This is an excellent article for probing the psychic realm of wilderness travel.

7. Indeed, such fundamental explorations of self, cuture and nature are abundant within the Canadian canoeing tradition. Just think of Grey Owl, Sigurd Olson and Bill Mason. Grey Owl offered his audiences in Britain only a single leaf; Sigurd Olson defined for us a way of the canoe in many books; Bill Mason shared his song of the paddle in books, film, painting and in an exuberance for life. See for example, James Raffan, *Fire in the Bones: Bill Mason and the Canadian Canoeing Tradition* (Toronto: Harper Collins 1996) 4.

8. Cleo Cherryholmes, *Power and Criticism: Post-Structural Investigations in Educations* (New York: Teachers College Press 1988), 179. Cherryholmes offers an interesting set of terms for what is typically thought of as realism and idealism that clarifies differences in teacher orientation. The "structurally pragmatic" teacher tends to be associated with realism and the "critical pragmatic" teacher with idealism but as he points out , it is "vulgar pragmatism" that clings to a status quo out of step with reality. For our purposes here, the reality in question is an ecological view.

9. Over a ten year period I have read well over 300 student canoe tripping journals. Though not evaluated, the journal is mandatory. All students receive the same participatory grade. Thus, it is intriguing that so many elect to act on the challenge of reporting descriptions of the richness of the subjective lifeworld of their travel experience as a comparison to the otherwise "everyday" day-to-day reality upon return to the city.

10. E.F. Schumacher, *A Guide for the Perplexed* (New York: Harper Colophon 1977) 1.

11. Paulo Freire, *Pedagogy of the Oppressed* (New York: Continuum 1989) 23.

12. Brian Fay, "How People Change Themselves: The Relationship between Critical Theory and its Audience," in *Political Theory and Praxis*, ed. Terrence Bell (Minneapolis: University of Minnesota Press 1977) 200-233.

13. Patti Lather, *Getting Smart: Feminist Research and Pedagogy with/in the Postmodern* (New York: Routledge 1991) 72.

14. Fred Bodsworth, "Our Threatened Heritage," in *Wilderness Canada*, ed. B. Spears (Toronto: Clark Irwin 1970).

15. The excerpts are from the journals of senior Physical Education students at McMaster University, Hamilton, Ontario.

16. Nils Faarland, "Nils Faarland," in *Wisdom in the Open Air*, eds. Peter Reed and David Rothenberg (Minneapolis: University of Minnesota Press 1993), 158. Friluftsliv is a central concept for the understanding of guiding advocated here. While common to an understanding of Outdoor Education in Scandinavia, it is virtually unknown within a North American understanding. However, similarities can be found with Aboriginal as well as Eastern traditions of thought. Friluftsliv is employed as a descriptor because it is clearly defined and understood within a tradition that is readily applicable to a Canadian contemporary content.

17. Arne Naess, *Ecology, Community and Lifestyle: Outline of an Ecosophy* (Cambridge: Cambridge University Press 1989).

18. Tim Cahill, Jaeguar Ripped my Flesh (Penguin 1989) 304.

19. Douglas Coupland, *Generation X: Tales from an Accelerated Culture* (New York: Martin's Press 1991) 5.

20. Bert Horwood, "The Influence of Outdoor Education on Curriculum Integration: A Case Study," in *Coaling for Education in the Outdoors, Second Research Symposium Proceedings*, eds. Leo.H. McAvoy, L. Allison Stringer, Alan Ewert (Indiana: Bradford Woods 1994).

21. Noel Gough, "Learning with Environments: Towards an Ecological Paradigm for Education," in *Environmental Education: Practice and Possibility*, ed. Ian Robottom (Deakin: Deakin University 1987).

22. Paulo Freire, *Pedagogy of the Oppressed* (New York: Continuum 1989), 23.

23. Brian Fawcett, *Public Eye: An Investigation into the Disappearance of the World* (Toronto: Harper Collins 1990), IX.

13. HISTORIC CANOE ROUTES OF THE FRENCH RIVER
(TONI HARTING)

1. Toni Harting, *French River: Canoeing the River of the Stick-Wavers* (Toronto: Stoddart-Boston Mills Press, 1996) 33-38.

2. Harting, 127.

3. Doris K. Megill, "Underwater Finds in the French River," *Canadian Geographical Journal*, (August 1963); Robert C. Wheeler, et al., *Voices from the Rapids* (Minnesota Historical Society, 1975); Harting, 98-99.

4. Alexander Henry (the Elder), *Travels and Adventures in Canada and the Indian Territories between the Years 1760 and 1776* (1809); Alexander Mackenzie, *Voyages from Montreal* (1801); John Macdonnell, "The Diary of John Macdonnell," in *Five Fur Traders of the Northwest*, Charles M. Gates, ed. (Minnesota Historical Society 1965); Provincial Archives of Ontario, Diary, Mackintosh Papers (MU 1956), Angus Mackintosh, *Journal from the Enterance of the French River . . .* ; Provincial Archives of Ontario, Robert Seaborne Miles, "Journals," Box 7-10 (MU 1391); John J. Bigsby, *The Shoe and Canoe* (1850); Nicholas Garry, *Diary of Nicholas Garry*, Proceedings and Transactions of the Royal Society of Canada, 2, 6 (May 1900); Frances Ramsay Simpson, "Journey for Frances," *The Beaver* (Dec. 1953; March 1954); Harting, 69-83.

5. Eric W. Morse, "Voyageurs' Highway," *Canadian Geographical Journal* (May-July-August 1961); Eric W. Morse, *Fur Trade Canoe Routes / Then and Now* (Toronto: University of Toronto Press, 1969); Eric W. Morse, *Freshwater Saga* (Toronto: University of Toronto Press 1987).

6. These aboriginal peoples included the Algonquins, Ojibwa, Nipissing and Huron, see Harting, 43-45.

7. Robert Seaborne Miles.

8. Frances Ramsay Simpson.

9. Angus Mackintosh.

14. THE DARK SIDE OF THE CANOE, (GWYNETH HOYLE)

1. Jamie Benidickson's book on the history of recreational canoeing, *Idleness, Water and the Canoe: Image, Symbol and Experience*, has a chapter and bibliography on this topic.

2. Eric Sevareid, *Canoeing with the Cree* (St. Paul: Minnesota Historical Society 1968) 165-7.

3. Christopher Norment, *In the North of our Lives* (Camden, Maine: Down East Books 1989) 32-33.

4. George Grinnell, *A Death on the Barrens* (Toronto: Northern Books 1996) 5, 26.

5. Ibid.

6. Victoria Jason, *Kabloona in the Yellow Kayak* (Winnipeg: Turnstone Press 1995) 36

7. Don Starkell, *Paddle to the Arctic* (Toronto: McClelland and Stewart 1995) 72.

8. Robert Cundy, *Beacon Six* (London: Eyre and Spottiswoode 1970) 21.

9. Gontran de Poncins, *Kabloona* (New York: Reynal and Hitchcock 1941) 187.

10. Elliott Merrick, *True North* (Lincoln: U. of Nebraska Press 1989), 332-3.

11. James Davidson and John Rugge, *The Complete Wilderness Paddler* (New York: Random House 1983) 209.

12. Margaret Atwood, *Strange Things: the Malevolent North in Canadian Literature* (Toronto: Oxford University Press 1995) 12.

13. Sevareid, *op. cit.*, 7.

14. Sevareid, *Not So Wild a Dream* (New York: Knopf, 1947): 17.

15. Sevareid, "Return to God's Country," *Audubon* (Sept. 1981),45.

16. Moffatt's diary in *Sports Illustrated* (March 9, 1959) 72.

17. Cundy, *op. cit.*, 3.

18. M.T. Kelly, *Into the Whirlwind* (Toronto: Stoddart 1995).

15. THOUGHTS ON THE ORIGINS OF THE CANOE
(KIRK WIPPER)

1. Archival material on William McBride and the connection with Daniel Herald was located by Mary Fleming and Robert Collins McBride, descendants of McBride. They carefully researched the life and work of McBride through investigation of tax rolls, official records, letters and other material with the aim of writing his story.

16. CANOESCAPES AND THE CREATIVE SPIRIT
(BECKY MASON)

1. Bill Mason, *Canoescapes* (Toronto:Boston Mills Press 1995) 16.

2. Ibid, 10.

3. Ibid, 136.

17. THE CANOE AS CHAPEAU: THE ROLE OF THE PORTAGE IN CANOE CULTURE
(BRUCE W. HODGINS)

1. Bill Mason, *Song of the Paddle: An Illustrated Guide to Wilderness Camping* (Toronto: Key Porter 1988), 4 but also note 1-10 and 166-68.

2. James Raffan, *Fire in the Bones, Bill Mason and the Canadian Canoeing Tradition* (Toronto: Harper Collins 1996), 1.

3. Andrea Mueller on the Wanapitei Camp Folder for 1996 and Bruce W. Hodgins, *Wanapitei on Temagami: A Story of Adventures* (Peterborough, 1996), back cover.

4. Donald S. R. Barry, "The Canoe in Canadian Art," doctoral dissertation, University of Alberta, 1993, especially pp. 142, 151, 170, 171, 178, 181, 192, 267, 284, 291. The same can be said for the photographs which Gwyneth Hoyle and I were able to obtain for *Canoeing North Into the Unknown: A Record of River Travel, 1874 to 1974* (Toronto:

Natural Heritage 1994), see especially pp. 6, 21, 70, 77, 93, 122, 170, 174, 216, 241.

5. Toni Harting, *French River: Canoeing the River of the Stick-Wavers* (Toronto: Boston Mills 1996).

6. Craig Macdonald, "Nastawgan: Traditional Routes of Travel in the Temagami District" in Bruce W. Hodgins and Margaret Hobbs, eds. *Nastawgan: The Canadian North by Canoe and Snowshoe* (Toronto: Betelgeuse 1985) 183-88.

7. James Raffan and Burt Herwood, *Canexus: The Canoe In Canadian Culture*, OGS. (Toronto, Betelgeuse 1988) pp 45-58.

8. Courtesy of Labatt's *Blue*, recent advertisements.

18. R.M. PATTERSON'S PADDLING PASSION

(DAVID FINCH)

1. R. M. Patterson, *Far Pastures* (Sidney, B.C.: Gray's Publishing 1963) 287.

2. R.M. Patterson, *The Buffalo Head* (New York: William Sloane Associates 1961) 54.

3. R.M. Patterson, *The Dangerous River* (London: George Allen & Unwin Ltd. 1954) 14.

4. R.M. Patterson Diary, 1927, August 19, British Columbia Archives and Records Service (BCARS), Victoria, B.C., Add. MSS. 2762, Box 4, file 1)

5. Ibid.

6. 1955 12 23, RMP letters to George W. Pocaterra: Papers at Glenbow Archives, M6340, f. 14.

7. 1963 3 7, RMP letters to GeorgeW. Pocaterra: Papers at Glenbow Archives, M6340, f. 111.

8. R.M. Patterson Diary, Sunday, October 23, 1927.

Adney, Edwin Tappan and Howard I. Chapelle, *The Bark Canoes and Skin Boats of North America*. Washington, D.C.: Smithsonian Institution 1964 and 1983.

Arima, E.Y. "A Report on a West Coast Whaling Canoe Reconstructured at Port Renfrew, B.C.," *History and Archaeology* 5 (1975).

Arima, E.Y. "Inuit Kayaks in Canada: A Review of Historical Records and Construction," *Canadian Ethnology Service Mercury Series* Paper 110 Ottawa: National Museums of Canada 1987, pp. 98-100

Bailey, Alfred G. *The Conflict of European and Eastern Algonquin Cultures 1504-1700*. Toronto: University of Toronto Press, 1969.

Bandi, Hans-Georg, *Eskimo Prehistory*. College: University of Alaska Press, 1969.

Barry Donald S.R. "The Canoe in Canadian Art," doctoral dissertation, University of Alberta, 1993.

Benidickson, Jamie Idleness, *Water and the Canoe: Reflections on Paddling for Pleasure*. Toronto: University of Toronto Press, 1997.

Bergsland, Knut, "Aleut Kayak Terminology." In Contributions to Kayak Study. Ottawa: Canadian Museum of Civilization Mercury Series 122, 1991.

Bigsby, John J. *The Shoe and Canoe*. Published in 1850.

Bishop, Charles A. *The Northern Ojibwa and the Fur Trade: An Historical and Ecological Study*. Toronto: Holt, Rinehart and Winston, 1974.

Brand, John. *The Little Kayak Book*. Colchester: John Brand, 1984.

Braund, Stephen R. *The Skin Boats of Saint Lawrence Island, Alaska*. Seattle: University of Washington Press, 1988.

Bringhurst, Robert and Ulli Steltzer, *The Black Canoe: Bill Reid and the Spirit of Haida Gwaii*. Vancouver: Douglas and McIntyre, 1991.

Buijs, Cunera, ed. *Continuity and Discontinuity in Arctic Cultures: Essays in Honour of Gerti Nooter, Curator at the National Museum of Ethnology. 1970-1990*. Leiden: Centre of Non-Western Studies 1993.

Calloway, Colin G., *Crown and Calumet: British-Indian Relations, 1783-1815*. Tulsa: University of Oklahoma Press, 1987.

Colwell, F,. *Riverman: A Romantic Iconography of the River and the Source*. Kingston: McGill-Queen's University Press, 1989.

Corey, Peter, ed. *Faces, Voices and Dreams*. Juneau: Alaska State Museums, 1987.

Davidson, James and John Rugge. *The Complete Wilderness Paddler*. New York.: Random House, 1983.

Dickason, Olive P., *Canada's First Nations: A History of Founding People from Earliest Times*. Toronto: McLelland and Stewart, 1992.

Dowd, John, Sea Kayaking: *A Manual for Long Distance Touring*. Vancouver: Douglas and McIntyre, 1997.

Duff, Wilson, *Thoughts on the Nootka Canoe*. Victoria: British Columbia Provincial Museum, 1965.

Durham, Bill, *Indian Canoes of the Northwest Coast*. Seattle: Copper Canoe Press, 1960.

Dyson, George. *Baidarka*. Edmonds, Wash.: Alaska Northwest Publishing Co. 1986.

Franks, C.E.S., *The Canoe and Whitewater: From Essential to Sport*. Toronto: University of Toronto Press, 1977.

Gates, Charles, ed., *Five Fur Traders of the Northwest*. Minnesota Historical Society, 1965.

Gibbon, J. Murray, *The Romance of the Canadian Canoe*. Toronto: The Ryerson Press, 1951.

Giddings, J. Louis, *Ancient Men of the Arctic*. New York: Alfred A. Knopf. 1967.

Grønnow, Bjarne. "Prehisory in Permafrost: Investigations at the Saqqaq site, Qeqertasussuk, Disco Bay, West Greenland." *Journal of Danish Archaeology* 7 (1988): 24-39

Harting, Toni, *French River: Canoeing the River of the Stick-Wavers*. Toronto: Stoddart-Boston Mills, 1996.

Heidenreich, Conrad, *Huronia, A History and Geography of the Huron Indians, 1600-1650*. Toronto: McLelland and Stewart, 1971.

Henry, Alexander, *Travels and Adventures in Canada and the Indian Territories Between the Years 1760 and 1776*. New York: I. Riley 1809, reprinted by Reader Microprint Corp. 1966.

Hodgins, Bruce W, *Wanapitei on Temagami: A Story of Adventures*. Peterborough, 1996.

Hodgins, Bruce W. and Gwyneth Hoyle, *Canoeing North Into the Unknown: A Record of River Travel 1874-1974*. Toronto: Natural Heritage, 1994 and 1996.

Hodgins, Bruce W. and Margaret Hobbes, eds., *Nastawgan: The Canadian North by Canoe and Snowshoe*. Toronto: Betelgeuse Books, 1985.

Hornell, James, *Water Transport: Origins and Early Evolution*. Cambridge: University Press, 1946.

Jason, Victoria, *Kabloona in the Yelllow Kayak*. Winnipeg: Turnstone Press, 1995.

Kellogg, Louise Phelps, ed., *Early Narratives of the Northwest, 1634-1699*. New York: Barnes and Noble, 1967.

Kent, Timothy, *Birchbark Canoes of the Fur Trade*, 2 volumes. Ossineke, Michigan: Silver Fox Enterprises, 1997.

Laughlin, William S., John D. Heath and Eugene Arima, "Two Nikolski Aleut Kayaks." In *Contributions to Kayak Studies*. Canadian Museum of Civilization Mercury Series 122 (1991): 163-209.

Le Rossignol, James E., *The Flying Canoe (La Chaisse Galerie)*. Toronto: McLelland and Stewart, 1929.

Lister, Kenneth R., "Water for the Phalarope: Kayak Design and Cultural Values among the Tununirusirmiut," Museum Small Craft Association Transactions 1995 2 (1996): 49-51.

Marsh, John S. and Bruce W. Hodgins, eds., *Changing Parks: The History, Future and Cultural Context of Parks and Heritage Landscapes*. Toronto: Natural Heritage, 1998.

Mason, Bill, *Path of the Paddle: An Illustrated Guide to the Art of Canoeing*. Toronto: Van

Nostrand Reinhold, 1980.

Mason Bill, *Song of the Paddle: An Illustrated Guide to Wilderness Camping.* Toronto: Key Porter , 1988.

Mason Bill, *Canoescapes.* Toronto: Boston Mills Press, 1995.

Maxwell, Moreau, *Prehistory of the Eastern Arctic.* Orland:Academic Press, 1985.

Merrick, Elliott, *True North.* Lincoln: University of Nebraska Press, 1989.

McKenzie, Alexander, Sir., *Voyages from Montreal.* Norman: University of Oklahoma Press, 1966.

Morse, Eric W., *Fur Trade Canoe Routes of Canada: Then and Now.* Toronto: University of Toronto Press, 1969.

Morse, Eric W., *Freshwater Saga.* Toronto: University of Toronto Press, 1987.

Neel, David, *The Great Canoes: Reviving a Northwest Coast Tradition.* Vancouver: Douglas and MacIntyre, 1995.

Niemi, Judith, ed., *Rivers Running Free: Stories of Adventurous Women.* Minneapolis: Bergamot Books, 1987.

Norment, Christopher, *In the North of our Lives.* Camden, Maine: Down East Books, 1989.

Patterson, R.M., *The Dangerous River.* London: George Allen and Unwin Ltd., 1954.

Peterson, H.C., *Skin Boats of Greenland.* Roskilde: Viking Ship Museum of Roskilde, The National Museum of Denmark and The National Museum of Greenland, 1986.

Pope, Richard, *Superior Illusions.* Illustrated by Neil Broadfoot. Toronto: Natural Heritage, 1998.

Raffan, James, *Fire in the Bones, Bill Mason and the Canadian Canoeing Tradition.* Toronto: Harper Collins, 1996.

Raffan, James, *Summer North of 60.* Toronto: Key Porter Books, 1990.

Raffan, James, ed., *Wild Waters: Canoeing Canada's Wilderness Rivers.* Toronto: Key Porter Books, 1986.

Raffan, James and Bert Horwood, *Canexus: The Canoe in Canadian Culture.* Toronto: Betelgeuse Press, 1988.

Roberts, Kenneth G., and Philip Shackleton, *The Canoe: A History of the Craft form Panama to the Arctic.* Toronto: MacMillan, 1983.

Seton, Ernest Thompson, *The Arctic Prairies: A Canoe Journey of 2000 Miles in Search of the Caribou.* 1911.

Sevareid, Eric, *Canoeing with the Cree.* St. Paul: Minnesota Historical Society, 1968.

Sevareid, Eric, *Not So Wild a Dream.* New York: Knopf, 1947.

Starkell, Don, *Paddle to the Arctic.* Toronto: McLelland and Stewart, 1995.

Stephenson, James R., "John Stephenson and the Famous Peterborough Canoes." Occasional Paper 8 (Nov. 1987) Peterborough, Ont: Peterborough Historical Society.

Stewart, Hillary, *Cedar: Tree of Life to the Northwest Coast Indians.* Vancouver, Douglas and McIntyre, 1984.

Taylor, J. Garth, *Canoe Construction in a Cree Cultural Tradition.* Ottawa: National Museums of Canada, 1980.

Tyrrell, James W., *Coast and Harbour Surveys in Hudson Bay and Strait.* Toronto: C. Blackett Robinson, 1980.

Wylie, Liz, *In the Wilds: Canoeing and Canadian Art.* Kleinburg: McMichael, 1998.

Zimmerly, David W., *Oajaq: Kayaks of Siberia and Alaska.* Juneau: Division of State Museums, 1986.

Zoltvany, Yves, ed., *The French Tradition in North America.* Columbia: University of South Carolina Press, 1969.

VISUAL ACKNOWLEDGEMENTS

FRONT COVER:
Early Morning on the French River (canoe from a Temagami outfitter). Photographer: Toni Harting.

BACK COVER:
Top: High water on the French River. © Artist, Neil Broadfoot. Lower left: Nootka whaling dugout. Photographer Michael Cullen. Lower right: Western Arctic baidarka model. Photographer David Rankin.

PREFACE:
Montreal canoe. Credit: *Peterborough Examiner*.

DEDICATION:
Bill Mason. Credit: Paul Mason.

FOREWORD:
Fall paddle. Credit: Toni Harting.

1. THE CANADIAN CANOE MUSEUM AND CANADA'S NATIONAL SYMBOL (JOHN JENNINGS)
p. 3 Haida Canoe. Credit: Michael Cullen.
p. 4 The *Black Canoe*. Credit: John Jennings.
p. 11 William Walker. Credit: Per Trige Johei.
p.14 Canoe bow "Oro." Credit: Skip Deane.

2. BEING THERE: BILL MASON AND THE CANADIAN CANOEING TRADITION (JAMES RAFFAN)
p. 16 Bill Mason. Credit: John Jennings.
p. 18 Pierre Elliott Trudeau. Credit: Ray Webber.
p. 23 Tom Thomson. Credit: Ontario Archives, Toronto.
p. 26 Grey Owl. Credit: Ontario Archives, Toronto.

3. EXTREMELY CRANKY CRAFT: THE JAMES W. TYRELL KAYAK,
BIG ISLAND, HUDSON STRAIT (KENNETH LISTER)
p. 32 Views of Tyrell kayaks. Credit: Heritage Toronto.
p. 34 Map of Observation Stations. Credit: Kenneth Lister.
p. 35 Tyrell. Credit: Royal Ontario Museum, Toronto, Canada.
p. 39 Chart. Credit: Kenneth Lister.
p. 41 Drawings of Kayak. Credit: Kenneth Lister.

4. BARKLESS BARQUES (EUGENE ARIMA)
p. 46 Inuit umiak. Credit: Geological Survey of Canada
p. 47 Sketch of umiak. Credit: Borguras 1904-09: (128 Fig. 44)
p. 49 Sketch of Kayak rib. Credit: Gronnow, 1998
p. 51 Kayak models. Credit: From the top and left to right, Zimmerly 1986. 3; Arutyunou et
       al: 344; op. cit. plate 83 no. 5; Ibid.no.4; Canadian Museum of Civilization Wa-Pi-2-29.15;
       Ford 1959: 157.)
p. 54 Aleut design relations: Credit: Eugene Arima

5. THE DAO OF PADDLING (BERT HORWOOD)
p. 64 Sketch of tai ji diagram. Credit: Bert Horwood
p. 66 Canoe contours. Credit: Bert Horwood
p. 73 Logo of Canexus I. Credit: Bert Horwood

6. TRADITIONAL LONGBOATS OF ASIA PACIFIC (ADRIAN LEE)
p. 75 Dragon boat race. Credit: Kirk Wipper.
p. 85 Two teams, Tapei. Credit: Kirk Whipper.
p. 87 Team practice, Toronto. Credit: Kirk Wipper.

7. THE CANOT DU MAÎTRE - MASTER OF THE INLAND SEAS
(PETER LABOR).
p. 94 Bowhead design. Credit: John Jennings.
p. 96 Alexander Mackenzie voyage. Credit: Peter Labor.
p. 98 On Peace River. Credit: Peter Labor.

8. MANUFACTURE OF BIRCH BARK CANOES FOR THE FUR TRADE
IN THE ST. LAWRENCE (TIMOTHY KENT)
p. 103 Map of Native and French settlements. Credit: Timothy Kent.
p. 108 Map of birch tree route. Credit: After Brisbin and Sonderman.
p. 109 Kahnawake, 1752. Credit: After Franquet.
p. 116 Quebec Canoe. Credit: Richard Nash.
p. 126 Royal Canoe. Credit: Timothy Kent.
p. 139 Map-Region of Domaine du Roi. Credit: Timothy Kent.

9. THE REPRESENTATION OF ABORIGINAL CULTURE WITHIN THE
CANADIAN CANOE MUSEUM (SHANNA BALAZS)
p. 146 Dugout canoe exhibit. Credit: Donald Rankin, Canadian Canoe Museum.

p. 149 William Commanda and drum. Credit: Canadian Canoe Museum.
p. 150 Birchbark exhibit. Credit: Donald Rankin, Canadian Canoe Museum.
p. 153 Kayak exhibit. Credit: Donald Rankin, Canadian Canoe Museum.
p. 158 Madeline Katt (Theriault) Credit: Ontario Archives, No. 12564.
p. 160 Objibwaw canoe headboard. Credit: Timothy Kent.

10. CANADIANS AND THE CANADIAN CANOE IN THE OPENING OF THE AMERICAN MIDWEST (RALPH FRESE)

p. 163 Joilliet-Marquett expedition. Credit: Ralph Frese.
p. 165 La Salle expedition. Credit: Ralph Frese.
p. 168 Bell of the West. Credit: Ralph Frese.
p. 169 Menard House. Credit: Ralph Frese.
p. 172 Fort de Chartres. Credit: Ralph Frese.

11. PADDLING VOICES: THERE'S THE POET, VOYAGEUR AND EXPLORER IN ALL OF US (ALLISTER THOMAS)

p. 177 Stillness, an Alberta river. Credit: Canadian Recreational Canoeing Association.
p. 179 Canoe, landscape. Credit: Alister Thomas.
p. 180 George River. Credit: Gino Bergeron.
p. 181 Canoe in whitewater. Credit: Alister Thomas.
p. 182 Canoes on shore. Credit: Canadian Recreational Canoeing Association.
p. 183 Kayak, Alsek River. Credit. Ken Madsen.

12. THE CANOE AS A WAY TO ANOTHER STORY (BOB HENDERSON)

p. 187 Guitar player. Credit: Bob Henderson.
p. 189 Journal writing. Credit: Bob Henderson.
p. 197 Individual. Credit: Bob Henderson.
p. 198 Group shot. Credit: Bob Henderson.

13. HISTORIC CANOE ROUTES OF THE FRENCH RIVER (TONI HARTING)

p. 200 Map 1: French River system. Credit: Toni Harting
p. 201 North canoe in rapids. Credit: Toni Harting
p. 203 Map 2: Chaudière area. Credit: Toni Harting
p. 204 Map 3: Five Mile Rapids area. Credit: Toni Harting
p. 205 Map 4: Main Outlet, French River. Credit: Toni Harting
p. 206 Map 5: Western Outlets, French River. Credit: Toni Harting
p. 210 Evening. Credit: Toni Harting

14. THE DARK SIDE OF THE CANOE (GWYNETH HOYLE)

p. 214 Jason and Starkell. Credit: Victoria Jason.
p. 218 Sevareid and Porter. Credit: Audubon Society, September, 1981.
p. 222 Cundy, Gordon-Dean and Challis. Credit: John Lentz.

15. SOME THOUGHTS ON THE ORIGINS OF THE CANOE (KIRK WIPPER)

p. 225 Kutenai canoe. Credit: Michael Cullen.

p. 226 Amur Valley canoe. Credit: Skip Deane.

p. 227 Welsh coracle. Credit: Skip Deane.

p. 228 Mandan bull boat. Credit: Skip Deane.

p. 229 Peterborough Canoe Co. factory. Credit: Canadian Canoe Museum.

p. 230 Canoe as wedding present. Credit: Canadian Canoe Museum.

16. CANOESCAPES AND THE CREATIVE SPIRIT (BECKY MASON)

p. 234 Bill Mason. Credit: Bill Mason Productions Collection.

17. THE CANOE AS CHAPEAU: THE ROLE OF THE PORTAGE IN CANOE CULTURE. (BRUCE W. HODGINS)

p. 240 Carol and Bruce Hodgins. Credit: Carol Hodgins.

p. 244 French River. Credit: Ria Harting.

18. R.M. PATTERSON'S PADDLING PASSION (DAVID FINCH)

p. 250 Virginia Falls. Credit: R.M. Patterson.

p. 253 R.M. Patterson. Credit: David Finch.

INDEX

A

"A La Claire Fontaine," 97

Abenaki(s) (First Nation), 105, 117-120, 137, 138

Abenaki canoe, 138

Abitibi, Lake, 113

Abitibi River, 107

Aboriginal(s), 10, 144-154, 225, 226, 228, 231, 242, 245
- Indian(s), 101, 104, 105, 109, 115, 116, 119, 122, 141-143, 162, 164-166, 171, 173

Across the Sub-Arctics of Canada: A Journey of 3,200 miles by Canoe and Snowshoe Through the Hudson Bay Region, 31

Adams, Victor, 232

Adney, Edwin Tappan, 103

Akun Island, 55

Akun Island, *iqyav,* 55

Alaska, 46, 48, 90, 243
- West Alaska, 50
- Southwest Alaska, 52

Albany (NY), 122, 118

Albany River, 92, 154, 220

Alberta, 92, 154, 177, 226, 240, 248-250

Alderville (First Nation), 157

Aleut kayak (see kayak)

Aleut umiak (see umiak)

Aleutian Islands, 55

Aleuts, 48

Algonkin (First Nation), 62, 93, 104, 110-1112, 144, 115, 117, 138, 162

Algonkin (language), 123

Algonquin Park, 23, 24, 178

Alpine Club of Canada, 175

Alton (IL), 162

Alsek River, 182

Amazon River, 221

American Bottoms (flood plain), 166

American Colonies, 5

American Fur Company, 171

American Midwest (Corn Belt), 161, 162, 165, 168, 173, 174

American Revolution, 168

American West, 6

Amur River Valley, 225, 226

Anahareo (wife of Grey Owl), 242

Anima Nipissing, 243

Ancienne-Lorette (see Lorette)

Archer, Sheila, 177

Arctic (the), 31, 38, 44, 56, 81, 90, 221, 226, 241, 244

Arctic Circle, 70

Arctic Forests, The, 248

Arctic Ocean, 250

Arctic Ocean Kayak (see kayak),

Arima, Eugene, 43, 66

Arkansas River, 163

Ashe Inlet, 34, 36, 37

Ashouapmouchouan River, 139

Asia, 48, 50, 76, 82, 84, 86, 91

Asian *long zhou* (see dragonboat),

Asians, 76

Asia Pacific longboats, 81, 82, 91

Assembly of First Nations, 151

Assinaboine River, 243

Athabaska, Lake, 200

Athabaska (region), 113, 125, 241

Athabaska River, 247-249

Atlantic Ocean, 19

Atwood, Margaret, 22, 217

Au Sable (IL), 171

Audubon Society, 219

Auger:
- Charles (Charles Le Maître), 117, 118, 120, 122-124
- Charles Jr., 117, 118, 120, 123, 124
- Étienne, 117, 120, 124
- François, 117, 120, 124
- Michel, 117, 120, 124

Auger canoe yard, 117, 118, 121-124

Australia, 43, 44, 89

B

Back River, 221, 222

Baffin Island, 28

Baie St. Paul, 138, 141

baidarka (Aleutian sea kayak), 75

Baker Lake, 220

Balazs, Shanna, 144

Bangkok (Thailand), 81

Bangladesh, 87

Bank of England, 248

Barlow, Joel, 24

Barren Grounds of Northern Canada, The, 248
Barren Lands (the Barrens), 31, 215, 219, 220
Bastille prison, 40
Bay of Fundy, 243
Beacon Six, 215, 221
Bear Island (Temagami), 158
Beauport (PQ), 105
Beaver, The, 251
Beauharnois (official of New France), 101
Beçcancour (Seigneury), 102, 117-120
Beechy Lake, 222
Beijing, 83
Belaney, Archie (see Grey Owl)
Bell, Robert (Dr.), 34
Bell-Portage, 243
Bella Bella (Waglisa), 231
Bella Coola oolachen canoe, 61
Bella Coola River, 60
Belleville (IL), 171
Beothuk canoe, 226
Bering Sea kayakers, 51
Bering Strait, 43, 48, 50, 52, 76, 225
Bering Strait Kayak (see kayak)
Berton, Pierre, 13, 17
Bice, Ralph, 178
Big Island (Hudson Strait), 34, 36
Birnik Culture, 52
Birnik model (see kayak)
Black, Samuel, 251
Black Canoe: The Spirit of Haida Gwaii, The, 3, 4, 90
Black Robe, 232
Black Watch (Regiment), 173
Blackwood's Magazine, 251
Bloody Falls, 241
Blondela, Lieut., 59
Blondin, Jacques (Jacques Leclair or Leclerc), 120
Bodsworth, Fred, 186
Bonnet Plume Lake, 72, 180
Borneo, 87
Bourbonnais (IL), 171, 173
Bourgault, Gille, 232
Bow River, 247Bow Lake, 251
Bowron Lakes, 178
Boyer, Louis, 132, 135
Boyer and Hawley (HBC agents), 135
Brantford (ON), 151

British, the, 5, 7, 102, 104, 223
British Columbia, 182, 225, 251-253
British Columbia Provincial Museum, 60
British Empire, 33, 243
British period, 201
Broadback River, 241
Broadfoot, Neil, 231
Brown Canoe Co., 230
Bruce Bay (see French River)
Brûlé, Étienne, 18
Buddhism, 64, 88
Buffalo Head Horse Ranch, 251
Buffalo Head, The, 252
Buldir/Round Island, 55
bull boat,
 - Mandan bull boat, 226, 227
 - Plains bull boat, 44
Burma (see Myanmar)
Burning Hills, 71
Burns, Philip, 113, 114, 127-137
Butler, William (Sir), 248

C
CBC (see Canadian Broadcasting Corporation)
CMA (see Canadian Museum Association)
CMC (see Canadian Museum of Civilization)
Cadet, Joseph, 140, 141, 143
Cahokia (Illinois Country), 111, 167
Calgary (AB), 154, 177, 250-252
California, 60, 78
Call of the Wild, 248
Callières, Louis, 101
Cambodia, 87
Cameron, Agnes Deans, 18
Camp Kandalore, 10
Campbell, Joseph, 22
"Canadian" (canoe race),
Canadian Arctic, 29, 31
Canadian Broadcasting Corporation (CBC), 17, 252
Canadian Canoe Co., 230
Canadian Canoe Museum, 10-13, 80, 144-147, 149, 150, 153-160, 229, 230, 239, 241, 242, 245
 - Board of Trustees, 12, 155, 157, 159, 160

- Hall of Honour, 11, 149
- National Heritage Centre, 12
- Millenium Centre, 12
Canadian Department of Marine and
  Fisheries, 33
- Observation Stations, 33, 34
Canadian Embassy (Washington), 3
Canadian Geological Survey (see
  Geological Survey of Canada)
Canadian Heritage River System, 7
Canadian Museum of Civilization
  (CMC), 13, 43, 76, 80
Canadian Museums Association (CMA),
  151-154
Canadian Outrigger Racing Association, 78
Canadian Pacific Railway, 32, 127
Canadian Recreation Canoeing
  Association, 7
Canadian Rockies, 251
Canadian Shield, 5, 21, 24, 25, 176, 183, 199
Canadian West, 6, 7
Canexus I, 244
Canexus Conference (1988), 63, 73
Canexus Conference (1996), 63
"Canoe Irony: Symbol of Wilderness and
  Harbinger," 24
Canoe Lake (Algonquin Park), 23, 24
Canoe Trip, 20
Canoescapes, 15, 234, 235, 237
Canoeing with the Cree, 212
canot du maître (Montreal canoe), 92,
  93-95, 97-99, 124, 203, 242
canot du nord (North canoe), 94, 125, 126,
  130, 201, 231
Cape Britannia (Chantry Inlet), 221
Cape Flattery canoe(s), 59
Cape Krusenstern, 48
Caribou Inuit (see Inuit),
Carleton Place (ON), 242
Carman, Bliss, 20, 21
Caron (notary at Trois-Rivières), 122
Carr, Emily, 231
Cartier, Jacques, 18
Cascade Falls (Lake Superior), 236
Cass, Lewis (Governor), 170
Canghnawaga, 114
Challis, Robin, 222
Champlain, Samuel de, 5, 161
Champlain-Huron 1615 commemorative

trip, 242
Chandun serpent boat(s), 87, 88
Chantrey Inlet, 221
Chang, (Yangtze) River, 84
Chao Phraya River, 84
Chapelle, Howard, 101, 102
Chauchetiére, Fr. Claude, 107, 108
Chaudière Portage (see French River)
Chaudière Rapids (see French River)
Chemong Lake, 243
Chester, Phillip, 17
Chestnut Canoe Co., 230
Chestnut canoe(s), 247, 249, 251, 252
- Chestnut Ogilvie Special, 252
- Chestnut Prospector, 249
Chicago (IL), 165-167, 170, 171
Chicago Portage, 164, 165, 170, 171
Chicago Portage National Historic Site, 173
Chicago River, 170
China, 76, 77, 84-86, 218, 243
Chipewyan (First Nation), 241
- birchbark canoe, 17
Chukotka, 46, 50
Chukchi (People), 51
Church of the Immaculate Conception
  (Illinois), 168
Church of the Kaskaskius, 168
Churchill (MB), 32, 35, 179
Churchill River, 35, 177, 241
Ch'ü Yüan (Qu Yuan), 75
Cinq Mars, Jacques, 43
Clachan site (1250-1420 A.D.), 53
Clark, George Rogers, 168
Clearwater River, 240, 241
Coast Salish canoes, 60
Cockburn's boatyard (see Pembroke)
Cochrane (AB), 250
Cody, Buffalo Bill, 8
Cody's Wild West Show, 8
Collins, Henry B, 50
Colwell, F., 24
Columbia River, 228, 247
Columbia Woods (IL), 173
Colville, Alex, 231
Commanda, William, 149
Communist Revolution, 81
Complete Wilderness Paddler, The, 217
"Confessions of a Know-It-All or Why
  Take A Clinic," 176

Cook, James (Capt.), 59
Copper Inuit (see Inuit)
Coppermine River, 70, 180, 241
coracle, 44, 45, 48, 49
  - Iraqui *quffa* ferry, 45
  - Irish *curach* or curragh, 45, 226
  - Welsh coracle, 45, 227
Coupland, Douglas, 193
coureur de bois (coureurs du bois), 17-19
Cowichan, Lake, 252
Craig, Martha, 72
Crawford, Isabella Valancy, 20
Cree (First Nation), 220, 241
Creue Coeur (IL), 171
Crevier, Jean, 118
Crevier, Madeleine, 118
Csikszentmihalyi, M., 68
Cumberland Sound, 28
Cundy, Robert (Rob), 215, 221, 222
Curve Lake (First Nation), 157

D

D'Artaguette, Diron (Intendant of Illinois
  Country), 167
Dablon, Fr., 162, 164
Dahlberg, Anne, 177
Dalles Portage (see French River)
Dalles Rapids (see French River)
Daigremont (official of New France), 101
Dangerous River, The, 247, 248, 250, 251
Dao, 63, 67, 70, 72, 73
Daoism, 64
Daoist literature, 69
Daoist philosophy, 63, 65, 67
Davidson, James, 217
Day of the Longboat (UBC), 79
de Poncins, Gontran, 216
de Tonty, Henri, 166
de Troyes, Chevalier, 107
Dean, William, 230
Dease River, 252
Death on the Barrens, A., 213
Deliette, Pierre, 166
Delta (see French River)
Dene (First Nation), 241
Denonville (Governor of New France), 117
Denonville Campaign of 1687, 104
DesPlaines River (St. Louis River), 165, 173

Des Rivières, Beaubien, 113
Digby (NS), 17
Disko Bay (West Greenland), 49
Dogrib, birchbark canoe, 17
Dollier, — (French missionary), 100
Dolphin, 53
Domaine du Roi (Domain of the King),
  128, 138-140, 142, 143
Dongting, Lake (China), 84
Dowd, John, 77
dragon boat(s), 75-78, 84, 87
  - Asian *long zhou,* 74
  - peirun (Japan), 87
Dragon Boat Festival, 76, 77, 86
Dragon Boat Racing Council, 78
Drayton, Reginald, 229
Driediger, Ric, 180
Drinking River, 180
Duff, Wilson, 59, 60
dugout canoe(s), 21, 56, 58, 60, 61, 83, 84,
  90, 146, 163
  - Haida sea-going dugout, 2
  - Melanesian, Micronesian &
  Polynesian dugouts, 226
Du Guay, (Duque), Antoine, 118, 125, 128-
  134, 137
Du Guay canoe yard, 128, 129, 132, 133
Du Puis, Charles, 122
Dundas Street (Governor's Road, Upper
  Canada), 244
Dundurn Castle (Hamilton), 31, 37
Dutch, the, 118

E

Early Punuk wooden kayak (see kayak)
East Canadian Arctic Kayaks (see Kayak)
East Channel (see French River)
East Greenland, 50, 52
Eastern North American Native people
  (see First Nations)
Ecomarine Ocean Kayak Centre, 77
Edmonton (AB), 74
Edwards, Jonathan, 27
Eighteen Mile Island (see French River)
Ekven site, 50
Elk Lakes, 251
Emerson, Ralph Waldo, 27
"En Roulant Ma Boule," (folk song), 98

"En Voyans de l'Avant," (folk song), 98
England, 22, 78, 167, 227, 247-249
English, the (Englishmen), 5, 117, 228
English, William, 230
English Bay (see Vancouver)
Erie, Lake, 100, 165
Eskimo (see Inuit),
"Eskimo Hunter (New Style)," 28
Eurasia, 44, 45
Europe, 5, 15, 33, 243
European(s), 6, 56, 139, 199, 228
Expo, 86, 76, 77

F

FCRCC (see False Creek Racing Canoe
    Club)
Faille, Albert, 249, 250
Fallis, Glenn, 242
Falls of the Nahanni (see Virigina Falls)
False Creek (see Vancouver)
False Creek Racing Canoe Club
    (FCRCC), 78
Far North, the, 179
Far Pastures, 252
Fawcett, Brian, 197
Feast of the Hunter's Moon, 173
Feldman, Seth, 17
Fiji, 78
Finch, David, 247
Finkelstein, Max, 178
Finlay River, 252
Finlay's River, 252
Finlayson, Mr., 134
First Nations, 2, 6, 9, 80, 145, 149, 151, 153,
    157
    - Aboriginal People(s), 5, 11, 19, 144-
    152, 155-160, 199, 202, 228
    - First People(s), 1, 89
    - Native People(s), 1-3, 5, 6, 150, 152, 155
First People (see First Nations)
Fisher, Hugh (Dr.), 78
Five Mile Rapids (see French River)
Flat River, 250
Florida, 164
Forks of the Thames, 243
Fort Channel (see French River)
Fort Chipewyan, 200
Fort Crevecoeur, 166, 173

Fort Churchill, 35
Fort de Chartres (Illinois Country), 167,
    171-173
Fort Dearborn, 170
Fort Massac, 173
Fort McPherson, 243
Fort McMurray, 249
Fort Snelling, 170
Fort Simpson, 249
Fort Smith (NWT), 223
Fort St. Louis, 166
Fort William, 115, 121, 126, 243
Fort Yukon, 243
Forsyth, Richardson & Co. (NWC supply
    agent), 120
Forsyth, Robert, 170
Fox Indians, 101
Fox River, 162, 170
France, 140, 141, 143, 165-167, 173, 249
France, Denis, 249
Franks, Ned, 72
Franklin, John (Sir), 221
Franklin expedition, 218
Franquet, Louis, 106, 109, 110, 115, 116, 120,
    121
Fraser, Simon, 228
Fraser River, 60
Fredericton (NB), 230
Freire, Paulo, 185, 197
French, the (Frenchmen), 5, 6, 93, 100-
    102, 107, 110, 115, 117, 124, 137, 161, 166,
    170, 172, 173, 228
French and Indian War, 102
French Canadian(s), 6, 93, 137
French Empire, 243
French River, 92, 165, 177, 199, 200-203,
    208-211, 243, 244
    - Bruce Bay, 202
    - Chaudière Portage, 202, 203, 209
    - Chaudière Rapids, 202
    - Dalles Portage, 205
    - Dalles Rapids, 205, 208, 209
    - Delta, 209
    - East Channel, 206, 207
    - Eighteen Mile Island, 203, 204
    - Five Mile Rapids, 203, 204
    - Fort Channel, 208
    - La Dalle (the Trough or Gutter),
    206-208

- Little Dalles Rapids, 205
- Little Pine Rapids, 203
- Main Channel, 202, 203, 205, 208, 209
- Main Outlet, 205, 208, 209
- Old Voyageur Channel, 205-209
- Ox Bay, 205
- Palmer Rocks, 206, 207
- Petite Faucille (Little Sickle), 206-208
- Portage Bay, 202
- Portage Channel and Dam, 202
- Recollet Falls, 200, 203, 204, 205
- Recollet Portage, 205
- Rock Circus, 206, 207
- Wanapitei Bay, 205, 206, 209
- West Cross Channel, 208
- Western Channel, 205, 206
- Western Outlets, 205, 206, 209
French settlements, 102
Frese, Ralph, 161, 163
Frobisher, Mr. (a NWC supply partner), 120
Frye, Northrop, 19, 22

G

Gagnon, Clarence, 231
Gale, Edwin, 171
Galinée, — (French missionary), 100
Gamelin, Ignace, 121, 122
Gambel archaeological site (Saint
    Lawrence Island), 50
- Old Gambel, 53
Gates, Harold, 230
Gathering on the Theatiki, 173
gatwaat (see Umiak)
Gaucher, Mr. (dit Gamelin) (see Ignace
    Gamelin)
Generation X, 193
Geological Survey of Canada, 34, 45, 221
George River (West Quebec), 179, 180
Georgian Bay, 92, 162, 199, 202, 205, 208, 243
Gergeron, Gino, 179
Germany, 78
Ghost River, 250
Giasson, Jacques, 125
Gibson, Dan, 24
Glenbow Foundation, 252
Glenbow Museum, 147, 150, 154
Glooskap (mik'maq), 17

God's Lake, 218
God's River, 219
Golden Lake Reserve, 62
Gordon, A.R. (Lieut.), 34
Gordon Thomas, 230
Gordon-Dean, David, 222
Gore's Landing (ON), 229
Gough, Noel, 195
Grand Kankakee Marsh Country Park,
    173
Grand Portage, 92, 93, 113, 243
"Grassy Lake Carry," (James Bay-Arctic
    watershed), 241
Great Lakes, 5, 92, 100, 122, 127, 161, 164,
    199, 243
Gramsci, —, 185
Greenway, Robert, 184
Green Bay (MI), 161, 162, 164, 170
Grey Owl (Archie Belaney), 18, 24-26, 69,
    242
Grey Owl, 232
Greenland, 46, 47
Greenland Inuit (see Inuit)
Greenland Kayaks (see kayak)
Griffin, 166
Grinnell, George, 213
Groseilliers, Médard Chouart Sieur des, 18
Group of Seven, 9, 17
Guinness Book of Records, 221
Gulf of St. Lawrence, 33, 140
Guizhou province (China), 84

H

HACC (see Hide-Away Canoe Club)
HBC (see Hudson's Bay Company)
Haida (First Nation), 58, 146
Haida canoe, 59
Haida sea-going canoe (dugout), 3
Haliburton (ON),
Haliburton region, 10
Halifax (NS), 74
Hall of Honour (see Canadian Canoe
    Museum)
Hamilton (ON), 31, 35, 37
    - hangard du Roi (King's canoe
    shed), 110
Hardesty, Richard, 131

Harp Lake, 178
Hart, Aaron, 120
Harting, Toni, 199, 244
Hawaii, 78
Hawaii Maritime Museum, 80
Hawaiians, 76
Hayes River, 228
"Head" canoe (war canoe), 58-60
Hearne, Samuel, 241
Heming, Arthur, 231
Henderson, Bob, 65, 183
Henry, Alexander (the Elder), 112
Herald, Daniel, 229, 230
"Herald Canoe," 229
Heritage River System (see Canadian
    Heritage River System)
Hery, Sieur, 122
Highwood River, 251
Highwood Valley, 251
"Hiawatha," 17
Hiawatha (First Nation), 157, 158
Hide-Away Canoe Club, 175
Hodgins, Bruce W., 67, 176, 239, 240
Hodgins, Carol, 176, 240
Hodgins, Shawn, 180
Holm, Bill, 59
Hong Kong, 75, 84
Hong Kong Tourist Association, 86
Honolulu (HA), 80
Hopkins, Edward, 113, 114, 130
Hopkins, Frances Anne, 17, 94, 113, 231
Hornby, John, 219
Hornell, James, 43, 44, 45, 83
Horton Lake, 70
Horton River, 70, 71
Horton Valley, 70
Horwood, Bert, 22, 62
Houdin, Mssr., 140
House of Commons (Canada), 33
Hoyle, Gwyneth, 178, 212
Hubbard, Gurdon Saltonstall, 170
Hubbard, Mina, 17
Hudson (ON), 35
Hudson Bay, 32-35, 124, 126, 179, 218, 219,
    221, 241, 243, 250
Hudson Bay kayak (see kayak)
Hudson River, 112
Hudson Strait, 31-34, 36, 40, 41

Hudson's Bay Company (HBC), 6, 33, 107,
    113, 124-129, 131, 133-135, 139, 202, 204, 251
Hudson's Bay Expedition, 33, 34
Hudson's Bay House, 113
Hudson's Bay Records Society, 251
Hull (PQ), 243
Hunters of the Great North, 248
Huron(s) (First Nation), 104-106, 111
Huron, Lake, 92, 100, 105, 117, 127, 165, 204

I

Iceland, 45, 227
Ievoghiyoq site, 51
Igloolik Inuit (see Inuit),
Ile aux Coudres, 138, 140
Ile aux Tourtes, 110
Ile d'Orléans, 105
Iles Jeremie (fur trading post), 139-142
Illes-t-noir, 119
Illini (Illiniwek) (First Nation), 171
Illini (language), 163
Illinois (brig), 171
Illinois Country, 111, 119, 165-173
Illinois (Prairie State), 167-171
Illinois River, 164, 166, 168, 171
Illustrated London News, 114
Imperial Navy of Thailand, 88
Impossible Dream, 231
In the North of Our Lives, 213, 219
India, 45, 84, 87, 218, 228
*Indians Settle at La Prairie de la Magdeleine
    Alongside the French, The,* 107
Indonesia, 84, 87
Inuit, 29-31, 36, 38, 45, 46, 52, 179, 241
    - Caribou Inuit, 30, 53
    - Copper Inuit, 53
    - Eskimo(s), 48, 51, 60
    - Greenland Inuit, 48
    - Igloolik Inuit, 53
    - Nattilik Inuit, 53
Inland Chikchi Kayak (see Kayak)
Inle, Lake (Myanmar), 84
Innis, Harold, 21
"Into the Heart of Africa," 147
Into the Whirlwind, 223
Iowa River, 162
Iraqui *quffa* ferry (see coracle)

Ireland, 44, 229
Irish *curach* (curragh) (see coracle)
Iroquois (First Nation), 102, 104-114, 117,
    118, 130-132, 165
Islands of the Four Mountains, 55
Isle a la Cache Rendezvous, 173

J

j-stroke (canoeing), 25, 75
Jade Canoe, 90
James, William C., 22
James Bay, 34, 107, 113, 241
Japan, 86
Jason, Victoria, 213-215, 221
Jefferys, C.W., 17, 231
Jefferson Barracks, 170
Jennings, John, 1, 159
Jeune-Lorette (see Lorette)
Jesuit(s), 108-110, 161, 162, 167
Jesuit Relations, 164
Jochelson illustrations (umiak), 54
Johnson, E. Pauline, 20, 232
Johnson, William (Sir), 104
Joliet (IL), 171
Jolliet, Adrien, 162, 165
Jolliet, Louis (Sieur), 5, 161-165, 174
Jolliet, Zacharie, 162
Journal from the Enterance (sic) *of the
    French River*, 201
*Journal of a Voyage from Rocky Mountain
    Portage in Peace River to the Sources of
    Finlays Branch and North West Ward
    in Summer 1924, A*, 251
Jutras, Joseph, 124

K

Kablouna, 216
Kablouna in the Yellow Kayak, 213
Kahnawake (La Prairie de la Madelaine,
    Sault St. Louis), 102, 106-110, 112, 113,
    115, 124
Kalm, Peter, 140
Kamchatka, 45, 48
Kanawa Collection, 11
Kanawa International Museum of
    Canoes, Kayaks, and Rowing Craft,
    10, 80, 229

Kane, Paul, 58, 231
Kanesatake (Oka), 102, 110, 112, 243
Kankakee River, 173
Katt, Madeleine (see Madeline Katt
    Theriault)
kayak(s), 2, 7, 10, 10, 29-32, 36-42, 48-56,
    76-78, 153, 221, 222, 224
    -Aleut kayak, 47, 53-55, 60
    - Arctic (Ocean) kayak, 31, 39, 153
    - Bering Strait kayak, 47, 52
    - Birnik kayak model, 51
    - Early Punuk wooden kayak, 50, 51
    - East Canadian Arctic kayak(s), 48,
    50, 52, 53
    - Greenland kayak(s), 52, 53
    - Hudson Bay kayak, 40, 41
    - Hudson Strait kayak, 31
    -Inland Chukchi kayak, 50
    - King Island kayak, 50
    - Kodiak kayak, 55
    - Koryak kayak, 49, 54
    - Maritime Chukchi kayak, 51
    - Old Bering Sea model, 50, 51
    - Punuk kayak, 51, 52
    - Seklowaghyaget model, 52
    - St. Lawrence Island kayak, 45
    - Thule kayak, 51, 53
    - Unalaska Aleut kayak, 55
    - West Alaskan kayak(s), 52
Karok (First Nation), 60
Kaskaskias (First Nation), 168
Kaskaskias (IL), 168
Kaskaskia Island, 168
Kaskaskia River, 168, 169
Kelly, M.T., 223
Keith, James, 127
Kent, Timothy, 100
Kerla State (India), 88
Kesting, Stephen, 179
Khmer Rouge Regime, 82
King of France, 100, 101
King's Domain (see Domaine du Roi)
King's Posts (French trading posts), 139
Kinzie, John, 170
Klondike River, 32
Kodiak Island, 47, 55
Kodiak Kayak (see kayak)
Kootenay River, 182, 247
Kootenay Valley, 225

Koryak *gatwaat* (see coracle)
Korukin's scale framework drawing, 54
Kotzebue Sound, 48
Krieghoff, Cornelius, 231
Kuskokwim delta dragon, 52
Kuskokwim-Nunivak Island, 46
Kuskokwim River, 52
Kutenai pine bark canoe, 225
Kwakiutl (Kwakwaka'wakw) war canoe, 58

L

L'Assomption (seigneury), 125
L'erable (IL), 171
"La Chasse Galerie," 17, 97
La Dalle (The Trough or Gutter) (see
    French River)
"La Guianne," 170
La Malabie (see Malabie Post)
La Prairie de la Madeleine (Kanawake),
    102, 106, 108
la Perouse, —, 59
La Petite Rivière St. François Xavier, 141, 142
La Salle, René-Robert Cavelier de, 5, 100,
    117, 166, 168, 173
La Salle expedition, 165
La Tuque, 131
La Vase portage (North Bay), 243
La Vérendrye, Pierre Gaultier de
    Varennes et de, 5, 122
Labrador, 34, 178
Lac des Deux Montagnes (Oka), 102, 110-
    112, 114, 243
Lac St. Jean, 139
Lac St. Pierre, 101, 120, 124, 127, 129, 133, 137
Lachine (Quebec), 92, 102, 106, 111, 112,
    114, 119, 123, 126-130, 133-136, 202, 243
Lachine Rapids, 5
Labor, Peter, 92
Lady Evelyn River, 176, 241
Lake of the Woods, 34
Lakefield Canoe Co., 230
Lamarque, M., 122
Lampman, Archibald, 20
Lancang (Mekong) River, 84
Landscape and Memory, 9
Laos, 87
Last of the Mohicans, 232
Laughlin, William (Prof.), 48, 55

Laurentian Mountains, 62
Leclerc, Antoine, 119
Leduchat, Capitaine, 106
Leechman, Douglas (Dr.), 252
LeBeau, Claude, 105, 106
Leclair, Jacques (dit Blondin) (see Jacques
    Blondin)
LePan, Douglas, 20
Le Maître: 93, 115, 118, 119, 124
    - Charles (dit Auger) (see Charles
      Auger)
    - Joseph, 118
    - Joseph (grandson of Louis), 124
    - Louis, 115, 117-122, 124, 125
    - Louis Jr., 120, 124
    - Marie, 119
    - Pierre (dit Lottinville) (see Pierre
      Lottinville)
Le Maître canoe yard, 115, 118, 121
Lemaître, Joseph (Dr.), 122
Lee, Adrian, 74
Les Éboulements, 140-143
Liard River, 247, 249, 252
Liberty Bell of the West, 168
Lister, Kenneth, 28
Little Dalles Rapids (see French River)
Little Pine Rapids (see French River)
Lituya Bay, 59
London, Jack, 248
London (ON), 244
London (UK), 124, 127, 221, 248
Long, John, 123, 124
longboat(s), 74, 78, 80, 82, 83, 87
    - *long chuan, (lung syhun),* 83
    - *long zhou, (lung jiau),* 83
Longfellow, Henry W., 17, 18, 232
Lorette (PQ), 102, 105, 106, 124
    - Ancienne-Lorette, 105
    -Jeune-Lorette, 105
Lottinville, Pierre (Pierre Le Maître), 118-
    120, 124
    - Pierre (Jr.), 124
    - Jacques (Jr.) 120
    - Jacques (Sr.), 124
Louis XV, 168, 171
Louise, Lake, 251
Louiseville (Rivière du Loup), 117-120,
    122-124
Louisiana, 167

Low, A.P., 45
"Low Tide on Grande Pré," 21
Lowie Museum, 44
Lubicon Lake Cree (First Nation), 150, 151
Lubicon land claim, 151
Luu Tas (Wave Eater), (Bill Reid), 2, 77, 80, 146
Lyon, G.F. (Capt.), 40

M

Macdonald, Jock (J.E.H.), 24
Macdonnel, John, 111
Mackenzie, Alexander (Sir), 11, 96, 201, 228
Mackenzie River, 32, 70, 241, 247, 249, 252
Mackintosh, Angus, 201, 208
MacLennan, Hugh, 21, 95
MacNab, Allan (Sir), 31, 37
Main Channel (see French River)
Main Outlet (see French River)
Main River, 180
Maine, 32
Maitland, Garden & Auldjo Co. (HBC supply agents), 125
Makah (First Nation), 147
Malabar (Kerala State of India), 84
Malaysia, 84, 85, 87
Malbaie Post (La Malabie), 139, 140, 142
Malecite canoe, 18
Mandan bullboat (see bullboat)
Mandan (First Nation), 227
Manitoba, 26, 32, 154
Manitoba Museum, 154
Manitoulin Island, 17
Manka canoe, 58-60
Maori (of New Zealand), 76, 89
Marchesseaux M. (merchant), 119
Marine Museum of Upper Canada (Toronto), 30, 31, 37
Maritime Chukchi Kayak (see kayak)
Maritimes, 243
Marois, Pierre, 134-137
Marquette, Fr. Jacques, 5, 162-164, 168
Marsh, George, 239
Mason, Becky, 233, 241
Mason, Bill, 1, 15-18, 24-27, 68, 80, 181, 231-234, 238, 241, 242
Mason, Michael H., 248
Mason, Paul, 179
Masson, Sheena, 176

Matisse, M. (missionary), 122
Mattawa (ON), 127, 138
Mattawa River, 92, 202, 243
Matthews, Gordon, 250
McBride, Charlton, 229
McBride, William, 229
McCully, Laura E., 20
McTavish, Frobisher & Co. (NWC supply agent), 120, 124
Meech Lake, 236
Melanesian dugout (see dugout)
Mènard, François, 118
Menard, Pierre, 169
Menominee (First Nation), 170
Meramec River, 167
Merrick, Elliott, 216
Merton, Thomas, 72, 73
Methye Portage (N. Saskatchewan), 241, 243
Métis, 6, 12, 93, 137, 157, 223, 243
Miao ethnic minority (China), 84
Michigan, Lake, 101, 161, 162, 164
Michilimackinac (Fort), 112, 118, 119, 171
Micronesian dugout (see dugout)
Mik'maq (First Nation), 94, 142
Mik'maq portage route, 243
Miles, Robert Seaborne, 202
Millennium Centre (see Canadian Canoe Museum)
Minneapolis (MN), 218
Minneapolis Star, 218, 219
Minnesota, 170
Minnesota River, 169
Mississauga (ON), 2
Mississippi River (ON), 242
Mississippi River (US), 5, 117, 161, 162, 164-170, 173
Missouri, 167
Missouri River, 163, 167, 227
Mitassini, Lake, 139
Miyowagh midden site, 50, 51
Mobile (AL), 167, 168
Moffatt, Arthur, 220, 221
Mohawk(s) (First Nation), 106, 107
Mohawk (language), 111
Moisie River, 138
Mongolia, 225
Monière, Alexis, 118, 121-123
Mont Royal, 110
Montagnais (First Nation), 104, 114, 139, 140, 142, 179

Montana, 226
Montreal (Quebec), 32, 93, 100-104, 106, 107, 110, 111, 113, 114, 117-127, 130, 133-135, 138, 169-171, 174, 200, 203, 222, 223, 243
Montreal canoe (see canot du maître)
Montreal Island, 92, 102, 107, 110, 112
Montreal River, 241
Moodie, Susanna, 18
Moose Factory (ON), 17
Moose Fort, 113
"Morning on the Lièvres," 20
Morse, Eric, 18, 24, 201, 243
Morse, Pamela, 18, 243
Morton, W. L., 21
Mounties (see Royal Canadian Mounted Police)
Muir, John, 26, 27
Museum of Anthropology (Vancouver), 76, 77, 81
Muskoka Lake, 79
Myanmar (formerly Burma), 84, 87, 88

N

NFB (see National Film Board)
NWC (see North West Company)
NWT (see Northwest Territories)
Naess, Arne, 190
Nahanni people, 248
Nahanni River, 219
Nanabozho (Algonkian), 17
Naskapis (First Nation), 179
National Film Board (NFB), 15
National Heritage Centre (see Canadian Canoe Museum),
Native People(s) (see First Nation),
Native Studies (Trent University), 10
Nattilik Inuit (see Inuit)
Neanderthals, 44
Neel, David, 146
Nelson, Edward, 50
Nelson River, 35
Nemiscou, Lake, 241
New Brunswick, 32, 230, 243
New England, 117, 118
New France, 5, 6, 101, 112, 115, 138, 140, 141, 161, 172
New Guinea, 43
New Orleans (LA), 167, 169, 170
New World, 44

New York (NY), 85
New York State, 78, 107
New Zealand, 76, 77, 80, 89
Newfoundland, 32, 180, 226
Niagara Falls, 165
Nicks, Trudy (Dr.), 153
Nicolet (Quebec), 119
nigilax (see Umiak)
Nipigon River, 241
Nipissing, Lake, 92, 199, 202, 209
Nipissing(s) (First Nation), 110, 111, 117
Nootka canoe (Southern), 58-60
Normandy, 167
Norment, Christopher, 213, 219
North, the (Canada), 9, 56, 176, 178, 223, 248
North Alaska, 52
North America, 2, 10, 27, 31, 64, 78, 89, 126, 138, 165, 171, 172, 200, 225
North Bay (ON), 243
North canoe (see canot du nord)
Northern canoe, 59
Northern River (Tom Thomson), 23
North West Company (NWC), 6, 111, 113, 118, 120, 125, 126, 128, 139, 208
North West Mounted Police, 7, 228
Northwest Coast culture area, 56
Northwest Coast war canoes, 57, 58, 74
Northwest Passage, 40
Northwest Territories (NWT), 70, 177, 180, 243, 249
Norway House (HBC), 167
Nova Scotia, 176, 243
Nouvel, Father, 117
Nunivak Island, 52

O

O'Dette Canoe Company, 230
Observation Stations (See Canadian Department of Marine and Fisheries),
Oceania, 80, 81, 89
Odanak (St. François du Lac), 117
Ohio Country, 100
Ohio River, 163, 173
Ohio Valley, 5
Objibwa (First Nations), 138
Ojibwa (language), 123
Oka (Lac des Deux Montagnes, Kanesatake), 102, 104, 110-114, 119, 124

Okhost Sea, 48
Okikendawt Island, 202
Okvik-Old Bering Sea Culture, 50
Old Bering Sea model (see kayak)
"Old Canoe, The," 239
Old Gambel (see Gambel archaeological
    site)
Old Crow River, 243
Old Voyageur Channel (see French River)
Old Whaling Culture (1800-1500 B.C.), 48
Old Woman Bay (Lake Superior), 238
Old Woman Bay,, Morning Mist, 237
Olson, Sigurd, 18, 24, 231
Onam festivities (Kerala), 88
Oneida (First Nation), 107
Ontario, 32, 34, 154, 199
Ontario Lake, 100, 104, 107, 244
Otonabee Region Conservation
    Authority, 12
Otonabee River, 242
Ottawa (First Nation), 165
Oregon, 78
Ottawa River, 62, 92, 102, 107, 110-114, 116,
    126-128, 162, 179, 199, 202, 241, 243
Ottawa Valley, 102, 116, 126, 137, 138, 243
Outboard Marine Coporation, 12
Outrigger canoe, 75, 77, 78, 89
    - Luli pau, 75
    - Polynesian va'a, 74, 89
Outward Bound, 219
Ox Bay (see French River)
Oxford-Cambridge collegiate boat race, 78
Oyukuluk, Andrew, 30

P

Pacific (Ocean), 19, 45, 74, 75, 80, 81, 90,
    228
Pacific Rim, 7, 80, 89
Paddle to the Arctic, 215
Paddle to the Sea, 232
Palace Museum (Beijing), 83
Palmer Rocks (see French River)
Panadis, Nicolas, 138
Papineau (IL), 171
Paris (France), 140
"Path of the Paddle," (series), 15, 68
Path of the Paddle, 15, 181
Patterson, Alan, 251
Patterson, Henry Foote, 247
Patterson, Raymond Murray (R.M.),

247-253
Peace River, 92, 98, 247, 251, 252
Peake, Michael, 175
Pedagogy of the Oppressed, 185
Pelly, David F., 178
Pembroke (ON), 62
    - Cockburn's boat yard, 62
Pengelly, William, 230
Penshina Bay, 49
Peoria (IL), 166, 167, 173
Peoria Indians (First Nation), 162
Perrault, Jean Baptiste, 111, 118
Petawawa Gorges (Tom Thomson), 23
Peterborough (ON), 10-12, 14, 80, 154, 178,
    229, 230, 242, 243
Peterborough Canoe Co., 229, 230
Peterborough (canvas and cedar strip)
    canoe(s), 80, 236, 244
Peterborough Centennial Museum and
    Archives, 154
Petersen, H.C., 48
Petit Lac St. Paul, 120
Petite Faucille (Little Sickle) (see French
    River)
Phillipines, 85
Pierre Menard House, 169
Pike, Warburton, 248
Place Portage (Ottawa River), 243
Plains bull boat (see bull boat)
Plains country, 5
Plains (First Nation), 2, 145
Plan of the Fort of Sault St. Louis, with the
    Iroquois Indian village, 109
Plateau culture area, 56
Pocaterra, George, 251, 252
Pointe au Gravois, 111
Pointe du Lac, 102, 114-117
Pointers, The (Tom Thomson), 23
Poliquin, Sophie, 136
Polynesian dugout (see dugout)
Polynesian va'a (see outrigger canoe)
Pond, Peter, 169
Pontchartrain (minister to King of
    France), 101
Pontiac (Chief), 173
Port, Walter, 218, 219
Portman, Marigold, 250, 251
Portage Bay (see French River)
Portage Channel and Dam (see French
    River)

Portage Place (Trent-Severn), 243
Post Oviatenon (Illinois Country), 167, 173
Prairie du Chien (Illinois Country), 169
Prairie du Rocher (IL), 167, 171
Prairie State (see Illinois)
Pratt, Mary, 212
Precambrian Reflections, 235
"Preserving Our Heritage: A Working
    Conference Between Museums and
    First Nations," 151
Prince Albert (AB), 35
Prince of Wales (1860), 114
Pukaskwa River, 234
Punuk Culture, 46, 50
Punuk kayak (see kayak)
Punuk people, 52
Purdy, Al, 28, 29

Q

Qeqertasossuk site, 49
Qing Shui river valley (China), 84
Quaife, Milo, 164
Quatuwas (the gathering), 231
Quebec, 6, 46, 232, 236
Quebec canoe, 116
Quebec City, 102-106, 117, 124, 126, 1?41,
    162, 164, 165, 167
Quebec City's Winter Carnival, 79
Queen's University, 63
Québècois, 9, 17
Quetico, 233
Quetico Park, 177
Qwi:stox (canoeing teacher), 57

R

RCMP (see Royal Canadian Mounted
    Police)
Radisson, Pierre-Esprit, 18
Raffan, James (Jim), 15, 67-69, 71, 175, 242
Rainy Lake, 113, 121
Randolph County (Illinois), 167
Rat Portage, 243
Recollet Falls (Sault au Recollet) (see
    French River)
Recollet Portage (see French River)
Red River, 243
Red Squirrel Falls Portage, 243
Redmond, Kevin, 180

Reid, Bill, 2, 3, 75, 77, 80, 90, 146
Relation, 106
Remington, Frederic, 8
Renault (IL), 171
Rice Lake, 229
Rice Lake Canoe Co., 230
Rich, E. E., 251
Richelieu River, 112
Rideau Canal, 17
Rideau River, 18
Riding Mountain National Park, 26
river canoes, 61
Riverin, Denis, 101
Rivière du Loup (Louiseville), 117, 122, 123
Rivières des Prairies, 110
Robertson, Colin, 113, 125
Robinson, Michael, 231
Rock Circus (see French River)
Rocks and Rock Minerals, (Pirsson), 248
Rocky Mountains, 5, 32
Rogers Rangers, 118
Roosevelt, Theodore, 8
Rose Marie, 232
Royal Barges of Thailand, 83, 88
Royal Barges Museum (Thailand), 81
Royal Canadian Mounted Police
    (RCMP), 228
- Mounties, 9
Royal canoe, 126
Royal Marines (UK), 221-223
Royal OntarioMuseum, 80, 147, 151
Rugge, John, 217
Rupert's Land, 241
Rupert River, 241

S

SAS (see Special Air Service)
S.S. Alert, 34
S.S. Neptune, 34
St. Ange, Commandant of Fort de
    Chartres, 173
St. Anne (Illinois Country), 167
St. Brendan's voyage, 45
St. Clair, Lake, 165
St. François du Lac (Odanak), 102- 117-
    119, 122, 124, 125, 128, 132, 133, 137, 138
St. François River, 117
St. Genevieve (Illinois Country), 167
St. Ignace (Jesuit mission), 162

St. Jean Port-Joli (Quebec), 232
St. Lawrence River, 79, 100-108, 110, 114,
    116-118, 120, 124-126, 128-130, 133, 137-
    142, 161, 165, 166
St. Lawrence settlements, 101, 120, 125, 128,
    137,
St. Lawrence Valley, 100-102, 103, 105, 106,
    116, 117, 125-129, 134, 137, 138
St. Louis (IL), 166, 168, 170
St. Louis River (see Desplaines River)
St. Phillipe (Illinois Country), 167
St. Regis, 113
St. Maurice district, 127
St. Maurice River, 104, 113, 114, 128-132,
    134-137
St. Maurice voyageurs (brigade), 131-134
Ste. Anne, 110, 112
Ste. Marie-Among-the-Hurons, 242
Saguenay River, 104, 139, 241
Saint Genevieve (IL), 173
Saint Lawrence Island, 50, 53
Saint Lawrence Island Kayak (see kayak)
Saint (St.) Maurice canoes, 132-135, 137
Salish (First Nation), 60
Santo Domingo, 167
Saqqaq Culture (West Greenland), 49
Sartre, Jean-Paul, 37
Saskatchewan, 32, 177, 240
Saskatchewan River, 35
Sault au Recollet (Recollet Falls), 110
Sault Ste. Marie (ON), 92, 162, 164
Sault St. Louis (Kanawake), 102, 106
Seal River, 179
Seklowaghyaget model (see kayak)
Seklowaghyaget site, 52
Self, Basil, 232
Senecas, (First Nations), 104
Sept Iles, 138, 139, 142
Seton, Ernest Thompson, 18
Sevareid, Eric, 212, 218, 219
Seven Rivers of Canada, 95
Severn River, 242
Schama, Simon, 9, 24, 25
Schoolcraft, Henry R., 17
Schumacher, E. F., 185
Scots, 6
Scott, Duncan Campbell, 20
Sharp Rock portage (Temagami), 243
Shefferville (PQ), 179
Shell Canada, 150

Shield country (see Canadian Shield)
Shields, James, 55
Shepherd, Paul, 184
Siberia, 90, 225
Silvie, Reverend Father, 108
Simcoe, John Graves (Lieutenant
    Governor), 244
Simcoe Lake, 244
Simpson, Frances, 18, 204
Simpson, George (Govenor HBC), 113,
    114, 126-135, 137, 204
Singapore, 85, 87
Sino-Japanese War, 81
Sir Sanford Fleming College, 10
Sitka (Spruce) canoe, 59
Slave River, 249
Snare River, 180
Snyder, Gary, 183
Spaniards, the, 164
Soldier's Settlement provision, 248
"Song of Hiawatha," 17, 18
Song of the Paddle, 15, 180
South Africa, 248
South Alaska-Kodiak umiak (see umiak)
South East Asia, 82, 85, 87
South Nahanni River, 177, 241, 247-252
Southern canoe (see Nootka canoe)
Southwest Alaska (see Alaska)
Special Air Service (Army) (SAS), 221, 222
Spirit of Haida Gwai, 75
"Spirit Sings, The: Artistic Traditions of
    Canada's First Peoples," 147, 150, 151
Starved Rock (Illinois), 166, 168
Stefansson, Vilnjalmur, 248
Stephenson, John, 230
Starkell, Don, 213-215, 221
Starved Rock (Illinois Country), 166
Stikine River, 247, 252
Straits of Michigan, 162
Straits of Michilimackinac, 118
Strange Things, 218
Stratford (ON), 74
Stringer, Omer, 24, 80
Sullivan, Alan, 20
Summit Lake, 243
"Sunnywater Carry," (Montreal River), 241
Superior, Lake, 19, 92, 99, 109, 122, 123, 127,
    165, 236, 238, 243
Sulpicians, 110
Suzuki, David, 2

T

Tadoussac (fur trading post), 139-142
Tai ji diagram, 64-66, 72
Taipei, 85
Talon, Jean (Intendant of New France), 162, 164
Tantramar Marshes, 243
Task Force on Museums and First Nations, 151-154, 157
Taylor, Elizabeth, 18
Te Papa Tongarewa Museum (New Zealand), 80
Tea Drum Lake (Tom Thomson), 23
Temagami, Lake, 191
Temagami Country, 243
Temagami River, 241
Teme-Augama Anishabai people, 158
Temiscaminque, Lake, 127
Texas, 166
Thailand, 81, 87
Thames (Isis) River (UK), 247
Thelon Game Preserve, 219
Thelon River, 178, 223
Theriault, Madeline Katt, 158
Thomas, Alister, 175
Thomson, Tom, 18, 23, 24
Thompson, David, 18, 228
Thorington, James Monroe, 175
Thoreau, Henry David, 26, 27
Thule Culture, 52
Thule Kayak (see kayak)
Tibet, 45, 46
Tigris River, 45
Times, The, 221
Tlingit (First Nation), 57, 58
Tlingit canoe, 59, 145
Todd & McGill (NWC supply agent), 120
Tomison, William, 124
Tonkin, 45
Toronto (ON), 17, 30, 76, 77, 85, 151, 244
Toronto Island, 87
Torres Strait, 43
Towasconton, Pierre, 137
Trail to the Interior, 252
Tremblay, 140
  - Ètienne, 141-143
  - Louis, 141-143
  - Jean, 141-143
  - Pierre, 142
Tremblay canoes, 143

Trent University, 10, 154
Trinque, François, 122
Trois-Rivières (Quebec), 93, 101-106, 113-121, 124, 127-131, 133-137
Trottier/Desonier family, 109
Trudeau, Pierre Elliott, 2, 7, 18
True North, 216
Tsimshian (First Nation), 58
Tununirusirmiut, elder, 30
Tunraluk, Tugaq, 30
"Turning the Page: Forging New Partnerships Between Mueums and First Nations," 151, 152
Turnor, Philip, 228
Tyrrell, James Willian (J.W.), 31, 32, 34-39, 41, 42, 220
Tyrrell, Joseph Burr, 31, 36, 37, 220

U

UBC (see University of British Colombia)
Uelen, 50
umiak, 44-48, 51-54, 60, 226
  - Aleut umiak (*nigilax*), 45, 46, 53, 54
  - Inuit umiak, 45
  - Koryak *gatwaat*, 45, 46, 54
  - South Alaska-Kodiak umiak, 46, 47
  - Unalaska Aleut kayak (see kayak), 55
Unalaska, 55
Unalaska Aleut kayak (see kayak)
Union Strait, 53
Ungava Bay, 179
United Kingdom, 247
United Nations, 13
United States, 4, 6, 14, 90, 169
University of British Columbia (UBC), 78, 79
Upper Canada, 244
Upper Chaudière Rapids (see Chaudière area)
Upper Palaeolithic (period), 43

V

Valders ice advance, 48
Vancouver (BC), 76, 77, 81, 85
  - Diamond Jubilee, 76
  - English Bay, 77

- False Creek , 77
Vancouver Island, 58, 251, 252
Vancouver Sun, 77
Vandalia (IL), 171
Verner, Frederic, 231
Vermillion River, 135
Victoria (BC), 74, 253
Viet Nam, 83, 85, 87
Village *des Iroquois* (see Oka)
Vincennes (Illinois Country), 167
Virginia Falls (South Nahanni River), 241, 250
Virginian, The, 8
Vokey, Daniel, 67
von Langsdorff, Georg H., 54
Voyages from Montreal, 201
Voyages et Mémoires sur le Canada, 115
Voyages and Travels of an Indian Interpreter and Trader, 123
Voyageur Canoe Co., 242
Voyageur Route(s), 9, 12
Voyageurs, The, 232

W
W.A.C. Bennett Dam (BC), 252
Wabash River, 173, 174
Wabash Valley,
wakataua (Maori), 89
Wakeham Bay (Quebec), 45
Walker, Walter, 11
Wanapitei Bay (see French River)
Wanapitei Wilderness Centre, 242-244
Warden's Grove (Thelon Game Preserve), 219
Washington (DC), 3
Washington State, 58
Watch That Ends the Night, the, 21
"Waterwalker," 27
Waterways (AB), 249
Watts, Alan, 64, 66
Webber, John, 59
Weld, Isaac, 116, 119, 129
Wellington (NZ), 80
Welsh coracle (see coracle)
West, the (Canada), 176, 178, 228
West Coast, the (Canada), 226
West Alaska (see Alaska)
West Coronation Gulf, 53
West Cross Channel (French River)

West Greenland, 48, 49
West Indies, 167
West LaFayette (IN), 173
Westcoast sealing canoe(s), 56
Westcoast whaling canoe, 57
Western Channel (see French River)
Western Outlets (see French River)
When the Wolves Sang, 15
Whitehead, Alfred North, 194
Wild North Land, The, 248
William English Canoe Company, 14
William Grant, Campion & Co. (NWC supply agent), 120
William Parry's Second Voyage of 1821, 40
William (Wm) Price & Co., 135
William River, 178
Wilmette (IL), 171
Wilson, Hap, 231
Winnebago (First Nation), 170
Winnebago, Lake, 162
Winnipeg (MB), 32, 154, 233, 243
Winnipeg, Lake, 228
Winter Olympics (1988), 150
Wipper, Kirk (Professor), 10, 18-20, 24, 66, 80, 149, 224
Wisconsin River, 162, 170
Wister, Owen, 8
Woodland Cultural Centre, 151, 154
World War I, 247, 248
World War II, 62, 76, 81

X
XY Company, 113, 125

Y
Yellow Sunsets (Tom Thomson), 23
Yonge Street, 244
York Factory, 124, 126, 218
Yurok (First Nation), 60
Yurok-Karok design, 60
Yukon, 180, 219
Yukon River, 178

Z
Zhu (Pearl) River, 84
Zybach, Paula, 180

CONTRIBUTORS

Eugene Arima is a Museum Ethnologist working mainly on Arctic and Northwest Native craft. He holds a doctoral degree from the University of Toronto and is currently research associate with the Canadian Museum of Civilization in Ottawa.

Shanna Balazs is pursuing doctoral studies in Anthropology at McMaster University. She is the recipient of a four year Social Sciences and Humanities Research Council of Canada (SSHRC) doctoral fellowship.

David Finch is a consulting historian based in Calgary. He writes about the history of the Canadian West and loves adventuring in its mountains and on its rivers.

Ralph Frese is a fourth generation blacksmith and an environmentalist with a special interest in issues of river conservation. He is also a collector of historic canoes with a collection of over 80 craft. Frese has built canoes for historic reenactments including the 300th anniversary of Louis Joliet's discovery of the Illinois region and the 300th anniversary of La Salle's expedition to the mouth of the Mississippi.

Toni Harting is the editor of *Nastawgan*, the quarterly journal of the Wilderness Canoe Association and a freelance photographer-writer with a special interest in canoeing topics. He recently published *The French River: Canoeing the River of the Stick-Wavers* (Toronto: Stoddart-Boston Mills Press 1996).

Bert Horwood, a retired professor of education, is active as a writer, ritualist and educator. He studied aspects of Daoism with Master Kenneth Cohen and applies the practice of tai ji xuan and Daoist meditation to canoeing.

Bob Henderson teaches Outdoor Education and Environmental Inquiry in the Kinesiology and Arts and Science Departments, respectively, at McMaster University. He also writes a regular column in *Kanawa*.

Bruce W. Hodgins is professor emeritus of History at Trent University and former director of the Frost Centre for Canadian Heritage and Development Studies. His writing centres on wilderness canoeing, the north and Aboriginal affairs. He is an avid wilderness tripper.

Gwyneth Hoyle is the co-author with Bruce Hodgins of *Canoeing North into the Unknown: A Record of River Travel, 1874 to 1974* (Toronto: Natural Heritage Inc. 1994) and has published a number of articles on northern travel and the fur trade. She is a Member of the Board of Trustees of the Canadian Canoe Museum and currently is working on a book about the Arctic explorations of a Scottish woman earlier this century.

John Jennings is an associate professor of Canadian and American history at Trent University and Vice-Chair of the Canadian Canoe Museum Board of Trustees. He specializes in the history of the Canadian and American frontiers and has written several articles on the subject of canoeing in the north. He is presently editing and co-ordinating the forthcoming book *The North American Canoe: The Living Tradition* in cooperation with the Canadian Canoe Museum and to be published by Firefly Books.

Timothy Kent is an independent scholar and lecturer living in Ossineke, Michigan. He recently published the two volume work *Birch Bark Canoes of the Fur Trade* (Ossineke, Michigan: Silver Fox Enterprises 1997). He is presently engaged in preparing for publication biographies of a number of his ancestors who were involved in the fur trade from about 1618 to 1758, as well as bringing to completion a detailed study of some five hundred dugout canoes from across the United States and Canada.

Peter Labor is the General Manager of Naturally Superior Adventures in Wawa, Ontario and has a masters degree from Trent University in Canadian Heritage and Development Studies. In 1989 he was a member and leader of Lakehead University's four-summer Alexander Mackenzie Bicentennial Expeditions, in which students paddled over 10, 000 km retracing all of Mackenzie's 1789-1793 "voyages."

Adrian Lee is the representative for the Americas to the International Dragon Boat Federation, the world sport governing body for dragon boat racing. He has a degree in Industrial Engineering from the University of Toronto and an MBA from the University of British Columbia. He has authored technical papers on Boat Rescue, Lake Rescue, Satellite Aided Search and Rescue and Rigid Inflatable Rescue Boats. Since moving permanently to Vancouver, Lee has been a racer, coach, regatta organizer and international level official of dragon boat racing.

Kenneth R. Lister is Assistant Curator of Anthropology at the Royal Ontario Museum, Toronto, Ontario where he is curator of the Subarctic, Arctic and Watercraft collections. His field research includes archaeological research in the Hudson Bay Lowland of northern Ontario and the Tununirusirmiut of northern Baffin Island. The main focus of his work is oriented toward understanding the role of material culture within the context of traditional cultures.

Becky Mason is an artist and canoe instructor. Every spring you are sure to see her out on Meech Lake breaking up the ice to get her first Classic Solo canoe course started. During the winter, she hangs up her paddle and returns to the studio where she paints her canoeing memories and experiences.

James Raffan lives and works in the Rideau Lakes north of Kingston, Ontario. He has written and edited several books on canoeing related topics including *Canexus: The Canoe in Canadian Culture* (Betelgeuse 1988) and a best selling biography of Bill Mason, *Fire in the Bones.*

Alister Thomas, a paddling enthusiast, often can be seen in the back eddies of Canada's magnificent rivers. He is manager editor of five oil and gas magazines in Calgary, Alberta.

Kirk Wipper is the founder and developer of the Kanawa International Canoe Collection. These craft, which represent nearly forty years of collecting, now form the basis of the holdings of the Canadian Canoe Museum in Peterborough, Ontario. He is past President of the Canadian Recreational Canoeing Association and is currently a Special Advisor to the Canadian Canoe Museum.

Doreen Small (co-editor) graduated from Trent University with a masters degree in Canadian Heritage and Development Studies in 1997 and is now a research associate of the Frost Centre at Trent.